LIBERTY RISING

One Cowboy's Ascent

The *why* behind the resolve
of one of the last sons of the West,
LaVoy Finicum,
as told by his daughter,
Thara Tenney

LIBERTY
ONE COWBOY'S ASCENT
RISING

THE MURDER OF LAVOY FINICUM
AS TOLD BY HIS DAUGHTER

THARA TENNEY

LIBERTY RISING: ONE COWBOY'S ASCENT
Copyright © 2019 Thara Tenney

All rights reserved. Without limiting the rights under copyright above, no part of this publication may be reproduced, stored in or introduced into a retrieval system, or transmitted, in any form, or by any means (electronic, mechanical, photocopying, recording, or use in motion pictures and otherwise), without the prior written permission of the publisher of this book.

ISBN: 978-1-950283-00-2 (Paperback)
ISBN: 978-1-950283-01-9 (Hardback)
ISBN: 978-1-950283-02-6 (Ebook)

Printed in the United States of America

Book design by Morgan Crockett | Firewire Creative

onecowboystandforfreedom.com
regaining.of.freedom@gmail.com

To all those who helped in the writing of this book, thank you.

The heart of this work is devoted to God the Father and His Son Jesus Christ who are the true Authors of Liberty. The ache and toil of telling this story is endured freely in honor of Robert LaVoy Finicum.

The finished work is for the posterity of Robert LaVoy Finicum, that they might read and discover the truth behind the story of their grandfather's murder.

TABLE OF CONTENTS

FOREWORD xi

AUTHOR'S NOTE xix

INTRODUCTION xxiii

CHAPTER 1 | *Read* 1

Murder Mayhem—Sacred Tutorials

CHAPTER 2 | *Laying Him to Rest* 5

CHAPTER 3 | *Murder Mayhem: Entering into the Rest of the Lord* 15

CHAPTER 4 | *Lords of the Message* 29

CHAPTER 5 | *A Force to be Reckoned With* 43

CHAPTER 6 | *Speaking the Language of Liberty* 53

Dad's Rubicon — Oregon

CHAPTER 7 | *History of Hammond Ranching Family* 69

CHAPTER 8 | *Dad Crossing the Rubicon* 81

CHAPTER 9 | *My Time at Ground Zero* 89

CHAPTER 10 | *Vindication* 93

Dad's Fundamentals —Before Oregon

CHAPTER 11 | *Blurring the Boundaries* 99

CHAPTER 12 | *Where the Rubber Meets the Road* 105

CHAPTER 13 | *Another Witness* 113

CHAPTER 14 | *Regional Government* 119

The Great American Experiment

CHAPTER 15 | *The Push and Pull Burden We All Face* 135

CHAPTER 16 | *Atrophy Tug of War* 139

CHAPTER 17 | *Atrophy Tug of War:*
People and Their System of Government 145

CHAPTER 18 | *Property Tug of War* 155

CHAPTER 19 | *Power Tug of War* 159

CHAPTER 20 | *Beautiful Yet Frightening Duty* 165

Dad's Core

CHAPTER 21 | *Dad's Choice Between Two Contending Forces* 183

EPILOGUE | *Dad's Day In Court* 193

Appendices

APPENDIX A | *Timeline of Events* 199

APPENDIX B | *Additional Materials* 209

APPENDIX C | *Extras* 275

GLOSSARY 295

RECOMMENDED READING 309

ENDNOTES 311

ABOUT THE AUTHOR 350

"Whilst the last members were signing [the United States Constitution], Doctr. Franklin, looking towards the President's chair, at the back of which a rising sun happened to be painted, observed to a few members near him, that painters had found it difficult to distinguish in their art, a rising from a setting sun. 'I have,' said he, 'often and often, in the course of the session, and the vicissitudes of my hopes and fears as to its issue, looked at that behind the President without being able to tell whether it was rising or setting: But now at length I have the happiness to know, that it is a rising, and not a setting sun."

—**James Madison**, Federal Convention of 1787

"The tree of liberty must be refreshed from time to time with the blood of patriots…."

—**Thomas Jefferson**, "Letter to William S. Smith"

FOREWORD

SCOTT N. BRADLEY, PHD
FREEDOMSRISINGSUN.COM

I am sorely disappointed that I never knew LaVoy Finicum. I only met members of his family after his assassination by government agents who seemed determined to silence his simple, eloquent, compelling message of liberty and proper government. Perhaps the government minions who were the trigger-men were simply "following orders" given them by superior bureaucrats. Perhaps they have never heard how compellingly flimsy that excuse was at the post-World War II Nuremberg Trials,[1] and the 1961 trial of Adolf Eichmann in Jerusalem.[2] Perhaps, if mortal justice is still part of American jurisprudence, they will yet come to that understanding. If not, we may be assured of justice before another venue wherein we are confident in the judgement of the Judge.

I have come to know LaVoy through interactions with his family members. I discovered LaVoy was not an impetuous man who took precipitous action without well-considered, deliberate forethought. As I watched his many YouTube videos, I could see he was a soft-spoken man of reason. He was not a belligerent man, not given to offer offense. He was a man who, when he saw his duty and was convinced of its justice, he did not hesitate to perform that duty. And he certainly was not a man that ever advocated sedition, rebellion, and violence. He was a man that felt certain that once people had a chance to review truth and principle, they would choose the correct path.

Nevertheless he was a man who was cut down by three assassin's bullets to his back while standing clear of his truck with his hands raised in the universal signal of surrender. He was killed in the prime of his life, leaving his wife a grieving widow and many children and grandchildren bereft of the honored and loving patriarch they relied upon for sustenance and sound counsel that should have been available for them for decades to come. During what should have been a long and worthy mortal life, he will miss the joy of watching his growing posterity blossom into good and honorable members of a free society that surely will perform many worthy tasks during their sojourn upon God's good earth. Words cannot possibly describe the magnitude of loss experienced by LaVoy's family and the diabolical machinations carried out with this this act by the minions of tyranny.

To avoid such tyranny, the Declaration of Independence was birthed. It eloquently captures, in a very succinct manner, the essence of the divine purposes of government:

> *"We hold these truths to be self-evident—that all men are created equal; that they are endowed by their Creator with certain unalienable rights; that among these are life, liberty, and the pursuit of happiness, that to secure these rights, governments are instituted among men, deriving their just powers from the consent of the governed..."*

In that brief sentence, the founders capture the Divine endowment of God upon mankind. God's involvement is mentioned twice: "all men are created equal" (creation speaks of a Creator) and "they are endowed by their Creator with certain unalienable rights." (In other words, the Creator placed upon mankind certain rights that were—-and are—-gifts from Him.) A few of those gifts are mentioned, but certainly the list is not the limits and bounds of His gifts, although "pursuit of happiness" could include quite an expansive list! The Declaration goes on to conclusively state the purpose of government: To secure God-given rights. It would appear that the American Founders firmly believed that the primary purpose of government is to assure that God-given rights remain sacred, un-infringed, and preserved.

During their era, the American Founders experienced the king's oppression and denial of God-given rights, so when they made their independence sure, they created a government that included assurances that their God-given endowment would be protected from government infringement, and they created a judicial system that favored the accused to protect to the greatest degree possible against the force of government from being imposed improperly, especially upon one who was innocent.

Among the many rights protected,[3] they specifically mentioned habeas corpus,[4] prevention of bills of attainder,[5] prohibiting the creation of ex post facto laws,[6] and, of course, the entire list of God-given rights vouchsafed by the Bill of Rights.

Tragically, and to the shame of the current powers who hold the reins of government, virtually every activity on the highway the day of the assassination of LaVoy Finicum was a violation of the original intent of the American Founders. He was instantaneously denied God's great gift of life, his liberty to choose a path that would bring liberty of conscience and his pursuit of happiness.

He was never allowed to experience a judicial system biased in favor of the accused and intended to render justice. He was summarily shot and killed without any effort to incarcerate and allow the courts to independently review whether or not he was properly jailed or guilty. He was assumed to be a criminal without any review except the prior arrangements made by the perpetrators and the impulse between their brain and trigger finger. His freedom of speech and peaceable assembly, which he was travelling to exercise when he was killed, was denied with extreme prejudice, as was his right to petition the government for a redress of grievances. He was denied indictment by a grand jury for his supposed and presumed offenses. He was deprived of life without due process. He never enjoyed the right to a speedy and public trial. He never experienced a trial by an impartial jury in the state or district wherein his supposed crimes occurred. He was never informed of the nature and cause of accusations against him. He was never able to confront witnesses that might have been brought against him. He was never able to bring witnesses in his favor. He never had the assistance of counsel for his defense.

It has been said that "dead men tell no tales," but in spite of the extrajudicial summary execution (conducted without the customary legal formalities) of a man never convicted of a crime in his life, this event MUST be heard before an earthly tribunal, and certainly WILL be heard before a heavenly tribunal.

Most Americans, today, cannot even begin to contemplate representatives of their government operating in the darkness of a netherworld that subverts the foundational principles upon which the United States of America was established, as was manifested in the coldly planned and executed extrajudicial execution of LaVoy Finicum. Perhaps some element of the cabal seeking to overthrow America as a land of liberty felt they had to silence him because his earnest expressions of liberty and proper government were so compelling that it was feared that these ideas might take root and spread among the many Americans who heard them.

The one-way violent and deadly exchange on the highway was never intended to be an operation by "peace officers" hoping to resolve a situation in a manner that protected life, liberty, and property, but, rather, was a finely-tuned ambush carried out as a military operation. Leadership had a deadly plan with a foregone outcome and likely selected the personnel in the operation that they were certain would not flinch from their orders and bring about a peaceful closure. Apparently, Hosea's ancient observation, "My people are destroyed for lack of knowledge,"[7] and Isaiah's second testimonial warning, "Therefore my people are gone into captivity, because [they have] no knowledge: and their honourable men [are] famished, and their multitude dried up with thirst,"[8] may be applied in modern America. Sadly, it seems that far too many Americans have come to take the blessings of liberty and proper government for granted and have become more like the proverbial boiled frog than most would ever dare to suppose.

Perhaps we could have predicted this circumstance. Anciently, Paul warned of what we must expect in our day: "For we wrestle not against flesh and blood, but against principalities, against powers, against the rulers of the darkness of this world, against spiritual wickedness in high [places],"[9] and John foresaw "under the altar the souls of them that were slain for the word of God, and for the testimony which they held."[10] Would we expect that "so celestial an article as freedom should not be highly rated"[11] and come at a steep cost?

Some will possibly read this book and become incensed to the point that they agitate for violence and revenge. Perhaps, the cabal seeking the overthrow of every last vestige of Americanist liberty will even promote this response through provocateurs to give excuse to what will surely be their devastatingly overwhelming reaction.

Surely, it is wise to consider the path the American Founders pursued in their quest for liberty. They exhausted all avenues before armed rebellion. The Declaration of Independence reminds us that they were wise and well-considered statesmen, not wild-eyed radicals bent on burning the nation to the ground in their quest to overthrow injustice.

After reviewing the offenses of the king within the Declaration, the American statesmen wrote,

> *"In every stage of these oppressions we have petitioned for redress in the most humble terms: our repeated petitions have been answered only by repeated injury...*
>
> *"Nor have we been wanting in attentions to our British brethren. We have warned them, from time to time, of attempts by their legislature to extend an unwarrantable jurisdiction over us. We have reminded them of the circumstances of our emigration and settlement here. We have appealed to their native justice and magnanimity, and we have conjured them, by the ties of our common kindred, to disavow these usurpations, which would inevitably interrupt our connections and correspondence. They too have been deaf to the voice of justice and of consanguinity."*

The American Founder's actions were not taken precipitously, but were deliberate and temperate.

In addition, there were two things the founders did not have that we have, and which may be wisely exercised and applied to restore the nation's foundation without violence:

> The vote and
> The United States Constitution

It is foolish and dangerous to promote armed rebellion because it would be welcomed by those who seek to overthrow liberty and proper government. It would give would-be tyrants (in their perverse agenda) justification to impose universal oppressive sanctions that an ignorant citizenry would be powerless to effectively resist.

There is a just God in Heaven who hears and answers prayers in accord to Divine wisdom if a faithful people seeks Him.

Hopefully, the people of the nation have not been so willfully stubborn and proud and so slothful in preservation of our God-given blessings, that He will allow an extended chastening before He intervenes.

How Might We Avoid Further Spilt Blood?

First, we must again bring our will into conformance with the will of God—as individuals, families, congregations, communities, states, and even the nation. The founders of this nation came here for the privilege of worshipping their God in accordance with their conscience. They brought the Holy Scriptures with them and largely sought to abide by the principles therein. They looked to God, they worshipped God, and they sought to please Him. When Tocqueville visited America in the early 1800s to observe the mores of the nation,[12] he was impressed that the general citizenry was motivated by an individual internal compass-system, which was driven by an almost universal belief that God's will and justice would ultimately be dispensed by an eternal, all-knowing God. Therefore, the people needed very few laws to bring order to society. Early America did not require a law and punishment for everything, because most Americans conformed themselves and their actions to the universal truths they found in the Holy Scriptures, and, therefore, society generally was stable and prosperous under the well-established and soundly-founded government set forth in the United States Constitution.

Interestingly, religious liberty became the first God-given right protected in the First Amendment. Perhaps that is altogether fitting because the awakening of the human spirit that occurred when people gained access to the scriptures and became literate to allow them to study and consider the truths found therein brought about a renaissance of not only science and art, but also an awakening to the concept of God-given rights and the hope of a form of government that would not only allow a people to worship as they pleased, but also to be prosperous and free under a form of government that allowed them to blossom to their full capacity. Retaining religious liberty, and exercising it as was done early in America's founding era, is essential to restore and preserve our liberty and proper government.

Second, we, the people, must restore to our national consciousness our understanding of the original principles that allowed this nation to become the greatest, freest, most happy, and most prosperous nation upon the earth. We can bring this understanding of the American Founder's "original intent" by studying and considering the plain English words of the United States Constitution. Those words have meaning, those meanings may be known, and they may only mean what they meant in the day they were written.[13] Then we must begin again to purely apply the words as they were originally set forth. We may come to understand the founder's original intent by carefully studying their words, as found in their foundational writings.[14]

Third, once we have embraced the founder's original intent, we must become actively engaged in the political process to assure that the representatives we elect keep their actions within the bounds originally defined in America's founding principles. The proper role of government must be maintained.

And fourth, we must actively teach others and vote in accord with the established bounds of proper government, so we may influence understanding and apply the wonderful principles the nation was so graciously gifted by God.

Following this approach, we may restore the nation to its once-great foundation without the shattering pain associated with losing innocent lives like LaVoy's. The tyranny-violence cycle that unwise nations suffer so regularly does not have to be the fate of America. But we must not be so foolish, naive, and shortsighted to assume that our "land of the free" is exempt from the dangerous swing of the political pendulum if we do not actively engage in the restoration and preservation of the gift of liberty and proper government that was granted to us at such a great cost.

In one of his letters to Thomas Jefferson after their reconciliation, John Adams wrote of his perspective about the American Revolutionary War, saying that the war was merely incidental to the true revolution that had captured the hearts and minds of Americans in their era. In his view, the true American Revolution occurred 1760-1775, before a drop of blood was spilt at Lexington Green. He felt that there had been an almost universal awakening in the hearts and minds of Americans during that 15-year period that had created within them a feeling that liberty was more precious than life itself and that they were compelled to separate from the king and England in order to more fully enjoy the blessings they hoped for.

It would seem that for liberty and proper government to be renewed and restored in modern America, a renaissance of similar nature must move upon the nation in our day. Sound understanding of proper principles of liberty and sound government must be widely understood and restored before the nation can be healed. LaVoy toiled to accomplish this.

After suffering for many years at the hands of officialdom for seeking to promote correct principles, in 1678 John Bunyan published his Christian allegory Pilgrim's Progress. Therein Bunyan documents the growth and progression of one man through his mortal challenges to his eternal reward, and the subsequent parallel path of his family as they follow the wisdom he lived by.

Liberty Rising: One Cowboy's Ascent is, perhaps, a modern allegory of a similar story, lovingly and devotedly told by the daughter of a man who saw the glory of liberty and unyieldingly and heroically pursued it, regardless of the mortal costs associated with it. It is a compelling story that, if read and understood by enough Americans, the "revolution" of liberty may again begin to be planted in the hearts of the nation and the Americanist form of proper government may have a re-birth in the land—with an outcome similar to what John Adams and Thomas Jefferson observed nearly 250 years ago.

AUTHOR'S NOTE

I am the oldest child of the LaVoy and Jeanette Finicum dozen. Growing up, I remember our family was often stopped in public by curious spectators who asked my parents, "Are all these children yours?" Mom and Dad would always laugh at the different responses they would get. Mom eventually designed Dad a t-shirt for Father's Day that read, "Yes, all these children are mine."

When we were young, Dad developed a system to quickly ensure no one was ever left behind. Upon receiving direction from Dad, we children would sound a number roll call from oldest to youngest, one to ten. Wait, you must be thinking, ten is not a dozen! That is correct. Two more finished off the Finicum flock years after the number roll call system was retired.

While Dad was not one to physically express affection, he had a way of capturing our hearts. I think I'm safe to speak for all twelve in that our hearts desire has always been to bring honor and not disappoint. This is part of what compels me to write this book, despite the deep unrest I suffer with being vulnerable. This feeling has been the driving force for me to discover answers to my many questions. I wanted to understand what drove my dad to the point where he was yelling at, who were at the time, unknown agents, "You want my blood on your hands?"

Writing is a practice I have participated in for years; however, I have never entertained the idea of sharing my heart and mind with others, let alone complete strangers. My husband always jokes with me about communicating and says if I give up the ghost before him, the first thing he will do is read all my journals. Yes, I don't even let my husband read my writings. They are mine. I am a very private person and he graciously respects me, which I love so very much.

After Dad was murdered, I was so angry with the world. Strangers spewed hatred toward our family. Some of our friends and even family ostracized us. I could not believe the lengths people would go to insult another whose political views are not the same as theirs.

In commenting on the hatred our family had to suffer due to iniquity and ignorance, I do not wish to neglect to mention the many individuals who reached out in tender love and respect. Each person's unique, kind gesture and service to our family provided the much needed healing balm to our broken hearts. We will forever be grateful to the many people who ministered to us in one of our most vulnerable time. It is these kind acts that helped us to rise above the despair toward humanity that could have consumed our hearts.

Being a very private person and understanding the very public ugliness I have already waded through on the topic of my father, the idea of publishing a book on the matter was very scary. Yet, I was compelled. My mind did not rest until the manuscript was done. While writing, I wrestled with deciding between writing in first person or third person. Of course, third person was much more appealing to me. I bet you can guess why. It was appealing because I didn't have to open my heart to readers while sharing that which I was compelled to share. Unfortunately, my protective boundary of writing in third person presented a huge caveat.

No one can relate to a brick wall!

I wrestled with this some more and concluded that a compromise to the safety of my third person boundary was necessary. The compromise is this: Half the book will be more personal in nature, telling our tragic story. The other half will be more academic. I have chosen to structure my book this way with the hope you will connect the dots. I want you to find answers to your questions and then begin powerfully applying civics.

A friend who helped me through moments of deep discouragement while writing provided me with a helpful perspective. She suggested I envision the sharing of my first person voice to be my offering to you. She said that I must lay my vulnerability on the alert. While pondering this imagery, I found myself deeply desiring to be successful at the idea, yet, I still feared.

I do plead with you to be patient as you read. Imagine it being your father who was murdered, your family that was publicly slandered, ridiculed, and libeled. I ask this of you because I know as you seek to be in my shoes, your disposition will be more tender toward my words. Resist the temptation to skip the parts where I am a brick wall writing academic. While I know most will be left yearning for more personal stories of Dad and me, I strongly believe the academic section of my book is very important for the future preservation of freedom and liberty. In reading my book, in its entirety, (I recommend reading the chatty endnotes as you progress through the book—this will give you a story within the story), you will more likely gain a greater understanding into what developed the conviction of my Father and how such a tragic murder as his could take place in the land we call *"the free."*

I can only assume why you picked up this book. My guess is it may be for one of four reasons. One, you love the man, LaVoy Finicum, like so many others out in this world and desire to financially support his family's efforts to fundraise for our wrongful death by purchasing this book. Two, you are on the opposite side of the Finicum family fan club spectrum and could not satisfy your curiosity by simply looking at the cover. Three, perhaps you only vaguely know of the Finicum family and want to know more. What better way to do that than by reading his daughter's book? Or finally, maybe happenstance led you to this book while not knowing anything of the Finicum's and yet here you are reading.

Whatever your reason, thank you for your time. This truly is where the rubber meets the road in getting to know my dad, LaVoy Finicum. Wherever you are on the Finicum family fan club spectrum, my appreciation for your time is deeper than you can comprehend.

INTRODUCTION

Regardless of which political side you might fall on, this story is so compelling, tragic, and iconic that once your journey of discovery begins, the hope is you will be moved by the details.

Everyone who was there with Dad on that fateful day was acquitted in an Oregon Federal Court. Today my Dad, the "*dead man,*" has his day in court. You, the readers become the jury—reviewing his side for the first time.

Dad said, "I'm just a redneck doing the right thing… was never one to poke people in the eye or cause trouble. I always stood in line, rose my hand, and never had a parking violation." He definitely did not fit the description of a "loose cannon" or "hothead." Interviews with his family and footage from his own home videos bear witness that he was a family man and ranching cowboy, not a closet criminal as the media portrayed him.

So what changed in Dad's life? Why did he begin his public political activism in 2014 by attending the Nevada Bundy Standoff understanding he may be labeled as a domestic terrorist? Why did he go to Burns, Harney County, Oregon and participate in the Malheur Wildlife Refuge occupation in 2016? Why, on his way to a political symposium in Oregon did he end up stepping out of his truck into a hail of bullets?

As you read the academic section of my book you will be introduced to many of the great minds that helped shape the resolve of my father. To me this section is so much more than a dry dissertation of quotes from a bunch of old dead guys who today may be perceived as outdated, difficult to understand, and irrelevant.

My stories and the organized academic sources will not only give you a good feel of who Dad was, but it will also be a witness of what the painful results are when a people's system of governance is not understood or maintained. For this reason, I say don't just read my stories about Dad and I and don't just read the dry academic chapters. Read it all, including the endnotes and appendix, and really let it sink in and then get to work.

Our family's deepest desire is for our story to be told in its entirety, void of misrepresentations, while also teaching principles of sound government. Amongst the complexity, we press forward in ways appropriate to right that which has been wronged. This has required more than a mere published manuscript. The first few years after Dad's murder, my Mom, a few of my siblings, and I traveled the nation orating at events of all kinds. While traveling had its place in righting wrongs, I believe this book also has its place in that process.

The mission of our family's work is to correct the distorted image of our family's husband and father, cultivate discernment between truth and error, and promote positive change in the destiny of this Nation. Fate has it for any martyr to become the spectacle of debate as to whether or not such person was a villain or a hero. And now, as for LaVoy Finicum, my father, was he an American villain, fool, or hero?

This manuscript being a labor of love, it's important to me for you to understand its mission is best accomplished when working in conjunction with a documentary series titled, *LaVoy: Dead Man Talking*. Same goes for the documentary series. Its mission is best accomplished when working in conjunction with this book. The two work hand in hand and I believe they are both incomplete by themselves.

The documentary series is a professional compilation of the most pertinent clips from Dad's very own YouTube channel, interviews he participated in during the Oregon occupation, and the fallout of the different court cases after his murder. If this book was not a book/documentary series bundle, the documentary series can be purchased from our family website: *onecowboystandforfreedom.com*.

My hope for this book and documentary series is that they together will inspire you to ask hard questions of yourself with the intent to seek difficult-to-find answers. My Dad's story can't help but stir a need to embark on the challenging endeavor to discover the delicate line that separates preserving and losing our unalienable rights as outlined in the American Declaration of Independence.

To begin, it's important to recognize how the iconic, tough as rawhide, Western way of life is giving way to modern 21st century. Putting that into perspective, a very high percentage of the current American public does not own a cow, let alone know what "grazing rights" are. In a world of city life and virtual existence, it may be difficult to visualize family life on an open range, spotted with cows, a cowboy, and his dog.

In understanding the 21st century's demographic transition from its roots, it is no surprise that what came to be known as the April 12, 2014 Nevada Bundy Standoff, which was Dad's first public political expression, was widely condemned by citizenry of most American urban areas.[15]

Dad was *One Cowboy* who stood to uphold and defend the United States Constitution against domestic adversaries. The series of events that led up to that tragic day, January 26, 2016, in Oregon, where his right to life was taken, are grossly misunderstood by a vast amount of Americans.

This is your journey of discovery to decide, was he the villain, fool, or hero?

CHAPTER 1

READ

As I prepare to read a book, I often flip the pages back and forth with my thumb. Most often I bring it close enough to my face to feel the breeze from the pages as they flutter by the tip of my nose. I admit, I do enjoy smelling the pages. Each book, new or old, is unique and everything about it, even its smell, has a story to tell.

While I do consider myself a proud member of the unofficial universal book nerd club, I am often guilty of skipping over the introduction of the books I read. The only reason behind this silly sin of omission is my desire to just dive into the story. I guess I could blame this on my subconscious convincing me to not bother with reading the forerunner.

I'm sure through the years I have missed many golden nuggets of insight and wisdom as I have freely bypassed the introductions and authors' notes of the many books I've read. While I never aspired to author a book of my own, I now have a new sorrow for what I have missed, knowing the thought and energy that went into writing my author's note and introduction. For this reason, I have decided to dedicate the first chapter of my book to extend the invitation to you to now turn back and read the overall author's note and introduction. If you are anything like me, I know it is highly likely you have bypassed them.

CHAPTERS 2-6

MURDER MAYHEM— SACRED TUTORIALS

CHAPTER 2

LAYING HIM TO REST

*"Pippin: I didn't think it would end this way.
Gandalf: End? No, the journey doesn't end here. Death is just another path, one that we all must take. The grey rain-curtain of this world rolls back, and all turns to silver glass, and then you see it.
Pippin: What? Gandalf?...See what?
Gandalf: White shores...and beyond,
a far green country under a swift sunrise.
Pippin: [smiling] Well, that isn't so bad.
Gandalf: [softly] No... No, it isn't."*
—**Tolkien**, *The Return of the King*

AUTHOR'S NOTES

This moment was so difficult. It was all I could do to stand there and not fall apart. Just moments after this captured photo (see below), I put my overwhelming energy to work as I shoveled scoop after scoop of red sand to bury my Father, deep in the Cane Beds, Arizona earth.

The days, hours, and moments leading up to the funeral were full of experiences our family would have rather never had to face. We simply wanted our innocent father and husband alive.

The wish was in vain. He was dead!

Nothing was going to bring him back. All we could do—and must do—was pull through together. This was the only way planning a politically-charged funeral would prove successful.

The house was full. Never a quiet moment, much like it always was when our big family gathered, except this time anguish permeated the spirit in the home. Each heart was still stunned by murder's stark reality. Death haunted us all.

Often my imagination would hear the jingle of Dad's spurs. He regularly wore his boots. Despite our never-ending full house, I always knew when it was Dad walking around. His firm step reverberated energy and purpose. He always wore his keys hooked to his hip belt loop, which contributed to the serenade of his walk. These all too familiar sounds were no more. His flesh was gone.

When home, we would always expect late night board games at the dinner table with plenty of chips, salsa, and homemade guacamole with extra salt. Not this time. Our cherished games stayed tucked away in the closet. It seemed no one wanted food. Sleep felt impossible. Sudden weight loss and dehydration began its damaging toll upon me.

Despite my human body screaming for rest, the process of healthy grieving took a back seat. Our family life became a national fishbowl within just a few weeks. To me it seemed many felt it their duty to peer in with unrighteous scrutiny. As a result, it felt as if everything required additional energy notwithstanding the great need for my soul to slow down.

While typical, grieving families gather to spend private, peaceful time together, I resented our family's required marathon that had just started. There was crucial evidence to gather, brainstorming with lawyers,[16] and press releases to generate on top of the typical duties of organizing an obituary, funeral program, life slideshow, and a pleasant meal for those who traveled to attend the funeral.[17] Yet there were additional things demanding additional attention. There were national media interviews to organize. We packaged and delivered orders of Dad's novel.[18] We had sheriffs to coordinate with, social media trolls to ban and delete, devastated people to comfort, ecclesiastical leaders to negotiate with, and a professional track of our *Freedom's Cry* song to record.[19]

The most dismal task was driving to the state of Oregon to bring home, in a cardboard box, my dear Father's lifeless body.

From Oregon, the body was delivered straight to medical professionals hired by the family to perform a second, independent, evidentiary autopsy. We strongly felt this second autopsy was absolutely necessary, as the government agencies had repeatedly broken our trust.

Upon opening the cardboard box for the first time, it was discovered the body was left filleted open by the previous autopsy medical personnel in Oregon. Whether or not such a practice is customary, this seeming disrespect filled us with revulsion and pain. Osama bin Laden was given greater respect then Dad and he *was* a terrorist mastermind who sanctioned murder for heaven's sake![20]

The next destination for the body was the Kanab, Utah Mosdell Mortuary. This is where his body would be prepared for the funeral. This was the first time my siblings and I saw our Father's lifeless body. Though his body lie on the steel table intact, there was no glow. Daddy's spirit was gone. What lay before me was a preserved tabernacle of clay, cold, stiff, and void of life. Each person, one by one, took their turn "render[ing] some of the last acts of service that one could give to another" in preparing the body for viewing.[21]

Upon returning home, we all were high strung, each coping in our own way. Within minutes of our return from the mortuary, we were informed media was scouting the location of our home. We were grateful our good neighbors sent them on a wild goose chase by telling them our home was in the opposite direction. Not only were they knocking on doors looking for our home, but they were also camped outside the homes of family members of Dad's ex-wives. At that moment I experienced overwhelming rage. *Why couldn't they just leave our family alone? Haven't they done enough damage with their putrid lies?* In my rage, I immediately went into a frantic mode of trying to prevent the media from having success with their malicious scout.

I straightaway called specific family members to inform them of the new development. While on the phone, we quickly reviewed what the response would be should media approach them at their door.[22] As these conversations came to an end, I felt dread about approaching a few of my grieving siblings.[23] My intent was to encourage and invite them to reach out to their family who also needed the information. I wanted so badly to just crawl in a hole. I hated the idea of bothering my suffering siblings during this raw, delicate time. Panic filled my mind. I had to somehow halt those reporters. I would have gladly called their family members myself. Unfortunately, I had no contact information. Nor was there any rapport between me and their other parent. I feared if I were to call, it would hinder success in the message being fully received.

My frantic mind decided I had no choice but to approach specific siblings to see that the message was successfully delivered. My nagging resulted in a family meltdown. My husband tenderly held me as all the stress, pain, agony, and anger inside my mind and heart overboiled. My arms and legs flailed uncontrollably. My voice wailed.

In looking back, I can see that this meltdown was bound to happen at some point or another because we were all ticking time bombs. The place had been a heating powder keg since the day of Dad's murder. But at that moment, I painfully embraced all responsibility hoping for just a small degree of peace.

That night as I lay awake in bed, my body still shot agonizing tension in my neck, shoulders, back, and legs just like it did during the drive to the ranch the night of Dad's murder. My mind was now frantic with fear and anxiety wondering what assaults on our family would be next. I was stiff and could not get comfortable and fall asleep. My eyes were swollen and dry. There were no more tears. My stomach was sick. My mouth was dry and my lips cracking. I don't think I ate or drank all day. I was a mess. The thing that repeated in my mind before I finally drifted into sleep was how repugnant Dad's cold stiff hand was to me. I tried to warm it by holding it. I tried.... I hated that it didn't work.

As the commotion kept rampaging on, local community members provided food for our *large* family for an entire week. While I wasn't eating much, it was so nice to be able to go to the kitchen and just put something in my mouth without having to prepare. Also being able to simply send my children to the kitchen to microwave a plate of food when hungry, was exactly what I needed.

For about a week, kind-hearted ladies from church helped watch the children while each daunting task was tackled. This was no small feat. I think at the time there were at least ten kids all under the age nine. The yard was completely renovated. Church members and friends even went to the extent of painting the plywood chicken coop and weathered swing set to match the house.

The outpouring of love began to replace our numbness with swellings of gratitude. This divine emotion helped us endure the deep ache. Our heavy burdens were made lighter as our disposition transitioned from deep sorrow and anger to refreshing appreciation. Christ like love had begun its healing work.

> "Do not pity the dead, Harry. Pity the living, and, above all those who live without love."[24]
> —**J. K. Rowling**, *Harry Potter and the Deathly Hallows*

Amongst what could be called true chaos, thousands reached out to our family from all over the world expressing their condolences. Cards from complete strangers started coming through the mail in mass quantities to show love, respect, and support. The sting of injustice forced upon our family was felt by many in this nation and worldwide. Countless, heartfelt expressions had a unanimous theme: how could an innocent American's right to life and due process be destroyed by American federal, state, and local law enforcement? Such a travesty is not American!

Given this outpouring of love, we decided to welcome all who wanted to show their respects to Dad the day of his funeral. We were unsure what to expect in regard to attendance. The mortuary quickly became overwhelmed with over 300 flower arrangement orders. The local flower shops felt the rush as well, resulting in their stock being sold out. The mortician did not realize this funeral would become the largest in his career. The small tourist town of Kanab, Utah flooded with newcomers. At least 2,300 people attended the funeral. The chapel, cultural hall, stage, hallways, and classrooms filled, leaving standing room only. Unfortunately, the line for the viewing became too long for everyone to be admitted.

Off Church property, outside the viewing, siblings were interviewed by the media. This was nerve wracking as we were uncertain as to whom was adversarial. Prior false characterizations of Dad by the mainstream media had created a deep sense of skepticism. Trust certainly had not been earned. To have to share the last moments with our beloved father with individuals and organizations whose propaganda had contributed to the unnecessary escalation of the occupation felt cruel. Our souls just couldn't muster the perfect political strategy that day! We understood, however, the need for future allies in our wrongful death case and thus sacrificed privacy.

After the funeral, Tierra-Belle and I, as the oldest daughters, addressed the media one last time in a press conference. This was foreign to both of us. The script was drafted the night before through red eyes and edited by Utah's KTalk radio show host, Cherilyn Bacon Eagar, who for a time, graciously managed media for our family, pro bono.[25]

After the press conference, family and friends rode in a three-mile memorial horse ride. The ride started in the Church parking lot, went down W Kanab Creek Drive to where the road came to a T at 89 A. It finished back at the Church. Dad's empty saddle was led by his father, David Finicum. Over 50 cowboys silently rode horse that day. Cliven Bundy, the man, who Dad said "spoke to his soul," was found among the riders that day in Kanab, Utah.

Just days after Dad's murder, Jordan Page, a musician whose work is dedicated to promoting liberty knew he received help from an unseen force in writing what he called *The Ballad of LaVoy Finicum: Cowboy Stand for Freedom*.[26] Jordan was so kind to perform that evening at the local middle school in Kanab, Utah with the hope of raising money for Mom.

That same evening, my sisters and I sang our song, *Freedom's Cry*, which received an overwhelming standing ovation. Again, the consensus was that an unseen hand had assisted in organizing the language of *Freedom's Cry*.[27]

As nightfall approached, everyone was fully spent. While we had been indisputably sustained by the hand of Providence through that long day, rest now became the imperative.

The day of Dad's burial was set aside just for family. Mid-morning, everyone gathered at the Finicum homestead where the simple pine casket was loaded in the old family wagon and pulled by a team of horses with David and Nelda, Dad's father and mother, at the reins. Diamond, Dad's trusted cattle dog, rode atop the casket for the mile-long journey to the cemetery. Mom followed behind on foot leading Dad's empty saddled horse. Many walked the trek with her, some rode horse flying the American flag, and some drove the distance. It was a quiet trek.

The family ranch has a private cemetery. To enter the unsuspecting graveyard, you enter through a small picket gate left unpainted. On both sides of the gate are tall posts. At the top, a wire runs from the top of one post to the other. Upon entering, we turned a slight right and walked a few hundred yards up a slight incline through the red sand and cedar. Dad's grave rests upon the crest.

Just as his pine casket was handcrafted by family, without the use of any power tools, his grave was also dug by hand by his father, brothers, and sons. "Digging a grave for a fallen loved one is the final act of love and service that can be rendered in this world."²⁸ Dad would not have had the preparation of his burial done in any other way, and neither would we.

Upon arrival, the casket was carefully suspended over the perfectly-dug hole. My oldest brother, Robert (Tell) presided over the many heartfelt sentiments shared at the graveside. Family mustered enough courage for pictures before that pine box was lowered into the ground with lasso ropes.

The scene was vibrant with color despite the anguish and exhaustion apparent in the eyes of those present. The backdrop for the family photos was cutting. It was the four-foot pile of freshly hand dug Cane Beds sand, deep red in color. The heap of damp earth was peppered with flower arrangements from the day's funeral, a flying American flag, and the Canaan Mountains.

When time came to move that fresh pile of red earth to close the open grave, the four-foot mound seemed to quickly shorten as we girls each took turns expressing our "final acts of love and service." We covered the pine box one shovel at time. My sister and I then carefully arranged the flowers neatly over the grave mound. This ground was now sacred. Only the breeze could be heard moving the sagebrush and cedar, causing the peaceful smell of country to permeate. The troubled unearthed spot had now become home for Dad. This was his final resting place until his body, one day, would reunite with his spirit.

Slowly people trickled back to the homestead to join in a meal. For the living, life still had to be sustained. For me the trek back felt unruly. I was one of the last to return. I didn't want to return to life. I couldn't help but kick up dust while walking that long dirt road, wondering how I could go on. In that raw moment, I struggled to remember Dad's hopeful perspective publicly expressed on a radio show months before he found himself in Oregon. He said, "It may cost you everything, but that's okay! It may cost you your life. That's okay. We all die. Die for something good. Let your children and your posterity know where you stood. Don't disappoint your ancestors. This is the day and the time to stand."[29]

Indeed, "to the well-organized mind, death is but the next great adventure."[30]

CHAPTER 3

MURDER MAYHEM: ENTERING INTO THE REST OF THE LORD

"A day may come when the courage of men fails,
when we forsake our friends and break all bonds of fellowship…."
—**J.R.R. Tolkien**, *Return of the King*

AUTHOR'S NOTES

Dad never was fond of modern Christmas tradition. Rather than gifts and packaging, his focus seemed to be honed on the birth of Jesus Christ. While he was tone deaf, he loved singing the Christmas hymns. As we girls got older, it seemed he relied more on our voice to lead the melody. Nevertheless, he sang with just as much vigor as he did when we were little.

A go-to classic during the Christmas season for our family was the black-and-white production It's A Wonderful Life. I love the message of that film and now carry on the tradition in my own family.

It never was an uncommon sight to see dad sitting quietly in his rocking chair reading scriptures, but it was only on Christmas morning that his reading included beef jerky, his one anticipated stocking tradition.

On December 19th, 2015, my parents traveled to my home in Utah for a pre-Christmas white elephant gift exchange for the grandkids. True to form, the gifts were silly in nature. I prepared a box of chocolates, ensuring each chocolate had been partially eaten. I remember chopsticks and other silly things like that. We all had a good laugh. The kids were sure to eat that box of chocolates.

After all the lightweight fun, dad in all seriousness said the only thing he wanted for Christmas was to hear us sing a few Christmas hymns. So, we did. We ended our chorus with Dad's request of I Heard the Bells on Christmas Day. Typical of young people, my kids were distracted but we adults kept singing with vigor. We joyed in the Christmas spirit that hymns bring.

We then read scriptures as a family before putting the kids to bed. I can still see Dad sitting on the carpet with his back against the couch and his legs outstretched and crossed. He wore his wool cox's.

As the kids' young bodies relentlessly wiggled, we read the story known as The Tree of Life, found in the Book of Mormon. This story has many themes but the one most crowning is how we can more readily feel of God's love. Dad cheerfully said this story was one of his most cherished.

After the kids were tucked into bed, Dad went further into why this scripture meant so much to him. He said feeling of God's love was a powerful motivation to him. He expressed how he had found in his life that God's love was one of the only things that tempered his strong will. He expressed gratitude for this love, because this was the force that helped him meekly submit his will to that of Gods.

On Tuesday, January 26, 2016, thirty-eight days later, I had what would be my last conversation with Dad. The purpose of the call was to discuss the progress of scheduling interviews with different media outlets. We worked diligently to be transparent during the Malheur National Wildlife Refuge occupation, amidst many obstacles.

I was quite frazzled by the false disseminated narrative and lamenting to Dad as I sat in my car waiting for the people who were viewing my home to finish. Back then, my house had been on the market for about a month. We knew we needed to move our little family but knowing where to was yet unknown.

While our time together on the phone that afternoon was short, I'll forever hold onto his last words to me before ending the call. With his voice possessing all the tenderness a father can have, he said, "I am so proud of you." The call ended and I was on with my crazy day.

It was not until late that evening that I learned he had been murdered shortly after our call.

Within an hour's time of getting the news, my family got in the car and headed to the ranch to be with Mom. As we rode, I cried out in convulsive gasps for a time. Then I felt a tensing of my neck, shoulders, back, and legs built into agony. My mind had no control. Quickly, I became stiff yet could not help trembling. My eyes couldn't focus or shut. My stomach was sick and my mouth dry.

I had never before experienced a physiological state of shock, but I'd venture to say, I was there.

It was not until the next year's Christmas, twelve months after Dad was taken from me, that I attempted to sing his requested hymn again. Even after a year's time, I could not utter the words to its melody. I remember my throat, gut, and muscles tightening in agony as I read the words through tear-filled eyes, "And in despair I bowed my head: There is no peace on earth, I said, For hate is strong and mocks the song Of peace on earth, good will to men."

Now, as I write this almost three years after his murder, my soul finds rest in the truth I always knew—Christ has won victory over the grave. While the sting of his murder will forever haunt my mind, I now sing his hymn with all the energy of my soul, "Then pealed the bells more loud and deep: "God is not dead, nor doth he sleep; The wrong shall fail, the right prevail, With peace on earth, good will to men."

On January 26th, 2016, Dad was still alive and staying in Oregon. He and others were preparing to address a large crowd of residents from John Day, Oregon who were anxiously awaiting the arriving cowboys' message about why federalism is so important.[31] The cowboys were occupying the Malheur Wildlife Refuge to petition the government for a redress of grievances.[32] No one that day anticipated the premeditated mayhem American agents would instigate.

From day one of the petition, the occupiers came and went freely from the refuge tending to business, both personal and pertaining to the occupation. The cowboys took every opportunity available to peaceably share their message, including initiating contact with federal, state, and local law enforcement. The goal from the beginning was transparency. Great care was taken to bridge any gaps of understanding due to lack of information or confusion from false media reports. Traveling to the adjacent county to address a gathering of over 300 was a great opportunity with no associated worry.

Caravanning to the event seemed logical when considering all who desired to go. The needed projectors, screens, and sound equipment were also in tow. When all was said and done, there were six vehicles in the convoy, two of which were ultimately ambushed.

For most of the previous negotiation and speaking engagements, it became customary for Dad to stay back at the refuge. He felt it his obligation to ensure the property be well maintained and respected. Nothing was going to be damaged on his watch. In his mind, trust was a hard commodity to come by. He was not naive enough to believe all who showed up at ground zero to "help" had goodwill. His suspicion and lack of trust was substantiated nine months after his murder. The Oregon federal trial revealed fifteen paid government informants whose only mission was to criminalize the occupiers, then leave.[33]

For reasons unknown, Dad decided to attend the John Day event. Maybe others were pressing him to attend. Hindsight gives rise to some speculation. Shawna Cox, an eyewitness to Dad's murder, revealed in an interview just subsequent to her release from detainment that Mark McConnell, the driver of the vehicle behind them, "kept aggressively pushing everyone to get going and to stay together, insisting he (Mark) be the driver of his expensive vehicle."[34] It was not until months later that the Oregon courts discovered Mark McConnell to be a government-paid informant whose mission was to assist in the ambush that day. He was also tasked with giving FBI continual updates prior to the ambush.

Maybe Dad's willingness to attend the John Day event was due to the occupation's progress. At this point it had been about a month since residents organized into what they referred to as their Committee of Safety. The name given this coalition was like unto other groups in American history who organized in times of political infamy: *The Committee of Safety*[35]. Ammon Bundy, who was the occupation's tip of the spear had traveled to Burns, Oregon a few times, all months prior to the occupation. His aim was to speak with the Hammond family about how he could help. Ammon communicated with the residents and elected officials in an effort to advocate for the Hammonds. In a later chapter I will take you through the history of the Hammond family up to the point of the occupation's beginning. For now, it is enough to know it was their being sentenced to report to the Bureau of Prisons for confinement a second time that sparked enough outrage for people to rally at their front door to show support and respect before they reported back to prison.

The aim of the *Committee of Safety* was that of old:[36] to actively maintain the system of local government to ward off the governing who abuse delegated control. It took great courage for each member to publicly join the newly formed coalition, understanding the tenure of local leadership had been to target and silence anyone in the way of their agenda.[37]

In addition to the committee, perhaps Dad's nerves were calmed just enough to join the traveling crew this time as result of the Grant County, New Mexico cowboy Adrian Sewell, who traveled to Harney County, Oregon for one purpose only. Sewell arrived just three days before the John Day event. His aim was to spearhead a movement that Oregon Senator Ron Wyden likened to a spreading virus.[38] Sewell publicly addressed the U.S. Solicitor General to announce the cancellation of his contractual relationship with the Bureau of Land Management (BLM). He declared he was now taking full responsibility for the management of his ranch including all range improvements.[39] Another cowboy that very night also signed the same declaration. There was an additional family who were residents of Harney County, Oregon scheduled to sign the following Friday. The spirit of freedom was indeed spreading. This momentum possibly put to rest some of Dad's initial concerns that had influenced him to stay back in the past.

Dad's decision to join the group's caravan perhaps came from a number of factors. Whatever the reason, he drove his truck on the roadway. He carried with him as passengers Ryan Payne (right front), Ryan Bundy (rear left), Victoria Sharp (rear middle), and Shawna Cox (right rear).[40]

Shawna Cox communicated later that it was not her intent to accompany them that day. But, due to an immediate need for a videographer for the event, she decided to offer the service. Eighteen-year-old Victoria Sharp was also not expected to be in Dad's truck. Her family had arrived at the refuge a few days prior hoping to provide an element of peace through their performing gospel music. When the Sharp family decided to attend the John Day event to share their talent with the audience prior to heading home, the family started their journey leaving Victoria behind. This was because she was not ready to go. She would ride with Dad.[41]

The vehicle behind Dad was driven by the, at the time, undercover FBI informant Mark McConnell with passengers Ammon Bundy and Brian "Budda" Cavalier, who claimed to be Ammon's bodyguard.

The six vehicles drove U.S. Route 395 to reach their destination. The two vehicles ahead of Dad were the singing Sharp family in the lead, followed by local members of the Committee of Safety. Both vehicles left fifteen to thirty minutes prior to Dad's and Mark's vehicles. According to Shawna Cox, Dad and Mark's vehicles left together per Mark's request. Ten to fifteen minutes behind Mark were two more vehicles, one with media and the other with local residents.[42]

Being late January, the view on the chilly drive was a radiant white. The skies were clear. All anticipated the drive to be a peaceful visit through God's country as respite from the draining controversy.

Upon entering the pine-covered mountains, the road narrowed to two lanes with deep snow banks on either side. It was at this point that Dad and the passengers in his truck noticed a convoy of black unmarked SUVs entering the route behind Mark's vehicle from a shoulder in the road where they had been parked waiting. The shoulder had to have been plowed in preparation for this mission as the fresh snow was knee deep.

Mark's vehicle slowed to a stop behind dad. Ryan Payne, the front right passenger of Dad's vehicle, began urging Dad to stop his truck. He reluctantly slowed at which point Payne stuck his hands out the window to shockingly be fired upon. That was the first shot fired. Payne wasn't hit. The passenger side mirror took the blow. Red laser beads rested upon the heads of everyone in the truck. The agents were unknown to the passengers. All they knew was they were not playing around. Payne insisted on capitulating despite being shot at. Dad stopped the truck for him to get out. He was immediately taken into custody.

Tension was high. Those who remained in the truck felt frightened for their safety. They all wondered, who are these agents? Why had they stopped them? Why did they shoot? Trust was lost.[43] There was no warrant out for the passenger's arrest. No one had been indicted. No laws had been broken.[44] No aggressive behavior warranted the unknown agents' fire, nor the threat of the red lasers. While the controversy of their "legitimate political protest, using the lawful principles and rights pertaining to setting up and attempting an adverse possession claim" was in motion,[45] there was no need for the heavy hand they were experiencing at this moment.

I understand completely how any less informed spectator not knowing the nature of adverse possession law would look at this situation with great skepticism and legitimate questions. Had not they taken over a federal building and ejected personnel? Had not these men been asked to leave? "Commentators in and out of court seemingly boast[ed] in their professed inability to understand how [the occupiers] could possibly justify [their] actions at the Refuge as being within the bounds of law."[46] Why wouldn't they be guilty of conspiracy to impede federal officers by conspiring to use unlawful "force, intimidation, and threats" against government officers? Why wouldn't they be guilty of conspiracy "to overthrow, or to put down, or to destroy by force the government of the United States, or to levy war against the United States, ... or by force to seize, take, or possess any property of the United States"?

To help you understand, I quote Ryan Bundy, who was a passenger in dad's truck and, like all the defendants, was found not guilty of all charges, from one of the occupation trial memorandums. It was drafted seven months after Dad was murdered.

> [T]hese charges relate directly to our right to assert the constitutional fact that the federal government cannot own land within a state, except for specific purposes outlined in the Constitution, and to attempt adverse possession, to return – return it to the rightful owners, including under the Color of Title Act. ... I want to just focus on one particular piece of the law. The refuge – the refuge was empty when we got there on January 2nd. We made sure of that. The main buildings were unlocked. We checked all of the buildings and surrounding property because we did not want any confrontation or violence. Once we verified that the buildings were empty and that there was no one in the surrounding property, we staked

our claim. Some have mocked our efforts. Some have criticized that some of us had firearms in our possession, though we never used them for threats or violence.

... That is what we set out to do. We did it openly, notoriously, and hostilely.

... [But] we did not use violences [sic], and we caused no harm to anyone.

The only bullets that were fired were by the government, and the only force that was threatened and the only guns that were brandished were by the government.[47]

Let's return to the moments just before Dad was shot in the back. Ryan Bundy's cell phone video from the truck that day shows how after Payne exited the truck unidentified agents asked for the vehicle to be turned off. It's important to note here the details of an FBI agent's testimony in court during the previously mentioned trial of FBI agent W. Joseph Astarita. The FBI agent witnessed on the stand that those in the truck were complying with their demands before Payne exited the truck. It wasn't until a weapon was fired at the truck by someone whom the court referred to as Oregon State Police number two, that those in the truck began their nonconformity.[48]

After asking the others what they wanted to do, and receiving a unanimous consensus, Dad chose not to comply with their demands.[49] He then informed the agents who he and Bundy were. He communicated their intent to travel to Grant County to meet the sheriff. Dad, to emphasize the seriousness of their intent to not comply with out-of-control unknown agents who had proven their intent *was to shoot*, tells them to "back down, or stop wasting time and just shoot."[50]

The unknown agents insisted that the women exit the truck. Dad asked and neither Shawna nor Victoria dared exit. In Bundy's cell phone video, we see Dad and Bundy colored in the hue of red from lasers after Payne exited the truck as they asked who the agents were. Remember: the unknown agents had already fired their weapons. "Oregon state police," yelled the men in black with aimed guns.

Upon being apprised of who these agents were, Dad invited them to follow as they travel to John Day to speak with the sheriff. His offer was not well received and was returned with the explicit instructions: "Do as you are told!" The heated argument continued as follows:

> Dad to agents: *"Boys, this is going to get real. You want my blood on your hands, get it done because we got people to see and places to go."*
> Oregon State Police: *"Right now you need to do what you are told."*
> Dad and Ryan B. in unison: *"No, I don't. You need to back off."*
> Shawna, to passengers: *"Where in the heck is Ammon?"*
> Ryan B.: *"We should not have ever stopped."*
> Oregon State Police: *"Turn off your vehicle."*
> Dad, to agents: *"You're wasting oxygen, son."*
> Victoria, to passengers: *"Do they have Ryan P.? Did they arrest him?"*
> Ryan B. and Shawna: *"He should not have got out."*
> Dad, to passengers: *"I am not turning over. I am going to John Day to see the sheriff."*
> Shawna, to Dad: *"Well, if we duck and you drive, what are they going to do, try to knock us out? How much further do we got to go?"*
> Victoria: *"They would probably shoot your tires out."*
> Dad, to Shawna: *"We got about 50 miles."*
> Shawna: *"Tell them to approach the vehicle. Ryan P. is talking to them, right?"*
> Ryan B.: *"Are they talking to him (Ryan P.)?"*
> Dad: *"I can't tell."*
> Shawna: *"I can't even see him (Ryan P.), except the guy behind the door that's got his gun pointed at us."*
> Dad turns up music.
> Shawna: *"Say we have kids in here."*
> Ryan B.: *"Who can we call?"*
> Dad: *"Start calling. Call the sheriff."*
> Victoria: *"I don't have cell service."*
> Ryan B., to Dad: *"Turn that down."*

Dad: *"Okay"*

Dad turns down music.

Shawna: *"Where's my phone?"*

Dad, to agents: *"Boys, you better realize we have got people on the way. You want a blood bath? It is going to be on your hands. We are going to go see the sheriff."*

Shawna, to passengers: *"Call Joseph Rice."*

Ryan B.: *"I don't have his number."*

Shawna: *"I have it."*

Ryan B.: *"What is it? I don't have service!"*

Dad, to agents: *"Better understand how this thing is going to end. I am going to be laying down out here with my blood on the street or we are going to see the sheriff. We have got people en route."*

Shawna to passengers: *"We don't have any service!?"*

Ryan B.: *"I think they..."*

Shawna, to Victoria: *"...yes we do. Hold this camera and listen, take pictures, keep an eye on him, keep an eye on LaVoy."*

Dad, to agent: *"You're wasting your oxygen."*

Victoria, to Shawna: *"Can you take pictures and still have it recording?"*

Shawna: *"Yes, it is recording now."*

Victoria: *"Okay"*

Ryan B., to passengers: *"What is his number?"*

Shawna: *"Just a minute."*

Dad, to agent: *"You need to back down."*

Shawna, to passengers: *"We don't have any service. We have no service here!"*

Dad, to passengers: *"Start calling people. They did it here because there is no service here!"*

Ryan B., to Dad: *"Yeah."*

Shawna, to Dad: *"Yeah, there is no service here at all."*

Ryan B.: *"We should have never stopped. We should have never stopped."*

Dad, to passengers: *"I am going to keep going."*

Shawna, to passengers: *"We are going to have to duck, and what are they going to do with Ryan P.? If we take off, what are they going to do shoot your tires out?"*

Victoria, to passengers: *"We need to get Ryan P. back."*

Ryan B., to Shawna: *"Most likely."*

Victoria, to Dad: *"Why did they pull you over?"*

Ryan B. to Victoria: *"Just because."*

Dad, to passengers: *"Ryan, we are going to go get help. Are you ready?"*

Ryan B., to passengers: *"Well, where is Ammon—those guns?"*

Dad, to passengers: *"They have got him stopped (referring to Ammon's vehicle behind them) We can't get around. I am going to go. Are you guys ready?"*

Ryan and Shawna, to Victoria: *"Get down!"*

Shawna, to Victoria: *"Duck down and give me that camera, GO! Gun it, Gun it!*

Victoria: *"Are they shooting?"*

Shawna, to Dad: *"Keep going."*

Ryan B.: *"What about Ammon and those guys?"*

Dad: *"We can't get around them, I am going to go get help."*

Ryan B.: *"Okay"*

Shawna, to Victoria: *"Stay down."*

Victoria: *"I need my phone so I can call as soon as I get service."*

Shawna: *"Stay down, stay down. Keep watching the phone to see when you get service. I can't even get Joe Rice.*

Ryan B.: *"They are coming up fast."*

Shawna: *"Yeah, they are."*

Ryan B.: *"Okay, I don't know about numbers."*

Shawna: *"Well, I got numbers, but we can't call because we have no service. Mobile network not available."*

Ryan B.: *"Okay"*

Victoria: *"Do you have numbers for people here in town?"*

Ryan B.: *"Yeah, but…*

The truck was then shot at a second time.

> Dad, to passengers: *"Hang on…"*
> Shawna, to passengers: *"They are shooting!"*
> Dad to passengers: *"Hang on…!"*[51]

The truck was shot at a third time.

A "deadman's roadblock"[52] set on a blind curve jumped into view and Dad swerved the truck and slammed into the snowbank to avoid hitting it.[53] This is when the additional two shots were fired at the truck. (I believe these were meant for Dad.) The FBI agent W. Joseph Astarita's trial refers to these two as the disputed shots.[54] He immediately exited the truck with both hands in the air, trying to run away from the truck in knee deep snow.

For quite some time after his murder I would dream the same dream. In the dream I was in the truck with him that day sitting next to him. In every dream as he went to quickly exit, I would wrap my arms around his neck. When I'd wake up, I never could remember my intent in putting my arms around his neck in the dream. Whether it was to prevent him from getting out of the truck or a desire to stand by him until the bitter end, I don't know. In the dream his great strength would always pull us both out of the truck into the knee-deep snow. My legs always flung around his waist. The dream would always end there. I would wake up haunted with anguish wishing I could have preserved his life.

When he exited the snow, he was yelling repeatedly to the many agents surrounding him with aimed weapons dressed in war gear, "Go ahead and shoot me. You're going to have to shoot me. Go ahead and shoot me. You're going to have to shoot me."[55]

I was haunted with many questions for months after Dad was murdered. Why was he yelling this? Of all the things he could have yelled at that moment, for him it was, "Go ahead and shoot me." His *empty* raised hands in the universal sign of surrender communicated his intent of no aggression. The only weapon he ever employed was his powerful voice. Even in his last moments of great stress, he desperately used his voice to leave no doubt where his line in the sand was. In that moment he proved that no form of intimidation could cause his knee to bend.

While he had every right to defend his sacred right to life, for him, killing another human being was never an option. This is why he exited the truck with both hands in the air, *empty*.

Fate, that cold winter day, was the three bullets that penetrated his upper left back torso. The media reported, "Finicum was shot after reaching for a gun."[56] We will forever reject such an erroneous statement. Mom, upon viewing all video footage exclaimed,[57] "The FBI's aerial video was of poor quality, edited and provided no audio.[58] The family asserts that he was shot with both hands up and he was not reaching for anything at the time of the first shot. He was trying to run in knee-deep snow with his hands in the air, a symbol of surrender. When he reached down to his left, he was reacting to the pain of having been shot."[59]

Guy Finicum, Dad's brother, asked how it was that when agents "feel that when their lives are threatened, it justifies the use of lethal force. [Why does this apply only to law enforcement and not citizens?]"

Lasers had rested upon all the passengers' heads. As the U.S. Constitution puts it, "th[eir] right...to be secure in their persons, houses, papers, and effects, against unreasonable searches and seizures," was being violated.[60] Dad's vehicle had been shot at the first stop. He was again shot at two more times before and while he exited the truck at the roadblock. These agents were out of control. Why was fleeing for safety considered unjustified extremism? Why the double standard?

While the outcome of that day was a huge blow to our family, we will forever honor his sacred freedom of conscience. Dad's choices, moments before he was murdered, were the direct result of being threatened by federal and Oregon state law enforcement officers. They escalated the situation. As such, he sought to protect himself and the others in the truck by escaping the life-threatening scene. Their explicit intent was to flee to safety by meeting with the sheriff.

They were not "fleeing felons." There was no warrant out for their arrest.[61] No state or federal laws had been broken. They shot my father. They left him to bleed out in a snow. There was no medical assistance, no charges, no arraignments, no preliminary hearing, no indictment, and no trial by a jury! NO DUE PROCESS! Yet another victim's blood cries from the earth for justice.

The FBI's obscured aerial video of the murder scene seemed to leave many contemplating if this could happen to him, then it could happen to anyone! Our tragedy is the result of rogue governor's rampaging due to unmaintained political boundaries.[62] At the point when the political pendulum has swung too far, history testifies, *'Only by Blood and Suffering'* can lost freedom be regained.

CHAPTER 4

LORDS OF THE MESSAGE

*"Facts are stubborn things;
and whatever may be our wishes,
our inclinations, or the dictates of our passion,
they cannot alter the state of facts and evidence."*
—**John Adams**

AUTHOR'S NOTES

In my youth, for a season, we lived in an old ranch house we called the little white house. Dad inherited the house and a small plot of land from his parents. The house was originally built by his great-great-uncle Jake. If I remember correctly, Jake hand dug a well for the home, which had gone dry by the time Dad got ownership.

Dad, as a young adult, rebuilt the old rundown ranch house to live in. He lived there on and off throughout his life. I faintly remember Dad explaining how he too tried to redig, by shovel, the well. Unfortunately, his toil was to no avail.

To describe it as quaint would be an understatement in comparison to today's modern homes. The house's foundation was anything but 'up to code' and set upon a literal sandy foundation. To give you an idea of the type of sand I am talking about, it is helpful to note that just up the road is the Coral Pink Sand Dunes State Park.

The house has three bedrooms, one bath, and a loft. There originally was no power, (though the family now periodically connects and disconnects solar panels), and there is still no running water. This meant no showers, no blow dryer, no vacuum, no washer, no dryer, no microwave, no radio, and no television.

Don't get me wrong, we did have a tub, blue in color, where we took baths with strict water rations since all our water was hauled. Luckily, I was the oldest and got to go first. I always did feel bad for the younger kids who went last, honest! While I did have guilt, their attitude being much like unto any child who would just prefer to play rather than bathe did help my troubled heart. We even had a matching toilet, which was used only on super cold nights. Otherwise, we would trek out to what we called the cranny (cowboy outhouse), which was positioned about 100 yards south of the house.

While most peering in would think to themselves, "Those poor unfortunate people," I, on the other hand, cherish and am grateful for the time I had at the little white house.

You might ask, "How can this be?" after reading the brief description above.

Within those humble walls, I learned that true peace and happiness is not gained by luxury or from what current culture approves. For me, this was the place where I began to learn how to escape the noise of the world with all its smoke and mirrors to decide upon which Lord of the Message to heed.

"In times of universal deceit, telling the truth is a revolutionary act," said English novelist George Orwell. This condition of universal deceit is a travesty to truth and instigates painful collateral damage. In our case it was the loss of Dad's life.

The name Helmuth Hubener might be one familiar to some. This young boy, just like Dad, was a member of The Church of Jesus Christ of Latter-Day Saints who had unprecedented courage. Hubener's stand was in countering propaganda of the Nazi regime, while Dad's was in standing for the American rule of law against domestic adversaries. Different eras of time, countries, and forms of government, but courage to stand for the harder right just the same.

Hubener's story, just like Dad's, is one that shocks the conscience. At the age of 17, Hubener became the youngest opponent of the Third Reich to be sentenced to death. He was arrested, brutally interrogated, and later tortured in Gestapo prisons, and finally beheaded by guillotine for merely authoring, printing, and anonymously disseminating news he heard on forbidden radio broadcasts. He was charged and executed on the pretense of conspiracy to commit treason against the Nazi regime just as the Oregon occupation defendants were charged with conspiracy against the U.S. government. Many thank God for our current American jury system because Hubener's story is a type of what the fate would have been for the remaining occupation defendants if our jury system was not set in place. Instead the defendants were found not guilty by a jury of their peers.[63]

Hours before Hubener's scheduled execution, he shared his last thoughts on paper. He said,

> *I am very grateful to my Heavenly Father that my miserable life will come to an end tonight — I could not bear it any longer anyway. My Father in Heaven knows that I have done nothing wrong. I am just sorry that I had to break the Word of Wisdom at my last hour. I know that God lives, and He will be the Just Judge in this matter. I look forward to seeing you in a better world!*
> —*Your friend and brother in the Gospel, Helmuth"*[64]

Dietrich Bonhoeffer was a German pastor and theologian. He, just as the previously mentioned young Helmuth Hubener, had unprecedented courage to stand up against the Nazi regime. It was he who preached, "Silence in the face of evil is itself evil. God will not hold us guiltless. Not to speak is to speak. Not to act is to act."

Whether pastor Bonhoeffer's and Hubener's individual stand against the Nazi regime was inadvertently or deliberately aligned, we may never know. What we do know is their fate paralleled one another as Bonhoeffer, three years after Hubener's beheading, was sentenced to torture and execution by hanging at the age of 39.

While this type of conduct was the run-of-the-mill for the Nazi regime, why was the pastor Bonhoeffer worthy of execution? Why was young Helmuth's feeble dissemination of his foolhardy news reviews warrant *his head being cut off*? On a more personal note, why is the taking of my father's life considered by some as justified?

My agonizing soul wanted answers. I wrestled with many tense hours, days, and long nights engulfed in study. My mind could not rest. My digging eventually led me to a study of the spearhead of the Nazi regime. A leader who manipulates a people as an artist molds clay; this was Adolf Hitler in his time.

Hitler's autobiography, *Mein Kampf*, offers influence strategists a chance to be in the mind of the man who successfully controlled enough minds to make possible the execution of shockingly inhumane crusades. Within the pages of his book, Hitler says, "from the child's primer down to the last newspaper, every theater and every movie house, every advertising pillar and every billboard must be pressed into the service subjected to…one great mission."[65] The motto of his rule was the idea that controlling information is as vital as being in command of the military. The proverb 'control the mind, conquer a nation' is the slogan of any leader wishing for success. It is for this very reason America's first amendment sets a firm boundary clearly preventing Congress from making any law respecting "the freedom of speech, or of the press…."

The Nazis cut off the head of that young boy because Hitler was not able to seize control of his mind. The only way to control his voice was to literally cut it off. A critically-thinking mind and courageous voice seems to be enough to risk warranting swift action.[66] In his time, Hitler understood manipulated messages only have power when a populous is not able to conceptualize, analyze, and evaluate information to reach sound conclusions and then chose to defend truth.[67] It seemed Dad's voice was yet another that presented a great threat to modern influence strategists. My studies are showing that such folk truly believe the use of deadly force is justified.

Relying on ignorance, the message, therefore, becomes a means to an end.[68] Hitler said, "what good fortune for governments are people who do not think."[69] He knew every expression, non-verbal or verbal, causes or prevents action.

Such sophistry in messaging is not original to Hitler's malicious intellect. Nor are Dietrich Bonhoeffer, Helmuth Hubener, and my dad the only victims who became collateral damage to such messaging schemes. On the contrary, this destructive process of ill intended messaging and collateral damage began way back in Adam and Eve's day. Their son's tragic murder story is evidence of that.

As unpleasant as it may seem, this process of sifting through ill-intended messaging provides the needed opposition requisite for us to learn how to be an agent unto self, to act rather than be acted upon. Humanity has forever suffered vulnerability to schemes of malevolent messengers. Mankind's charge has forever been and forever will be, to discern who the lords of the messages are and choose loyalty to the lord of truth.

Dad taught me that such a feat is attainable despite being in a fallen world of endless voices. There are woven seeds of intelligence planted in the sinews of all people with the hope we will choose to apply the laws of nature that pertain to the development of intelligence.[70] It is decreed; "For behold, my brethren, it is given unto you to judge, that ye may know good from evil; and the way to judge is as plain, that ye may know with a perfect knowledge, as the daylight is from the dark night."[71]

Dad – Collateral Damage from The Driven Message

It never was an aspiration of our family to make national headline news or to become the spectacle of galleries full of shameful *mocking loud laughter*. We were all just fine with being nobodies. A quiet covenant life of loyalty to *'the laws of nature and of nature's God'* through study of truth, hard work, and personal sacrifice was quite alright.

Lamentably, not all who choose the "harder right instead of the easier wrong" in working to preserve life, liberty, and the pursuit of happiness get the luxury of altruistic privacy.[72] The more I study the more I clearly see the patterns of history unwaveringly showing an inseparable connection between making headway on liberty's journey with intense opposition. While in intense suffering, I have yet to possess the disposition of one hundred percent gratitude to the Lord for the experience. Each time I experience this, my gratitude is deepened for His mercy toward me as I learn line upon line, here a little, there a little.

Avraham Gileadi, in his own way, seconds such a notion. Gileadi is a Hebrew scholar, literary analyst, and author of ten books. His life's work has been dedicated to the study of the prophetic governing themes found in the Book of Isaiah. Gileadi's simplest way of describing the main theme of Isaiah's work is that his prophecies "express man's behavior and its consequences." Gileadi has literally dissected the widely-known complex chiasmuses written by Isaiah, verse by verse, chapter by chapter. As the readers of his ten books venture on the path of discovery with Gileadi in unfolding the meaning behind Isaiah's words, it is learned that "ultimately Israel's [each covenant individual's] destiny is to be humiliated or exalted... [and] in order to be exalted, Israel must first pass through a period of humiliation – for exaltation has a price.[73] ...The wicked of Israel, and all wicked entities... exalt themselves now, persecuting the humble, but in the end God humiliates them. In order to attain exaltation, Israel must exercise compliance and loyalty toward God [in the now]. As God's people prove themselves under duress, God delivers them."[74]

Dad said once, he was a "redneck just doing the right thing. ...never one to poke people in the eye or cause trouble, always stood in line, rose my hand, and [to the day of his last dying breath] never had a parking violation."[75] Never once had a lick of tobacco, nor a drop of alcohol entered his system. Unless ill, his white shirt and tie were religiously fashioned for Sabbath. Reading from scripture, the United States Constitution, and from many other great minds was habitual for him. His choice was God and family rather than idols and the good ol' boys.

Be that as it may, false sound bites delivered from the mainstream media during the 2016 occupation were chess moves in the ever-present political game. Americans repeatedly heard reports describing Dad using buzz words and insinuations such as but not limited to terrorist,[76] right-wing extremist,[77] racist,[78] virus,[79] anti-government,[80] welfare rancher,[81] and militia leader[82]. The occupiers were painted as the outsiders, invaders, and villains. But as you continue on your path of discovery, you will be introduced to a completely different perspective. In the case of Dad, using the word *humiliation* to describe the national attack on his character, might almost be an understatement. Only *every* American following headline news from mainstream media would have read and heard the libel.

Choosing to see life's experiences as sacred tutorials is comforting when recognized the parallelism of Dad's fate to that of Isaiah's prophetic governing theme of "humiliation – for exaltation." The comfort this perspective grants has been a source of power to us as we continue to wade through opposition.

During, and months after the Oregon occupation, we received countless hate letters.[83] There were even a few who went to the extent of sending packages with disturbing material inside. Such efforts seemed to accompany the same goal in mind, which was to intimidate, insult, and speak blasphemy. As disheartening as it was to be the recipient of such darkness, the results solidified three things for us.

First and foremost, these are the end of times as "the love of many [has] wax[ed] cold," just as Jesus Christ foretold would be the case before His second coming.[84]

Second, there is great power in the adage phrase coined by Joseph Goebbels, who ironically was Adolf Hitler's propaganda rockstar in Nazi Germany: "Repeat a lie often enough and it becomes the truth," thus influencing the listeners' behavior and ultimately their destiny. Today's world of psychology might refer to this concept as the *illusion of truth*. The many passionately rude responses we received were the direct result of the many lies told about us and about what the proper functions of government should be.

Thirdly, witnessing the great lengths people would go to discourage the progress of defending the rule of law was a sign indicating that this was a path truly threatening the device of those scheming for that which is contrary to the preservation of life, liberty, and the pursuit of happiness. Those behind conspiracy only become worried and act when truly intimidated. What else might explain the reasoning behind the uncanny resistance key players of the Oregon occupation received before, during, and after Dad's murder? The egregious putrid act of murder, as devastating and unfortunate as it was to lose his great life, was the crowning witness that the occupiers were on to something big. Their petition for a redress of grievance and attempt to stake a claim of adverse possession was pushing the hot buttons of big dollar, behind the scene, the '*powers that be.*'

The Connection of The Powers That Be and Those Driving the Message

Let's return to the idea of those driving the message, the resulting collateral damage, and those behind the scenes pulling the strings of the Oregon occupation.

The local, state, and federal agents took extreme measures to escalate the situation and, as result, those driving the message provoked fear, anger, and division not only in Burns, Oregon, but also across the nation.[85] This division created a well-prepared stage beckoning for a hero to step in and save the day. Make no mistake, the umbrella aim of the those behind the scenes were pushing those driving the message with the force that comes from seasoned relationships nurtured by the purse. The overall aim was dedicated solely to that "one great mission," which in this case, was to cloud political boundaries. Hopefully this book will be a strong witness of the unavoidable butterfly effect such a compromise to the system inflicts upon a people. Dad's murder is one small witness to the reality of the current wretched state of things.

Suggesting there is a connection between the *'powers that be'* and those driving the message is not to suggest journalists across the board cognitively schemed to mold minds with malicious intent to overthrow life, liberty, and the pursuit of happiness. However, the reality of an ever-present continuation of strategy by a select few to bring about a means to an end is being suggested.[86] Plato's *Republic*, which is Plato's leading work that has come to be one of the world's most read works of philosophy and political theory, refers to this select few as *philosopher kings* and labels the ignorant unwashed masses as *producers*.[87]

If we really took time to research independent or smaller media outlets who reported on the occupation, one would discover the man LaVoy, who was called anti-government by large mainstream media, to have actually been filmed during the occupation calmly expressing several times, "I believe in the federal government, we need the federal government, how else are we to protect our borders and keep commerce regular."[88] We would also find the man who was called racist to have said during the occupation, "freedom has no color, it is color blind, it belongs to all race, color, and creed."[89] These messages were not disseminated by large outlets. Why? Because the one beholden to the purse cannot serve two masters.

The FBI released blurry, aerial footage of Dad's murder just days after the fact, but no other footage though the agents were all wearing body cameras. The unanimous outcry of both the political left and right questioned, if it was so important to prove Dad was reaching for a gun to justify the agents use of deadly force, then why not also release the body camera footage of the agents as well, so as to leave no room for doubt?[90]

This was so because those who Plato referred to as philosopher kings understood the opportunity available to cement *their* narrative into a majority of America's minds was a very small window of time. Once the story had come and gone, the ability to disseminate, *in a massive way*, the false narrative to serve *their* cause, would have been lost. It was not until two years after Dad's murder that court proceedings would reveal the FBI agents ordered all in the field that day to turn off their body cameras.[91] Why not follow protocol? What were they hiding?

Facts point to the reality that the agents were seeking to hide details. But as vindicating as that small discovery was for us, most Americans who simply read the headlines still believe Dad to be that crazy rancher who sought suicide by cop. Most people still believe the American agents on duty that day were the heroes who saved the day. The modern-day philosopher kings understood this would be the case.

These modern-day philosopher kings were quite decisive to have made such a quick chess move. Only our echo chamber would follow the story to have unfolded before their searching eyes, years later, the unacceptable lagging details of the agents at play that day.

Lagging Details — Out of Control FBI Agent W. Joseph Astarita

Seventeen long months after Dad's murder, on June 28th, 2017, a federal grand jury in Portland, Oregon "charged W. Joseph Astarita, a member of the FBI's Hostage Rescue Team (HRT) based in Quantico, Va., with three counts of making false statements and two counts of obstruction of justice. Astarita was one of a number of FBI agents assigned to the armed occupation of the Malheur National Wildlife Refuge and was present during the shooting of Robert LaVoy Finicum on January 26, 2016, in Harney County, Oregon."[92]

This agent's trial was not until the summer of 2018, over 30 months after Dad was killed. Just a week before he was to be tried, the judge threw out two of the five charges against him.[93] Despite missing shell casings, agents' flippant conduct, and not following protocol, agent W. Joseph Astarita was acquitted by the jury because there was too much reasonable doubt.[94]

While this outcome came as no shock, the details of the case provided many necessary openings for further discovery in our wrongful death case. The post-verdict interview with the presiding juror was also very curious. This juror communicated being surprised he was even picked to be a juror in such a case. The presiding juror said, officers are always "Heroes.'" He went on to say in an interview with a reporter, "I will always tend to give them the benefit of the doubt. He continued expressing one of the troubling things was the apparent "us vs. them" tension between the FBI and Oregon State Police. He said this animosity came out in the trial testimony. For me the most interesting detail of this juror's interview was his comment that he felt, "it's possible someone is lying." He expounded by offering that he didn't "know which side, or who, or it could be both." He reminded the reporter that there was "still two unattributed shots," and that he felt the people would never know who shot them. The juror again expressed his observation of the "pendulum going back and forth during the trial—from 'oh man, he definitely did it' and then 'well, maybe, he didn't.'" He ended his interview commenting, "It's not my job to know who shot, it's my job to find out if these facts were proven beyond a reasonable doubt, and they weren't."95

Understanding my own pain and frustration as result of this political pendulum swing, I tried to put myself in this juror's shoes. I imagine it must have been incredibly frustrating to sit and watch the *"tension"* between the state a federal law enforcement, knowing in your gut someone was *lying*. Very aware of my suspicion of individuals who manage the delegated sacred controls within our system of government, I can only imagine the seeds of distrust that were planted in the hearts of each juror.

Again, only devout LaVoy Finicum groupies would put the pieces together as truth slowly surfaced. Only those following the story would see it come out in the court of law that law enforcement was colluding together to hide lies. Again, the philosopher kings knew this. The outcome of Astarita's case was of not real concern to those flipping the switch because their mission of creating a false illusion for the majority of Americans was already accomplished.

Lagging Details — Out of Control BLM Senior Law Enforcement Manager Dan Love

In August of 2017, about ten months before the previously-mentioned W. Joseph Astarita trial, Dan Love, senior manager with the Bureau of Land Management's (BLM) Office of Law Enforcement and Security was investigated by the United States Department of Interior for official misconduct. Many of the allegations were substantiated leading to his permanent termination.[96] "Utah's Representative Rob Bishop said he welcomed Love's exit from federal service."[97]

Dan Love is the special agent in charge who oversaw the Bundy standoff in 2014.[98] His alteration of the FBI threat assessment on the Bundy family for the Nevada 2014 situation was ultimately transferred to the Oregon FBI agent in charge, Greg Bretzing, for the Oregon 2016 occupation.[99] This falsified FBI threat assessment influenced the Oregon occupation, ending with my father's blood on the ground. The agents were trained to believe these men were highly dangerous, heavily armed terrorists who were ready to commit an act of domestic terrorism. Understanding this to be the language used to brief the local, state, and federal agents in Oregon about the people involved in the occupation explains why the agents were so amped up for war.

> "Let us remember that a traitor may betray himself and do good that he does not intend."
> —**Tolkien**, *The Return of the King*

Lagging Details — Out of Control Prosecution Team in the United States Vs. Bundy Nevada Case

Not long after Dan Love's exit from federal service and the not-guilty verdict in Oregon, the United States Vs. Bundy trial in Nevada began. After many days and hours of trial, Judge Gloria Navarro was compelled to decide upon a mistrial with prejudice on January 8th, 2018. Navarro's language to explain the reasoning for her decision included phrases describing the prosecutions team conduct as "especially egregious, grossly shocking behavior, constitutional violations, flagrant prosecutorial misconduct who has reckless disregard and willfully failing to produce" exculpatory evidence, therefore committing numerous Brady Act violations. She expressed a great "need to preserve judicial integrity and to deter future misconduct on the part of the government."[100]

While small sound bites from this Justice's language may have been included in written reports, among mountains of data on the web, ironically, her language calling out and condemning the conduct of the individuals involved in both the Bundy Standoff and Oregon occupation was not repeatedly megaphoned on national networks for months on end.[101] Why not? Doing so would have been absolutely appropriate, as the life, liberty, and pursuit of happiness of innocent people were on the line. If convicted, they would have been sentenced to over 100 years in prison. One of the acquitted defendants from the Oregon occupation case lamented by saying, "the media was to be the watchdog for the people but has become the lap dog for the federal government."[102]

Lagging Details — Whistleblower, Larry Wooten Divulging Details of His Out-of-Control Colleagues

Only searching eyes would connect the dots of whistleblower Larry Wooten. Just before the above-mentioned mistrial, Wooten, a lead BLM investigator, took a courageous stand in drafting a 16-page memo,[103] detailing the corruption of key players involved in the Nevada Bundy standoff. It cannot go without saying, the influence of the agents mentioned in this memo were also strongly involved in the Oregon occupation's outcome.

This memo was first shared with a high-ranking Department of Justice official. The previously-mentioned agent, Dan Love, was included in the memo, divulging how he kept and bragged about a 'kill list' of American ranchers whose death he contributed to. The memo explains further how agents on Love's team boasted about maltreating protesters before, during, and after the Bundy standoff. The memo also detailed several suspected violations of law and policy in addition to federal officials exhibiting religious bigotry against members of

The Church of Jesus Christ of Latter-day Saints, as well as extreme prejudice against the Bundy family and their supporters.[104]

Wooten was removed from the investigative team after he "raised concerns that the government was withholding discovery evidence involving Love. Wooten's removal came during the first trial stemming from the Bunkerville standoff. ...Wooten noted he was driven to send the whistleblower memo because his supervisor 'deceptively acted ignorant' and 'dismissive' about his concerns."[105]

Conclusion

While our husband and father was at the mercy of tyrants in government uniforms and a national *Lugenpresse* (German word for *lying press*) in a world of universal deceit, his countenance was calm and at peace. What others consider ultimate humiliation was of no worry to Dad. His peaceful resolve emerged from "it only matter[ing] if God was smiling."[106]

As the 'suits' ruthlessly sought to "exalt themselves" by "persecuting the humble," Dad and others triumphantly pass through their period of humiliation, "prov[ing] themselves under duress," while the tyrants humiliating destiny continues to unfold.

CHAPTER 5

A FORCE TO BE RECKONED WITH

"Courage is found in the most unlikely places."
—**Tolkien**, *The Fellowship of the Rings*

The day Dad was murdered, Mom was thrown into open, political warfare. Overwhelmed, unprepared, vulnerable, disadvantaged, and suffering deep grief, she was still thrust into play. As tempting as the thought of retreating into a private life of solitude was, good conscience could not allow this. Rather, her journey unknowingly mirrored the disposition of the famous patriot Patrick Henry as he expressed, "For my part, whatever anguish of spirit it may cost, I am *willing to know* the whole truth; to *know the worst*, and to *provide for it* [emphasis added]."[107] She, from day one, was determined to see that Dad got his day before a jury and my siblings and I daily stand as character witnesses.

Her selfless life, before the huge turn of events, must not go unmentioned, for it is what primed her to be the powerful force she has become in facing political Goliaths. Prior to the great tragedy, she selflessly went about seeing to the successful fulfillment of what she considered sacred family duties. Her ministering did not stop with just her family, but extended to many others in great need.

Often mothers are undervalued by the world. Thus, becoming one with courage to rise above prejudice demands eternal perspective, long suffering, and patience. While much of her life's work was unsung, her struggles were no less valiant. While very imperfect, she stood firm. She knew the success of society rests upon the backbone of healthy families. The family is the central unit of society. This was one of the many reasons why Mom and Dad chose to provide full time in-home therapeutic foster care. They helped to raise sixty plus young men, while raising their own ten children. Mom and Dad contributed to their communities by helping to mend, heal, and build young men with the hope they would enter their own families, where joy and strong societies are built.

Offering aid to the brokenhearted whose journey had been consumed by shattered dreams is anything but glamorous. Only one whose eye is fixed on the desired outcome would stay the long painful course, knowing full well happy endings are never guaranteed. Yet, for Mom and Dad, the hope for positive change was enough.

Many trying experiences while providing treatment built both Mom and Dad's character, preparing them for what was to come. They lived as if all things

were for their learning. They firmly believed duty called in whatever it was they worked on.

Rewinding further into Mom and Dad's history, their courtship was anything but conventional. In seeking to help interested spectators understand their relationship, Mom often referred to Dad as her Matt Dillon, and herself as his

Kitty from the classic western series *Gunsmoke*. Her analogy was brilliant satire as Dad, just as the character Dillon, was bred for the country dust and she, just as the character Kitty, was primed for the charm of city chandeliers. Dad said once that he moved three times during his entire upbringing and that was from one room to the next, whereas Mom was an army brat. His was a small-town mentality and hers cosmopolitan.

Dad must have somewhat agreed with her satire. To propose to her, he wrote on the back of a heart shaped *Beauty and the Beast* puzzle. He spelled her name wrong! He delivered the package to her work, where she, surrounded by friends, couldn't piece it together quickly enough. The time from their first legitimate date to their tying the knot was just two weeks!

They both had been previously married and carried the emotional scars that accompany divorce. Each had children from their prior relationships, who were, upon their union, joined into one big whole. Mom, who was a working mother of three, overnight became the stay-at-home mother of nine children. The age groups of the children practically meant three sets of twins with a few kids in between. This fresh romance was not the ideal recipe for success. Statistically speaking, the odds were most definitely not in their favor.

Often through the years, people would ask who belongs to whom. I always hated that. I still hate it because our family has toiled and suffered so much seeking to be unified. It is amazing how what can feel like a simple question to a bystander is actually insensitive and damaging. It is enough to know we are an eternal family with no empty saddles.

Despite the odds against them, they, together with their God, pushed through the many difficult days, weeks, months, and even years to eventually come out on top as a successful family. They beat the stereotype: their family would not become a negative statistic. Dad's brother, Guy, once described their relationship as an "unstoppable force [LaVoy] coming in contact with an immovable object [Jeanette]." To this day, their love story is a beacon of hope to many. Their story tells how happiness and healing in family life are possible even in circumstances that others consider impossible.

As mentioned earlier, they together chose a life of service to those they felt were fellow sufferers, with respect to the family unit. The many years of shared parenting in their own family provided a degree of refinement that they were most grateful for, which, when time came, enabled more success in foster care. It is interesting to contemplate when dealing with human relations and suffering how there is a camaraderie among folks who have trekked similar paths. True empathy fuels connection.

In time, Mom and Dad gave birth to a beautiful tradition. During the Christmas season, our family would host a celebration where *all* individuals involved in our journey of uniting families were invited to a gathering at our home to joy in the season. The house indeed almost burst its capacity. Those typically in attendance were child protective service workers (CPS), probation officers, in-home therapists, independent living specialists, licensing workers, foster children, the foster children's parents and siblings, clergymen, Mom and Dad's ex-spouses, neighbors, and Mom and Dad's children and grandchildren. The group would sing carols, exchange encouraging stories, eat food, and play games. On one particular occasion, the in-home therapist who had closely worked with our family and foster children for several years, said with great emotion that the scene before his eyes was one of the most beautiful he had been privileged to witness during his long career of laboring to mend families.

Dad expressed once, "life is about getting back up again and again in humble faith and hope for the joy that awaits those who keep pressing forward, looking to God." This was the legacy he and Mom lived together. The mantle now is left to her, to wear alone, without her helpmate, ...that is, until they meet again, in the life to come.

Just hours before Dad was murdered they shared their last embrace where he said to her, "Jeanette, I love you. Have faith, take courage: God is in charge."

A STRONG WOMAN VS. A WOMAN OF STRENGTH

A strong woman works out every day to keep
her body in shape, but a woman of strength
kneels in prayer to keep her soul in shape.
A strong woman isn't afraid of anything, but a
woman of strength shows courage in the midst of her fear.
A strong woman won't let anyone get the best
of her, but a woman of strength gives the best
of her to everyone.
A strong woman makes mistakes and avoids
the same in the future. A woman of strength

> *realizes life's mistakes can also be God's*
> *blessings and capitalizes on them.*
> *A strong woman walks sure-footedly, but a*
> *woman of strength knows God will catch her*
> *when she falls.*
> *A strong woman has faith that she is strong*
> *enough for the journey, but a woman of*
> *strength has faith that it is in the journey that*
> *she will become strong.*[108]

Jeanette: Liberty's Audrey Hepburn

Audrey Hepburn was a universal icon of beauty, elegance, class, talent, grace, and courage. Within the span of her career, she became one of only fourteen people to have received an Emmy, a Grammy, an Oscar, and a Tony Award. Many admired her.

While Audrey was an accomplished woman of her time, the depth of her character was much more than what met the eye. She was a stunning women of courage who stood for freedom's cause. In her youth, contrary to her parents' political views, Audrey supported the resistance to Nazi Germany. Her influence was felt as a courier for the Dutch resistance movement and a dance performer to raising funds for the cause. She was only eleven years old when the war started.

In her later years, Audrey chose a life of active philanthropy focused on assistance to children and mothers in developing countries. Fate had it that her life would be short as she died at the age of sixty-four. Her legacy of beauty, elegance, class, talent, grace, love of freedom, and courage was left for future generations to enjoy and glean from.[109]

What does this have to do with the Finicum story? Jeanette Finicum, widow of LaVoy, is a lot like her: courageous, gracious under fire, and dedicated to what's right.

After the funeral, we decided as a family that we were going to see to it that the meeting Dad was headed to the day he was shot and killed needed to happen.

We wanted to deliver the message that no form of intimidation could stop our peaceful voices. We called it the 'One-Year Event' because, at this point,[110] it had been a year since Dad's murder.

The tenor of the meeting was as expected. Emotions were elevated. The 800 plus guests came to the 'One-Year Event' with the same questions; how could an innocent, God-fearing man be shot in the back three times by American agents while his hands were up in the universal sign of surrender? The jury acquitting the Oregon occupation defendants just nine months after his murder fueled the fury behind the injustice. If Dad's right to life and due process had not been maliciously taken from him, he would have been home, a free, *living* man![111]

Angie Bundy, the wife of Ryan Bundy,[112] was a VIP guest. At this point, she had not seen her husband for months and endured the pain of knowing the cruel and unusual punishment he was suffering.[113] After the evening's events, she quietly commented that Mom was liberty's Audrey Hepburn.

The media reports prior to the 'One Year Event' used sensationalized language to make it appear that local citizens resented our family for returning to Oregon to host a reenactment of the event Dad was headed to the day he was murdered. The *Associated Press* suggested there was a buzz of fear about what the Finicums' presence could do to their town. Despite the frenzy, we pressed forward with the work of liberty that no form of intimidation could stop.

Amid the rising outrage, the one individual whose overflowing fury would have been completely understandable and who had the force and leadership to wreak vengeance was Mom. But the disposition of the widow of murdered LaVoy Finicum projected a calming influence upon that room full of outraged citizens. Surprising to some that evening, fire and brimstone was not the message. Mom clearly understood how "it is useless to meet revenge with revenge, [as doing so]... will heal nothing."[114] On the contrary, the Finicum matriarch delivered a truthful, credible, authoritative message. Her elegance penetrated the room, leaving tear-filled eyes. She embraced the audience as she gracefully and powerfully admonished all to take courage, get educated, and begin exercising their individual civic authority so as to stop tyranny's path of destruction.

That night, Mom's beauty, elegance, class, talent, grace, love of freedom, and courage was truly iconic. Angie Bundy calling Mom liberty's Audrey Hepburn rang true.

> "We've all got both light and dark inside us. What matters is the part we choose to act on. That is who we really are."
> —**J.K. Rowling**, *Harry Potter and the Order of the Phoenix*

The monumental 'One Year Event' was not the only time her influence had been felt. After Dad's murder, Mom received numerous invitations to speak across the nation. People wanted to hear this shocking story from the source. While she was the victim, often she was the one comforting inconsolable Americans whose devastation climaxed due to the current awful state of freedom and liberty. People were drawn to and trusted her self-effacing nature. There is no doubt strength was Mom's core.

She often started her speeches by expressing she was just the housewife who took care of the kids, made dinner, and cleaned, and how it was Dad who was keen on political issues of the 21st century. Despite her self effacement, the more she talked, the more the listener's hearts were won over. They could see her true colors. Her motive was not for fanfare or money. "It [truly] is a curious thing, ... [how] those who are best suited to power are those who have never sought it. Those who...have leadership *thrust* upon them, and take up the mantle because they must, and find to their own surprise that they wear it well."[115]

Not far into her liberty tour, it became apparent that FBI and BLM agents were attending her events with ill intent. For one particular event in Colorado, these agents went so far as to contact local law enforcement, trying to become deputized with the intent of raiding the event.[116] Luckily, the local law enforcement did not permit the raid. It would have been devastating for me as my children were in attendance, not to mention all the innocent citizens of that community.

The host of the Colorado event was not made aware of these agent's tactics until after the event. This host did her due diligence before approaching us with details, knowing how important it was to deliver verifiable information. After enough evidence was gathered, we were informed. Upon being informed of their chess move, it became our turn.

To us it was clear the focus of our move should be to peacefully communicate that intimidation tactics would not halt progress. I drafted a letter with the help of my applied civics mentors.[117] Mom and I both delivered this letter to our district's elected officials. A second event was strategically organized at that same location. The exact speech that was given at the previous event was again delivered, understanding that personnel with ill intent would be in attendance. The purpose of doing so was to show there was no conduct or language in the previous event that warranted a raid by the government agents.

Next, the host provided the audience with a detailed explanation of what had taken place prior to the last event. The audience was shocked to hear how FBI and BLM agents approached local law enforcement with the goal of raiding the previous event. They were outraged with their local governors' libeling them as sovereign citizens as defined by the FBI's lexicon.[118]

Our goal was threefold; first inform the local citizenry of the underground work taking place in their hometown; second, ignite applied civics to promote responsible government; and third, send a powerful message that tactics of intimidation would not silence the Finicum family.

During the second event,[119] news came out that the jury in Oregon had acquitted the Oregon occupation defendants. The audience cried with mom and me. We prayed together in gratitude. The moment was very bittersweet! The innocent men Dad stood with were vindicated-but Dad was still dead.

Once again, Mom's grace was on display. She shed tears for the victory of others despite her own great loss. The crowded room understood her tears of joy and sadness. There was a unanimous silent reverence and respect for the woman's dignity and courage to press forward. It would seem incredible that any undercover FBI or BLM agent who witnessed this moment would not have their consciences deeply seared!

Indeed, Angie Bundy was right, Mom was again liberty's Audrey Hepburn! She was then and continues to be an example of what a beautiful woman of strength is. Her life experience testifies that as she turns to God, nothing is impossible. Even if the very jaws of Hell in the form of corrupt out-of-control government agents refusing to be governed by the confines of the United States Constitution, "gape open the[ir] mouth wide after [her husband]," she knows "these things shall give...experience, and shall be for [her] good."[120]

CHAPTER 6

SPEAKING THE LANGUAGE OF LIBERTY

"Now the Lord is that Spirit: and where the Spirit of the Lord is, there is liberty."
—**2 Corinthians 3:17**

The very moment Dad found himself in Oregon, I was thrust into the world's most ruthless crash course on the raw nature of preserving—in a fallen world—life, liberty, and the pursuit of happiness. All at once, the delicate balance between preserving and losing these rights was no trifling matter. My Dad was occupying a federal building while local, state, and FBI agents prepared for an advance, for heaven's sake!

While Dad's judgment through the years had always proven sound, which nurtured for me a deep respect for him and his points of view, his poised participation in the occupation created in me an unyielding urge to find out for *myself* whether or not Dad had lost his mind due to some kind of midlife crisis. After all, Dad was mortal and not exempt from humanity's fallen state. As foreign as not just taking his word for it felt to me, this I could not, in good conscience, blindly accept.

I prayed. I prayed like I had never prayed before. I received no heavenly messenger, but over time my mind was gently guided. Here a little, there a little, I began to see and understand. I remember at one point I was distinctly directed to a scripture passage in 1 Nephi 11:1 of the Book of Mormon. I can honestly say I had read over this passage probably thousands of times through my many years of study, but, at this moment, its message burned in my mind and heart.

For those who may not be familiar with the context of 1 Nephi, Nephi was the son of Lehi, a man unshakably loyal to his God. Lehi was a prophet of his time who delivered warnings of what might become the downfall of his beloved hometown, Jerusalem. No one cared to listen. Actually, people thought he was a little on the crazy side. The opinion of the townspeople seemed to be that nothing could destroy the great city of Jerusalem. I'm sure they treated Lehi like he was a crazy, old man who should just go home and give it a rest. However, Lehi drew his firm line in the sand by doing and saying what the Lord would have him do and say.

One night, in a dream, the Lord advised Lehi to take his family and leave Jerusalem. Why? This was because Jerusalem's destruction was imminent, and the Lord always warns His faithful servants. So, Lehi took his family and obediently left his comfortable homestead. He, without hesitation, left his inheritance to wander in an unknown wilderness for many years. Eventually, they did arrive at the place prepared for them by God.[121]

At the beginning of this wilderness journey, Lehi was privileged to be given a symbolic vision of *the* tree of life. While Lehi's children wandered in the wilderness with him, not all were converted to what they perceived as *Dad's crazy ideas*. Some resented their father for making them leave their home, gold, silver, and precious things only to suffer in the wilderness. Not all could understand why they left. Nor could all grasp the symbolism of his vision, let alone its application in their life.

Despite some of his siblings' disbelief, Nephi's reaction, on the other hand, was one of love and respect. He trusted his father. Because of his humility (and the rapport father and son must have enjoyed), Nephi didn't quickly fall sway to discrediting his father on the pretense that he was old and senile. Rather, he desired to understand the things that his father so boldly witnessed of. He decided to approach God for help. Nephi wanted to understand.

This brings us right up to the point when Nephi said,

> *For it came to pass after I had desired to know the things that my father had seen, and believing that the Lord was able to make them known unto me, as I sat pondering in mine heart I was caught away in the Spirit of the Lord, yea, into an exceedingly high mountain, which I never had before seen, and upon which I never had before set my foot. And the Spirit said unto me: Behold, what desirest thou? And I said: I desire to behold the things which my father saw. And the Spirit said unto me: Believest thou that thy father saw the tree of which he hath spoken? And I said: Yea, thou knowest that I believe all the words of my father.*
>
> *And when I had spoken these words, the Spirit cried with a loud voice, saying: Hosanna to the Lord, the most high God; for he is God over all the earth, yea, even above all. And blessed art thou, Nephi, because thou believest in the Son of the most high God; wherefore, thou shalt behold the things which thou hast desired.*[122]

While the epic story continues on, with all its intrigue, ageless wisdom, and sweet doctrine, we will stop there for the purpose of my story. When I read this for the "nth" time, my soul was filled with much needed peace and comfort. I no longer felt utterly alone in my deep yearning for understanding. I was reminded how Nephi, a man I read about and highly respected, was once in the same dilemma as I. Reading Nephi's path of discovery provided me comfort and courage. Just as he did, I too had the great promise available if I chose to approach my God with real intent. So, I prayed, again and again and again.

In answer to my prayers, I never "was caught away in the Spirit of the Lord... into an exceedingly high mountain," nor did I receive any heavenly messenger.[123] What I did receive, in increments over a long period of time, was overwhelming feelings of peace, calm, and confidence that Dad was right. This peace was food for my soul. It silenced the *many* critics' voices in their debate as to whether or not my Father was an unhinged fanatic or a fearless hero.

I had done the work of the soul and found out for *myself*. This energized me. As result, I completely and very openly supported Dad's exercise of his sacred freedom of conscience despite the danger of the situation. This marked a point of no return in my life. In ways I never imagined, my new path opened unanticipated understanding of the eternal law of "opposition in all things" and the power available through the use of choice in response to opposition.[124] Despite the deep wrestle this has provided, I am forever grateful for the gifted refinement that has come.

As I mentioned briefly in a prior chapter, one result of my due diligence was my choice to travel to Burns, Oregon during the heated occupation to help with the occupation's media. While I will never regret that decision, the school of painful opposition in my personal life began as direct result of my choice. It was a crazy time that forever changed me. Be that as it may, I believe the blessings of peace came and continue to come in increments because the Lord understood the opposition I would face as I sought to support my father during the occupation and now my Mother after Dad's murder.

I openly supported Dad, though strange to some, after his murder. While some people believed and some even unsparingly vocalized their opinion that the tragic ending with him bleeding out in the snow was evidence of his extremist stand, I still am at complete peace and hold firmly that he was right and that his spirit is okay and clear of conscience before God. I had always heard the quote of the Prophet Joseph Smith,

> The time will come when the government of these United States will be so nearly overthrown through its corruption, that the Constitution will hang as it were by a single hair, and the Latter-day Saints—the Elders of Israel—will step forward to its rescue and save it.[125]

I just never dreamed my dad would be one of those "Elders of Israel" on the bloody front line.

As I pressed on, I continually found myself surrounded by myriad voices, all at war with their words. I felt like Mom and I were living the life of Katniss from *The Hunger Games* as we were unwittingly thrust into political warfare.

Depending on the voice, this sick game made our beloved husband and father either the most recent *poster boy martyr for liberty* or a *good-for-nothing dead terrorist*. No matter the truth, it was deep emotion that drove such statements and, again, another example of "opposition in all things."

As mentioned at the beginning of this chapter, the raw nature of preserving life, liberty, and the pursuit of happiness in a fallen world is no trifling matter. These issues affect real people. When life, liberty, and the pursuit of happiness are violated, naturally raw emotions erupt. The fate-determining question is then left hanging: will such emotions generate opposition to the spirit of *liberty or captivity?*[126]

My reality was my father being shot three times in the back and left to bleed out in the snow. I was bleeding; we were all bleeding! There was no way to escape the reality of our involuntary fishbowl life. The political red and blue, right and left watched to see what our response was going to be. What would we speak and perpetuate, the language of liberty or the language of captivity?

We were not perfect by any means, but I can honestly say we diligently sought to rise above the hell we felt, so as to be an honorable beacon for liberty. While every walk of life claimed to speak liberty's dialect, I could see an apparent lack of basic, foundational knowledge as to what preserving freedom and liberty requires. It seemed mindless reactional fear was the moving force for many. Fear's emotional comrades are always limiting, contentious, manipulative, discouraging, etc., which are often manifest in anger. We know it is these emotions that foster war. As we stumbled along seeking to rise above a captivity mindset, we were blessed with specific people who were prepared in unique ways to offer their rare support so that we might be as successful as possible in speaking the language of liberty to all whose paths we might cross.

Fear seemed to be a common theme for a majority of the liberty events we attended. From my perspective, the result of such events seemed counterproductive. Much focus and energy were spent in discussion about *national or global powers* that seek to destroy freedom and liberty. The audience could not help but be consumed with fear's comrades. While there is an argument to be made for understanding the tactics of opposition, "preoccupation with unworthy behavior can lead to unworthy behavior."[127] It seems fair to say a way to safeguard against this would be a shift of focus from obsessing about the reality of conspiracy to simply acknowledging it exists.[128] This shift will open up more time and energy that can be dedicated to learning sound principles of free government and more time for the necessary processes of check and balance and troubleshoot and fix that a free government requires. As we press forward with forward thinking and proper training, we naturally become a true leader who meets people where they are and patiently leads them higher one step at a time.

As I continued to attend different liberty events, I was deeply confused and troubled because I knew isolated painstaking research into legitimate conspiracy and the preaching of its reality was not going to change the destiny of this nation. In my mind, this conspiracy base technique to prick the hearts of Americans into action was extrinsic.[129] Rather than extrinsic fruits of skeptical fear driving motivation, I wanted hearts converted and driven by truth. My soul was screaming, "Don't just talk about the problems. Let's spend our energy learning how to apply principle to empower everyone in their effort to troubleshoot and fix."

Despite my understanding of where focus needed to be, I found myself stuck in this *time-sucking black hole* wondering why so many others were also stuck there. I was in great need of deliverance if I were ever to really make a positive difference. As time continued to pass, I found myself desiring less and less to attend *liberty*-themed events because the topics covered seemed to only prolong my stay in the *black hole*. I grasp how our story could be a shock to the conscience of those sitting on the fence in the audience. It may even have a force and effect to get them moving, hopefully in the right direction. Nevertheless, I hated sitting through hours of conspiracy talk with no time spent on fundamental political doctrine and how to apply its principles.

At first I was happy to represent our family at events as a witness of how nasty things had gotten. But as I began to recognize the low percentage of individuals actually willing to sacrifice their time and talent to learn how to effectively apply civics, I began to feel like an ugly showcased puppet whose job was simply to entertain the room full of blank-faced people. Each person who came to be entertained listening to our tragic story but was still unwilling to get out of their comfort zone and stretch themselves seemed a mockery of our family's pain. Often my heart was burdened with the temptation to resent the entire human race for complacency.

For several months after Dad's murder, this type of negative energy was very fierce. Try as I might to hold it all in, my intense emotions began manifesting themselves. I was unable to engage in conversation about politics without my heart rate dangerously rising and my skin flushing a deep red. While I never said so out loud, my soul projected fire and brimstone toward *any* elected, appointed, or employed governor.[130] My overwhelming grief blamed all of them for the murder of my father. I suffered from the pains that deep hatred cause. In my mind, I was also hostile toward select groups who abandoned me in my greatest time of need.

I knew my heart needed healing and changing. I was taught at a very young age and personally studied the doctrine of forgiveness my entire life. I knew it would be my love and loyalty to God that would allow my wounds and fears to be dispelled. I had the sure knowledge that, as I chose to refocus my sight upon the eternal perspective of my mortal life experiences, I would be blessed with peace and healing to endure and press forward on the covenant path.

While allowing myself time to be healed through the grace of God, I had several powerful experiences that taught me the things of God as well as the fallen nature of humankind. I am going to share one in particular that unveiled another element of my life that needed changing if deliverance from all captivity-stricken areas of my life was truly wanted. This event revealed the state of my subconscious with respect to my relationship with the governing to be very toxic. I am sure you are thinking, *No kidding. You unjustly blamed them all for the murder of your father.*

I realize that was completely discriminatory now that I have successfully ebbed and flowed through each step of the grieving process while suffering in a fishbowl. What I am saying is that the incident I'll relate helped me see deeper. What I gained from this specific occasion was insight into human behavior and its consequences in relation to personal captivity resulting in a perpetuation of captivity in communities, towns, cities, counties, states, and eventually nations.

When talking with a friend of mine about this experience, we noted how easy it is for anyone to become a contributor to the very thing they say they oppose- without even fathoming it.

It seemed my fate at this time was to go through the intense heat of the refiner's fire. (And to think, I had previously regarded sibling squabbles as extreme!) Nevertheless, I was willing to embrace the refinement. After all, I had prayed with real intent. I know I was strengthened to press forward in humility; otherwise, I would have crawled into a dark cave and died.

Shortly after Dad's murder, I attended one of Congressman Jason Chaffetz's meet-and-greets in Utah County. He was, at the time, my representative and just so happened to be a chairman of the United States House Committee on Oversight and Government Reform. I, as his constituent, knew I needed to establish some type of relationship with him as our family was collecting thousands of signatures for the purpose of petitioning for a congressional investigation into the murder of Dad. The emotions I experienced prior, during, and after meeting with him were very telling of my state of being. I will try to describe my thoughts as clearly as possible to help you understand:

First and foremost, I suffered from fear:

› He was superior while I was subordinate.
› He had power while I was powerless.
› He was part of the all-powerful system with an endless money supply that can take life while I could do nothing to preserve it.
› He could speak while I could not.
› He had mysterious charisma, while I felt timid, broken, and obnoxious.
› He had control while I did not.
› It was them against me.
› His clout and prestige made his voice more important while mine was silenced by label lynching.[131]
› The attitude projected that evening was as if he was smart and I was not.
› He was tall and I was short.

> Frankly, *he was a political god while I was just a person.*

I wish I could ask if this description is familiar to my readers. I think I'm safe to assume there are others out there who, just like me, have sought to connect with their political representatives about deep concerns associated with the preservation of life, liberty, and pursuit of happiness. I wonder how many of you walked away feeling the same as I had at Congressman Jason Chaffetz's meet-and-greet.

That evening, I walked away very discouraged wondering why I bothered to put myself out there. The big, bad government was too powerful. It didn't help that my representative seemed to struggle being human with a tear-filled, heartbroken person sitting right in front of him. While he heard what I had to say, he was impersonal and cold.[132] These emotions were very raw and real. I was defeated before I even showed up. Why?

A few months later, I discovered something that was alarming yet comforting in an absurd way. I found that my experience that day mirrored the observation of Frédéric Bastiat, a French economist who lived over 200 years ago. To describe the dynamic he witnessed, he said, "the relations between [governed] and the [governor] appear[ed] to be the same as those that exist between the clay and the potter."[133] Such a culture teaches the governed to become docile while the governors take "possession of omnipotence."[134]

As embarrassed as I am to admit it, this experience did indeed make clear to me my regard for the system and *its* agents as worshiped *golden calves* of old. Even as inadvertent as my state of being was, I felt pathetic months later when I realized exactly what my thoughts and actions were really doing. At that point, I was sick inside but couldn't quite put my finger on as to why.

If thoughts equal words, words equal action, and action equals destiny, what then was to be my destiny if my political paradigm did not change? After many sleepless nights wrestling with the results of this experience, a good mentor of mine said, "Remember, the governmental system and those *controlling it* are not a golden calf unless the people worship *it* and treat *it* as if *it* is superior and animate."[135]

For a time, I questioned how it was that I had become like the fallen Israelites from the Old Testament. Any student of the Bible knows their destiny was to be stricken with captivity as they continued to worship false gods in thought, word, and action. This new sense of awareness caused me great sorrow because I supposedly knew what the fallout would be if I did not watch myself continually as I had often read and pondered Mosiah 4:30:

> ...this much I can tell you that if ye do not watch yourselves, and your thoughts, and your words, and your deeds, and observe the commandments of God, and continue in the faith of what ye have heard concerning the coming of our Lord, even unto the end of your lives, ye must perish. And now, O man, remember, and perish not.

My experience with my congressmen burned a crater in my heart and brain. It was then that I realized I had a major paradigm shift to make within my conscious and subconscious if I really wanted deliverance from the *black hole* I was stuck in. That day I realized that I obviously did not understand the shared control system the founders established and entrusted to the hands of the American people. Nor did I understand my powerful role as a partner in shared control of the government system's function. I was, likewise, deeply humbled to recognize how I was also forgetting where power truly originates. I am not subordinate, and governmental agents are not superior. We are equal in power given by our Maker. The degree of control within the system might be different, but we are equal in power. They are to be public servants and I, a governmental system maintenance provider.

I had been speaking the language of captivity. This was devastating. What added weight to this new burden was my ability to now clearly see hundreds and hundreds of others I had thus come in contact with who valiantly voiced loyalty to liberty's cause, who were also dangerously and unknowingly speaking the language of captivity and thus perpetuating its ugly existence. This realization was almost too heavy for me to carry. I found myself wondering what was to be the destiny of a nation found with countless people who think, breathe, and act in captivity under the guise of liberty's sacred cause? What could I do to cure myself of this ongoing universal plague of captivity and influence others to do the same?[136]

To compound things a little more, at that moment in time, my interactions with the governed weren't much better than my described experience above. If I was not careful, my voice was what my husband likened unto a firehose, knocking well meaning, sincere, people over with unsolicited data. I understand clearly now how it is this very type of conduct that causes people to turn away and rant to their friends about our tin foil hats. For a short while, despite my husband's feedback, I didn't care that I was fire hosing people and driving them away. I was going to talk about my father's murder every chance I got because, in my mind, people needed to know the state this nation was in.

Only by the grace of God was I, in time, able to develop a healthy temperance, for the sake of myself, my loving husband, and others. This temperance has softened my voice and enabled me to be a little more patient, longsuffering, mindful, and respectful of others' path of discovery. However, I'm still a work in progress. Are not we all?

I was working through my process of grief while learning from the political muddy trench I was in. At least I was now very aware of my vulnerability to quickly shift from positively countering opposition to be a contributor to it. For this reason, my choice became to just sit back and observe. This was a powerful tool for me. I began to recognize patterns of human interaction. Either there was a true support of liberty or something quite contrary. I noticed the magnitude of loss of liberty was always dependent upon the amount of education, charity, brotherly kindness, and temperance each individual had. As I sat back and watched, it became clear that a safety boundary was necessary for me while I was yet vulnerable. I had to surround myself with those whose language spoke liberty. This was food to my soul. I wanted this. I craved this. I believe most others do as well.

Please know this is not to suggest I was choosing to re-enter the delusion that all was well and thus close my eyes to the active work of darkness. I don't think I could ever do that. My dead father will forever be the painful reminder that all is not well. What I am saying is positive, solution-based, hopeful, and forward-thinking language and action was what felt right. This type of positive energy gave me a sense of hope in what felt like a hopeless situation. I had to choose hope because I knew all too well what the antithesis was again, the *miserable, political, time-sucking black hole*. I was not going back. I was not powerless because my Maker breathed life into me.

As I pressed forward, my spirit constantly pled with God to be gifted the talents of longsuffering, brotherly kindness, charity, temperance, faith, and hope as I continually was confronted with people fixed upon problems rather than solutions. My mind can't help but compare this situation to the Israelites who lost life because of a fixation on the serpents advancing at their feet rather choosing a focus on the readily available solution.[137] My chosen path was and is one of "no aggression, no hate, but [a deep] willing[ness] to [competently] stand" as gently as possible but as firm as necessary in defense of life, liberty, and the pursuit of happiness (property).[138] I will do this forever seeking to truly speak the language of liberty.

I now direct my focus to you. Do you claim to work for liberty but inadvertently promote captivity?[139] I invite you to take a courageous honest look within yourself. Think for a moment the type of feelings you leave people with. Is your sole focus on negative energy? If so, this is a dangerous place to be. In such a state there's hardly much left for the work that forward-thinking, positive action requires.

> "You must be the change you want to see in the world."
> —**Mahatma Gandhi**

Please know my intent is not to lecture. You must understand by now that I, of all people, understand how easy it is to be found with contentious, divisive, manipulative, and contemptuous thoughts, feelings, and language about individuals and programs we believe to be key players in the downfall of freedom and liberty. However, if we truly are on liberty's side, our mission must be twofold:

yes, know the enemy, but most importantly, actively choose a relentless focus on positive solutions to see them realized. To accomplish such a feat, our system and forms of government must be completely understood and maintained.

For a comprehensive training on applied civics please visit: centerforselfgovernance.com

If you're from the state of Utah, consider subscribing to Defending Utah: defendingutah.org

---

FOOD FOR THOUGHT

"These things I have spoken unto you, that in me ye might have peace. In the world ye shall have tribulation: but be of good cheer; I have overcome the world."[140]

"Fear not, little flock; for it is your Father's good pleasure to give you the kingdom."[141]

"For they all saw him, and were troubled. And immediately he talked with them, and saith unto them, Be of good cheer: it is I; be not afraid."[142]

"Therefore, fear not, little flock; do good; let earth and hell combine against you, for if ye are built upon my rock, they cannot prevail."[143]

"And there shall be earthquakes also in divers places, and many desolations; yet men will harden their hearts against me, and they will take up the sword, one against another, and they will kill one another.

And now, when I the Lord had spoken these words unto my disciples, they were troubled.

And I said unto them: Be not troubled, for, when all these things shall come to pass, ye may know that the promises which have been made unto you shall be fulfilled."[144]

CHAPTERS 7–10

DAD'S RUBICON — OREGON

CHAPTER 7

HISTORY OF HAMMOND RANCHING FAMILY

*"Courage is being scared to death
but saddling up anyway."*
—**John Wayne**

The cowboy was once the great American icon. A picture of the open range and a cowboy represents the first settlements of this nation, which was the manifestation of a people not willing to be ruled by arbitrary authority any longer. Such a character embodied all the qualities that America was built on: love for country, self-governance, loyalty, fear of God, hard work, honesty, and self-reliance.

Be that as it may, current organizations tirelessly seek to extinguish the herdsman's way of life through regulation on the pretense that their lifestyle is detrimental to nature. On the contrary, the cowboy's stewardship of the land equates to much more than what is portrayed as the driving force behind organized language in modern legislation.[145] The shameful result of such language is that many plants and wildlife that share the land with cowboys now possess more rights in their habitat then the cowboy does in his. To be clearer, this is denying human beings their right to life, liberty, and pursuit of happiness. How can this be?

Let's discuss the Oregon cowboys Dwight and Steven Hammond.

Extreme controversy surrounded the United States v. Hammond case. These cowboys became a lavishing spectacle for cooperative federalist communities whose aim has been for decades to eliminate geographic county and state political boundaries.[146] The atrocious lengths taken to accomplish such a feat has been the cause of great suffering upon many across this nation. In the case of the Hammonds, not only did they suffer through egregious tactics of intimidation but blatant gross violation of the United States Constitution, and yet most people went on with their lives not skipping a beat.

Not Dad. He watched, diligently studied, and became all the more concerned for the freedom and liberty of this nation. Before deciding to travel to Oregon, he did not know a small group of acquaintances were also studying the Hammonds' case. He and his acquaintances were unknowingly and simultaneously growing all the more uneasy. Dad would have never guessed his fate would be to join these associates in protest. All he knew at the time was the Hammond family to be innocent victims of label lynching, intimidation, legislation abuse, and targets of "cruel and unusual punishment."[147] While it's debatable, some even suggest they were "subject for the same offence to be twice put in jeopardy of life or limb."[148]

To understand fully what got Dad to the state of Oregon in the cold winter of 2016, you must first review the long history of abuses that surrounds the Hammond family and Harney County, Oregon. Only after will you begin to understand why he, a quiet homebody, a family man, a ranching cowboy, and one willing to defend the Constitution would act upon the strong inclination to travel fifteen plus hours just to rally with a few acquaintances and mostly complete strangers.

There is definitely more than meets the eye in this story.

History of Hammond Family and Harney County, Oregon

In the mid 1800s people started settling in what they called the Blitzen Valley. This area is now the political boundary of Harney County, Oregon. The people were attracted to this valley because the soil was rich and there was water. Water meant life. The old saying often uttered by sons of the West was "whiskey's for drinkin', water's for fightin'."

Early settlers established what's now known as the Hammond ranch in the aforementioned Blitzen Valley. It was then that the people mixed their labor with the natural resources to establish a cutting-edge irrigation system to water the meadows.[149] This enabled several ranchers to run their cattle in the area. Word has it that the forage there was able to sustain over 300,000 head of "fat and sassy" cattle.[150] This meant delicious steaks, roasts, and ground beef for thousands of American families.

This water infrastructure not only improved the forage for the cattle but also attracted all other living creatures. The Blitzen Valley became what Little Foot in the well-known motion picture *The Land Before Time* called the "Great Valley." One 81-year-old local citizen, who was born and raised in Harney County, called the Blitzen Valley the jewel of the county. This jewel, by nature, became the stopping place for many migrating birds on their annual trek north. One in particular to frequent the area was the *red-crowned crane*. This particular bird is also known as the Manchurian crane or Japanese crane and is among the rarest cranes in the world. The land, with its water, was inviting to all.

In 1908, President Theodore Roosevelt created an "Indian reservation" around three Oregon lakes; Malheur, Mud, and Harney. In so doing the area was established "as a preserve and breeding ground for native birds." Later this "Indian reservation" became what is known today as the Malheur National Wildlife Refuge. This "Lake Malheur Reservation" was the "19th of 51 wildlife refuges created by Roosevelt during his tenure as president. At the time, Malheur was the third refuge in Oregon and one of only six refuges west of the Mississippi."[151]

The Hammond family bought an Oregon ranch in the Harney Basin in the year 1964. They acquired roughly "6000 acres of private property, four grazing rights on public land, a small ranch house, and three water rights.[152] The ranch is around 53 miles south of Burns, Oregon."[153]

Just six to ten years after the Hammond's purchase, a majority of the neighboring ranches next to Blitzen Valley were procured by the United States Fish and Wildlife Service (FWS). Ironically, the land the FWS acquired was joined with the Malheur National Wildlife Refuge. "The refuge consists of over 187,000 acres of habitat which include wetlands, riparian areas, meadows, and uplands. The refuge lands are configured in roughly a 'T' shape, 39 miles wide and 40 miles long."[154] Through the years, the aim of those directly and indirectly managing the refuge seemed to always be to expand its borders. Over time, the refuge grew and eventually surrounded the Hammond's ranch.

Despite consistent efforts to get the Hammonds to sell, the Hammonds and a few other ranchers refused every time they were approached by FWS. For this reason, Fish and Wildlife Service (FWS) and the Bureau of Land Management (BLM) aimed to increase deed transfer of privately-owned land to *federally owned* land for the purpose of increasing control, in a little more aggressive way. Those who had respectfully refused to sell were arbitrarily informed, "grazing was detrimental to wildlife and must be reduced," and as result 32 out of 53 permits were retracted, forcing many to seek a livelihood elsewhere. In other words, they were put out of business. For those who remained, grazing fees were substantially raised. At that point, the refuge maintenance team asserted claim upon the irrigation system that the early settlers established. I want to stop here and reiterate that such a property right cannot legally be taken without just compensation. The deed of this water property right had been transferred from one owner to the next through the years via purchase starting with those who had prior appropriation. The first settlers mixed their labor with the natural resources that had no existing claim, thus creating a water property right for themselves that legally could be sold.[155]

By the 1980s, strife began involving water distribution with respect to the nearby privately-owned Silvies Plain. Yet again, FWS had its eye on the privately owned Silvies Plain ranch lands. The tactic used to gain possession of ownership this time was egregious. Refuge employees deliberately rerouted water away from the large meadowlands, causing the flow to rise in the Malheur Lakes. They only had to wait 24 to 36 months for the lakes to double in size. As result, thirty-one ranches on the Silvies plains were flooded.[156] The abstract of the 1986 Malheur Lake Flood Damage Reduction Study in Harney County, Oregon clearly revealed the intended mode of how to manage "current and future flooding cycles. [It stated the option was a] diversion of water from the lake to the Malheur River; [followed by the] purchase of flooded lands."[157]

Never mind the people's lives and liberty spent in blood, sweat, and tears to build and improve upon their homes, corrals, barns, livestock, water, and forage. This was their sacred heritage, their pursuit of happiness. Nevertheless, the destiny for these Oregonians was penned by bureau agents with the intent to strategically rise waters and leach away their property. Why? Because the federal overlord said so. The ranchers who had kindly declined the previous FWS offer to purchase their land were shown who was boss and were drowned out. The ranchers now only had one choice, swallow their pride and grovel at the feet of FWS, entreating them to now buy the swamp land. In 1989, the waters began to recede and the once thriving privately-owned Silvies Plains became the boasted section of the Malheur National Wildlife Refuge.

By the 1990s, the Hammonds were among the few who held firmly onto their private property, which was adjacent to the refuge. The Hammond matriarch began digging through mountains of history in an effort to discover why it was that their right to property ownership was so deeply under attack. She found a study done in 1975 by the FWS hidden in a mountain of public record. Ironically, the study showed the "no-use" policies of the FWS pertaining to the refuge were resulting in wildlife leaving the refuge to find a more appealing habitat. As she continued to read, she could hardly believe the results of the study, confirming for her what she already knew to be true. The results of the research indicated how the private property next to the Malheur Wildlife Refuge generated four times more ducks and geese than that of the refuge, whose sole aim was to provide a safe appealing environment for birds. She read on to find the research indicating migrating birds were more inclined to land on private property rather than on the refuge. In her excitement hoping for some type of recompense, Mrs. Hammond brought this study to the FWS's attention. Unfortunately, the result of unveiling this study was reprisal from federal agencies.[158] Heavy-hearted, she tucked away the study in the three-ring binder where the many other pertinent documents to their case were organized.[159]

Around the same time that Susie found the study, the family obtained, from the State of Oregon, a new water right deed that bordered the Malheur Wildlife Refuge. The antics of the cooperating federal agencies at play when they learned of the Hammond's new water right were to challenge the family's right to the

water in an Oregon State Circuit Court. To the fed's dismay, the court found the Hammonds as the legal owners to that water right according to Oregon State law.

One small victory for the family.

However, the cooperating agencies began planning for their next chess move by plotting to have Oregon state law changed with respect to water, so as to favor their agenda. Their slow steps toward accomplishing their design came to fruition, as now, in the state of Oregon, "wildlife is considered as an accepted beneficial use for government agencies only."[160] Up until this beguiling chess move, *wildlife's* sporadic use of water and forage would not guarantee *any persons,* as defined by law, ownership of the water, forage, right of way, and land that the wildlife used.[161]

Looking at this scenario logically, it is insulting to realize how modern law is granting *wildlife* more rights than a *natural-born person* who is contributing to society by using their life and liberty in pursuit of happiness.[162] This change in Oregon law was a victory by circumvent, for the cooperating agencies.

While the law had not yet been changed, remember, that was a long-term goal for them that they did eventually accomplish. To complicate things for the Hammonds, in August 1994 after their small victory in court, the BLM and FWS started constructing a fence that surrounded the Hammond's water property right. Being the legal and rightful owner of this water right, the Hammonds peacefully sought to stop the fence's development as a way to defend their property right. Their intent was to remain true to *continual beneficial use* law. The family's aim was not to simply counter the federal agents' conduct in a defiant way as portrayed by media. On the contrary, their choice to prevent blockage to their water right was an effort to peacefully defend their property right. To prevent the fence development, they "parked [their] Caterpillar scraper squarely on the boundary line and disabled it, removing the battery and draining fuel lines.[164]

The Hammond family not only had the pressure of losing their water right for failure to have continual beneficial use, but their cattle were at great risk of dying due to dehydration. Dying cattle meant another great risk to their property. Their cattle relied daily upon that water. Without water, livestock dies. The old saying in the West, "whiskey's for drinkin' and water's for fightin,'" was no joke.

After the Hammonds sought to stop the fence development, the BLM and FWS contacted the Harney County Sheriff department insisting Dwight Hammond (father) and Steven Hammond (son) be arrested. Unfortunately, the County Sheriff was either ignorant as to whom the property owner was in conjunction with the element of continual beneficial use laws or he was beholden to the Fed. Whatever the reason, he allowed the cooperating federal agencies to influence him to violate the life, liberty, and pursuit of happiness of his constituents Dwight and Steven Hammond.[165]

The madness didn't stop there. FWS understood the only way for the Hammonds to access upper parts of their privately-owned ranch was by traveling on a road that they believed went through the Malheur Wildlife Refuge. You guessed it, the agents began barricading these roads, restricting the Hammond's access to their private property. The barricades were accompanied with threats as to what would happen if they drove on the road. Again, the Hammonds refused to be intimidated and peacefully asserted their right to access their private property by removing the barricades. That road proved to be owned by Harney County, Oregon, leaving the federal cooperating agencies to stew in their embarrassment.[166]

The next tactic used against the Hammond family was an arbitrary use of law, which was the demise to their cattle grazing on the land. First, one must have a little history.

Open-range counties within the state of Oregon include Grant, Harney, and Lake. This means no livestock districts exist in these counties and the livestock can legally run at large without need of any fencing or barriers.[167] Despite this reality, the Hammond's upper grazing permits were revoked by BLM and FWS without any given cause, court proceeding, or court ruling on the pretense that the family must build and maintain miles of fence or be restricted from the use of their property. At first glance, any who do not understand open range laws, the demand of the BLM and FWS to build fence would make sense. After all, why shouldn't the family be responsible for their cattle? But even if law dictated they were to build the fence, which it does not, what most don't realize is to build miles of fence in an unreasonable amount of time would demand thousands of dollars and many forty-hour weeks' worth of work. This would be enough to put the family under. They couldn't build the fence and thus lost. Confused as to why BLM and FWS were ignoring open range laws, the ranchers were simply informed the federal government didn't have to observe Oregon open range laws.[168]

Losing the ability to benefit from half of their forage brought financial devastation upon the family for many years. To simply feed the cattle, they had to sell their ranch and home. What little they acquired from that enabled them to obtain a different property with enough forage. The new property had two grazing rights on public land, which in time were also arbitrarily revoked. Around this same time, the individual who purchased the Hammond's original ranch died due to a heart attack. Circumstance and rapport enabled the Hammond's to take part in a fair trade for the original ranch back.[169]

As the Hammonds continued to wrestle with the local cooperating federal agencies in an effort to pursue their happiness, unbeknownst to them, the groundwork for developing the very tool that would be used to label and reconvict them to years in prison in the future was well underway. The legislative weapon was the Antiterrorism and Effective Death Penalty Act of 1996, (AEDPA), which was signed into law on April 24, 1996 by President Bill Clinton. The bill was introduced after the 1993 World Trade Center bombing and the 1995 Oklahoma City bombing as a way to deter terrorism in the form of bombing.

In 2012, sixteen years after the act's ratification, the Hammonds were accused by the United States Attorney's office of different crimes using the AEDPA act for the case's backbone. The prosecution claimed they were domestic terrorists for being in violation of section 18 U.S.C. 844 (f) (1) of the act. It reads,

> *(f)(1) Whoever maliciously damages or destroys, or attempts to damage or destroy, by means of fire or an explosive, any building, vehicle, or*

> *other personal or real property in whole or in part owned or possessed by, or leased to, the United States, or any department or agency thereof, shall be imprisoned for not less than 5 years and not more than 20 years, fined under this title, or both.*[170]

This move would prove to be the cooperative federalist's checkmate. They grossly circumvented the intent of AEDPA to accuse the Hammonds of arson for two specific occasions they used fire to manage the land in 2001 and 2006.[171]

Fast forwarding to 2012, just days before the statute of limitations for issuing a lawsuit from the previous 2001 and 2006 fire instances, is when the U.S. Attorney's Office made its chess move. Dwight and Steven Hammond were accused of "terrorism." The attorneys' offices referred to their setting fire as acts of arson that were in violation of the Federal Antiterrorism Effective Death Penalty Act of 1996, knowing there carried a minimum sentence of five years in prison and a maximum sentence of death.[172]

The defendant's argument in the district court proceedings was that the five-year mandatory minimum would be violation of the United States Constitution Eighth Amendment cruel and unusual punishment clause and that facts prove fire to be a means of land management to improve the land and shield forage property rights against wildfire.

It is interesting to note how the district court asked the prosecuting attorneys if they had any further understanding on the purpose for the five-year mandatory minimum incarceration associated with the arson violations from the AEDPA act on which the Hammonds were being tried. The court asked if anyone felt the intent of this act anticipated bringing before a court issues such as those brought forth by the Hammond case. The response was, "Congress does things that it's not intended…."[173]

In the court proceedings, we read the judge's response after the prosecution's argument. In "law and equity" the court said,

> *I am not going to apply the mandatory minimum and because, to me, to do so under the Eighth Amendment would result in a sentence which is grossly disproportionate to the severity of the offenses here. And with regard to the Antiterrorism and Effective Death Penalty Act of 1996, this*

sort of conduct could not have been conduct intended under that statute [to do so] it would be a sentence which would shock the conscience to me.[174]

The sentencing of Dwight and Steven Hammond was the last ruling for this Justice,[175] as he was due for retirement. Rather than the five-year AEDPA mandatory minimum, Dwight Hammond (father) was sentenced to report to the Bureau of Prisons for confinement for a period of three months. Steven Hammond (son) was sentenced to report to the Bureau of Prisons for confinement for a period of twelve months and one day.

While Dwight and Steven were grateful for the judge's sentencing not reflecting the five-year mandatory minimum, many believed the case should have been dismissed altogether. Rather than gloat about a willingness to show a degree of mercy by not convicting the Hammonds to the five-year mandatory minimum, this Justice could have powerfully ended his tenure as Justice by truly "ensur[ing] fair and impartial administration of justice for all Americans" by dismissing the case altogether on the backbone of USC 18-1855.[176]

The last sentence of this United States Code states an allottee is exempt of conviction for the exercise of their proprietary rights of the allotment! What does this mean? This means the Hammond family did not have to lose large portions of their life, liberty, and pursuit of happiness to the Bureau of Prisons. This means the Hammonds did not have to be labeled as domestic terrorists, and they did not have to be convicted as felons.

The United States Prosecution team knew what they were doing. They were not ignorant to the law. The aim was to put the family under further duress. Trying them under the AEDPA Act was a tactic used as a weapon to get a conviction so as to aid getting claim to the Hammond property. Such weaponry is no new thing to humanity. Similar tactics were employed in the Bundy, Hage, and many other cases.[177]

On January 4, 2013, Dwight and Steven reported to prison. The Hammond father and son served their time and then returned to ranching life as they knew it.

Dwight was released in March of 2013 and Steven in January of 2014 with the hope to quickly return to ranching life. However, with the track history thus far, it would be out of character for the powers that be to streamline their process back into business. True to form, the Hammonds were denied their application for grazing permit renewal.[178]

Pressing forward, the best they knew how, the father only being home for twelve months and the son for one, they were apprised of an appeal that had been set in motion. It seemed the United States prosecuting attorney saw it his obligation to assist in the digging of their grave. As Dad said, "the government came back demanding more skin off their back." It was in February of 2014, sixteen months after the district court's verdict, after they had served their time and returned home, that an appeal was filed in United State court of appeals for the Ninth Circuit by the prosecuting attorney. This attorney felt it his moral duty to follow the letter of the law in protest to the district court Justice choosing to follow the spirit of the law by not condemning the two men to the five-year mandatory minimum incarceration.[179]

As result of the appeal, the Ninth District Court forced the Hammonds to grant the Bureau of Land Management (BLM) first right of refusal to their property if ever sold, in addition to requiring them to pay over $400,000 in fines. It was also decided that they return to prison to fulfill the rest of the five-year mandatory minimum, as outlined in AEDPA. Dwight, 74, and his son Steven, 46, were scheduled to report to prison *again* on January 4th, 2016, leaving behind their wives and children once more to manage alone.

To answer your question as to why, these are the many reasons that moved hundreds of people from across the United States on January 2nd, 2016, to gather at the doorstep of the Hammond family. The aim was to show support to the Hammond family before they again turned themselves over to federal prison. Remember they had already served time for this so-called offense. As controversial as it was, many asserted this family was not only victims of label lynching, years of intimidation, legislation abuse, and targets of "cruel and unusual punishment" (violation of Amendment 8 of US Constitution), but now these victims were "subject for the same offense to be twice put in jeopardy of life or limb."[180]

CHAPTER 8

DAD CROSSING THE RUBICON

"Yet such is oft the course of deeds that move the wheels of the world: small hands do them because they must, while the eyes of the great are elsewhere."
—**J.R.R. Tolkien**, *The Fellowship of the Ring*

D ad felt so inclined to be in Oregon the New Year's season of 2016 because he understood that if the Hammond story was swept under the rug, it would become a type and shadow of things to come for many more Americans.

He personally witnessed the painful results of unmaintained political boundaries and federal overreach in his own county. He saw what was once a thriving, successful place become one that was stricken with widespread poverty and depravity. Yes—depravity![181] Dad once explained it this way:

> *No longer can a man bust his butt on the oil rig he has worked on for most of his bread-winning career. The joy and satisfaction of bringing home the bacon is gone because code dictates. Why? Because the federal government says the land and resources is not the state's, but theirs. The natural resources are taken and hid away on the pretense of potentially saving some crazy endangered species, as if the animal has dominion over the earth.*

> *Families are put in duress and then offered federal subsidy to barely scrape by. The people's livelihood is taken and in return they are offered free stuff. Time has witnessed this to breed anger, hostility, demoralization, laziness, a deep sense of entitlement, multigenerational poverty, and eventually a morphed worldview of natural law and the proper role of government.*

For Dad, it was clear what caused the decline of his own stomping grounds. He recognized the parallelism between Harney County, Oregon and his own.[182] Much like Dad's own county, Harney County was once the wealthiest county in the state of Oregon before large operations were regulated out of business. But now, as one lifelong resident of Harney County put it, "they [the fed] took the jewel of the county and turned it into a weed patch."[183] This sentiment has proven to be both literal and figurative.

Harney County is 10,228 square miles (26,490 km²) in size, the largest in Oregon, and one of the largest in the United States and yet it's unemployment rate is the second highest in the state.[184] It is interesting to consider how "Oregon's largest county by area [is also the] smallest by population, [therefore] economic development is fleeting. Harney County, like many rural counties, struggles to hold onto jobs, which come and go with each economic cycle.[185]

Dad truly embraced Bonhoeffer's words: "Silence in the face of evil is itself evil. God will not hold us guiltless. Not to speak *is* to speak. Not to act *is* to act." Dad left the comfort of his home because stalwart people defend others' liberties together with defending their own. The backbone for his arriving in Oregon was the original intent of America's founding document. On a more personal note, he said in an interview,

> *What is our objective? Why are we here? Maybe I can use the parable of the Good Shepherd. In the parable, the Good Shepherd left the ninety and nine and went out to rescue the one. ...we do not live in a democracy; we live in a republic wherein the rights of the individual are protected against the tyranny of the majority.*[186]

Dad firmly believed that the supposed majority, dictating by fiat, would mean the economic ruin of entire communities in several states across the union. That would be unethical and contrary to the original intent behind the nation's rule of law. He knew tyranny never was satisfied and rural America was under attack.[187]

> ## "All I'm for is the liberty of the individual."
> ## —**John Wayne**

He proclaimed the original intent of the rule of law was for the federal government to leave the things of the state to the state, and for the state to leave the things of the county to the county. There is no such thing as national or federal supremacy. Yes, Article 6 of the U.S. Constitution talks about federal supremacy but let us not assume it means full supremacy.

> *Article 6 is often referred to as the article that contains the supremacy clause. This demonstrates the provisions in which the federal law is supreme. It says that "this Constitution, and the laws of the United States which shall be made in pursuance thereof; and all treaties made, or which shall be made, under the authority of the United States, shall be the supreme law of the land; and the Judges in every State shall be bound thereby, anything in the Constitution or laws of any State to the contrary notwithstanding."*
>
> *In other words, the federal government has legislative supremacy within the confines of its specific and defined powers in the Constitution. Notice that Article 6 does not state that the federal government has supremacy in all matters. This becomes an important distinction in regard to the rights and powers of the states.*[188]

Dad knew it was through the practice of regionalism that state and county boundaries were dissolved.[189] He saw how the people's rights being successfully meddled with was direct result of these destroyed boundaries. He understood the perpetrator wearing the mask of big government purposely set up its victim to feel as if they're up against unbeatable odds.

Dad arrived in Oregon not knowing he would end up choosing to stay long-term. All he had was the clothes on his back and his 'bugout' bag he took on every long road trip. At a local diner after, the idea of beginning an occupation of the wildlife refuge with the intent to practice adverse possession law upon the property while petitioning the government for a redress of grievance was presented to a group of individuals.[190] Dad was included in this company and this is what he said:

> Dad: *It might be helpful for me to kind of...in your understanding of what you'd like to see happen today and tomorrow.*
> Dad: *For a long time, we've just tried to stand and hold our ground. This is… this is maybe the first time that now we are stepping forward, and we are pushing forward to stand and no longer being defensive but we're going to be proactive. Claim and reclaim. Do I have it right?*
> Ammon Bundy: *That's right, that's correct.*
> Dad: *I'm in. I'm with you.*[191]

His decision to participate in the occupation was not the result of fanaticism, however he understood his decision to be a "crossing [of] the Rubicon."[192] Dad cognitively "counted the cost and was willing to pay it" to help restore what had been taken.[193]

> *He said shortly after the occupation started, I'm doing this for my kids. My 20 grandkids, daughters and sons…. I want them to be free. I want the Constitution to be upheld in its original intent. I want freedom to be restored to our country. And, unfortunately, our liberal class does not have the will. Their entrenched and they won't do it. So, here in this little place, we will uphold the Constitution. We'll return these resources to the people. It belongs to the people of Harney County, these good folks. And so, I'll stand here, with my friends.*[194]

His choice to stay was partly due to understanding local people could not, while consumed in fear, duress, or ignorance, defend their invisible geographic political boundaries. Someone had to take courage, no matter the risk, to firmly stand amidst the county's crisis and use an unwavering voice to bring the issues to the forefront. While many local citizens of Burns voiced that they did not agree with the occupiers' strategy, they also expressed gratitude and appreciation for the occupation bringing rural poverty issues to the forefront. Dad and other occupiers worked diligently with members of the community at ground zero on a daily basis, interfacing with them on how to defend their rights. Dad said in interview, "I want to get back to taking care of my own ranch, and so me personally want to leave as soon as possible, but I will stay here as long as necessary to help these ranchers resolve their plight, just as a neighbor to another."[195]

To expect a people to firmly stand in fear or ignorance is insanity. A true leader is one who gently steps in for a people, who, at first, cannot do it for themselves or who are so debilitated, thus not able to act at all. In the case of the occupation, both circumstances applied. The Hammonds—for years—had been squeezed dry; they were emotionally, physically, mentally, financially, and spiritually spent and much of the local citizenry did not fully understand the extent of the corruption.

This is not to suggest Dad was of the opinion that all were uninformed. On the contrary, he expressed several times how he quickly became acquainted with many local citizens who understood the dire situation of the county. Be that as it may, there is opposition in all things, thus daily he worked to vanquish ignorance.

Helping the American people outside of the agriculture and ranching communities understand how the plight of these communities affects the freedom and liberty of all Americans proved to be very strenuous. Misleading soundbites delivered by many of the present Associated Press, who themselves did not fully understand the nature of law in relation to property rights, seemed to fuel the heated divide amongst the American people. Despite this, Dad found great joy in witnessing a change of disposition in reporters who spent time in discussion. He could see light bulbs turning on in their eyes! Notwithstanding the rapture in these experiences, the pressure of a massive disconnect between most Americans was an ever-present burden.

There are several reasons for this disconnect. As mentioned in the introduction, a very high percentage of the current Americans do not own a cow or know what "grazing rights" are. In a world of city life and virtual existence, it is difficult to empathize with the open range, spotted with cows, a cowboy, and his dog.

Statistically speaking, how are the masses to understand the important connection between the plight of the Hammond family to the protection of property rights of individuals who live a more modern lifestyle? Because not everyone has water, forage, and right-of-way property that extend over wide landscapes, it is difficult to understand the role invisible geographical political boundaries play in safeguarding personal property.

Regardless of human nature's tendency to patronize and threaten the inalienable rights of those who are not part of the current trending majority, all people are equal in their right to life, liberty, and pursuit of happiness, as well as equal under the law. The teeth of this nation's protection is in the rights of the individuals against the tyranny of the majority. How is this done? Through well-maintained divided and subdivided political boundaries. If such boundaries are compromised, then everyone's rights are at risk.

The Co-Founder and President of Center for Self Governance said in an interview what he believed was the *why* behind Dad's participation in the Oregon occupation:

> *The issues found within the Hammond case are not just about cows, grass, water, and fire but about how liberty hangs by a delicate thread when it comes to political boundaries. There is a reason the founders set up a nation with its respective separation of county, state, and federal controls. LaVoy tried to teach this.*[196]

Dad calmly went to do the uncomfortable work that liberty's preservation demanded when the political pendulum had swung too far in Oregon. He was willing to turn the wheels of the world with his small hands while a majority were blinded with contempt or apathy. All the while, elected aggrandizing individuals' hearts failed in supporting liberty's cause. In weighty matters as this, Dad's serene sentiments were these: "That's okay. We will each have our reward in the end."[197]

CHAPTER 9

MY TIME AT GROUND ZERO

There were many uncertainties in venturing to ground zero.[198] Be that as it may, needing to be there was the only certain thing. Disapproval from others was of no concern. I had approached God seeking confirmation of my decision to go and I felt peace in that decision.

It had only been a few days into the occupation. At this point, smear campaigns from the left and right were proving very successful. Even American comedians foolishly jeered about Dad to rooms full of *loud laughter*.

The aim in journeying to Oregon was to facilitate a shift in the occupation's current public relations but, most importantly, to bring Dad home. Before hitting the road, we contacted the Oregon State Police to ensure the family's arrival would not bring about unpleasant results. Family and friends caravanned from Arizona, from Utah, and from Idaho for a scheduled mid-morning press conference in Oregon on January 8th. Mom stayed back to tie up loose ends with their foster children.

It being the beginning of January, the view of the drive was absolutely beautiful. Rolling hills of white blanketed pine top mountains covered in thick fog was the view for most of the drive. At any other time, such surroundings would invite mystical nostalgia and magical emotions. But this time it was quite different. As I drove on those Oregon wintery roads, it felt like we were under an evil spell. While there was no question as to whether or not I should go see Dad, the cold outside my car seemed to penetrate the raging climate within my heart. I think somehow my inner subconscious knew this would be the last time I would get to see him.

We rolled into the refuge midmorning. My sister Brittney and her daughter had carpooled with me and my boys. A few hours prior to our arrival at the refuge, our caravan had stopped at a hotel, hoping to get much needed rest. Sleep was of no avail. So there we were, red eyed and tired.

The road into the refuge was iced over. To reach the main building we had to take a steep downward sloping path. There was a checkpoint set up at the top of the hill with men who would alert those down below in the buildings via radio.

The snow- and ice-packed parking lot down below was almost vacant. It seemed as if no one was there. This was quite contrary to the frenzied media reports telling of heavily armed and dangerous militia men. Upon exiting the vehicle, I could hear soothing sounds of small birds. While these birds were not the refuge's famous red-crowned crane, I didn't mind. I guess these little birds were either brave enough to weather the winter or accustomed to surviving. Whatever the reason for the small birds' serenade in the dead of winter, I was grateful for their song.[199]

The place seemed like a ghost town. We didn't know where to go. We slowly began to walk down the sidewalk toward a building. Only a few moments passed before Dad joined us outside. He immediately embraced each one of us. The expression felt driven with deep sentiment, again cementing in my subconscious that this would be the last time we would embrace. After everyone was greeted, it was back to business. There was no time to waste—the press conference was within an hour's time.

My siblings and I waited while Dad planned a strategy with his team. To pass the time, I tried to play cards with my kids. That was a joke. I couldn't focus. So, we walked around outside so the children could play in the fluffy snow. It was so quiet. I could hear every drop of snow from the barren trees. It was as if we were in a twilight zone. According to the wire this place was supposed to be crawling with flamboyant anarchists.

Showtime arrived. We gathered in a circle and prayed, imploring for the powers of heaven to distill upon the reporter's hearts that we might be represented honestly. We then, together with Dad, began the *ascent* up the ice-packed slope to the entrance of the refuge where the many media outlets were stationed.

Reporters waited for our arrival. It was the most unreal thing to be walking while several complete strangers shot thousands of photos at various angles. Some fell to their knees in the snow and ice right in front of us to take photos as we continued to walk past. My face was smiling, but my heart was raging. Raging because of the lies from past reports. The false representation of my father created the dynamic of me versus them.

Dad powerfully spoke his sentiments and points of law into the bundle of ready microphones. In all, the press conference took about 20 minutes, at which point we headed back down that slippery hill. During the descent, Dad shared with us the experience he had when deciding whether or not he was going to stay and participate in such a protest of adverse possession.[200] He knew we needed to understand. Without us needing to pry, he willingly offered the details.

His voice was full of energy and optimism. He expressed how he understood and pondered the butterfly effects if he were to stay. He said it would be a crossing of the Rubicon for him. There would be no turning back. Grasping the gravity of the situation, he said he offered a silent prayer asking God what to do. Upon opening his eyes, he looked into the winter sky. Again, he silently prayed for strength and guidance. At that moment, his eyes caught hold of a large bald eagle expanding its wings for flight. The beautiful bird circled back and forth for quite some time. He said it was close enough for him to see the different colors in its wingspan. He said it was at that moment that he was overcome with peace. He said there was an odd assurance that all would be well. Dad witnessed to us how our Maker is into the details of our life and current situations.

The bald eagle was the answer to his heartfelt prayer.[201] Just after receiving this peace, the words of the late prophet of God, Ezra Taft Benson, came to his mind: "The fight for freedom is God's fight. ...So long as a man stands for freedom, he stands with God."[202] It was then that he knew, despite uncertainty, it was his duty to meekly stay the course. He was to help the residents of this area assert their rights with the aim to pass the baton to them after they had been strengthened.

Upon arriving back to the building, we ate lunch together, compliments of my sister's crock pot.[203] After lunch, I witnessed local residents arrive to provide supplies for the occupiers' sustainment. Others arrived with questions seeking better understanding. Dad eagerly spoke and welcomed them with open arms.

I remember feeling anger toward those who kept showing up. It felt as if they were robbing me of my last moments with my Dad. So, I tried the old trick I use with my kids: close proximity while Dad communicated with others. I thought maybe my message— "hey, I was here first!"—would somehow be delivered. As the conversations continued, I silently stamped out a three-foot heart in the fresh snow. It still hurts today wondering if Dad was able to see it.

The day would have continued on with my unspoken efforts to draw his attention to me while others pulled him away. Not long after the press conference, amidst an unfamiliar emotion during a moment when no one was around, Dad said it was time for us all to return home. Strangely, he was very adamant that, once we walked out the door, we did not return. I think I heard him say softly under his breath "because it's too difficult."

Respecting his wishes and holding sacred his freedom of conscience, we each took our turn for a father's blessing and one by one had our last daddy embrace. We were sure to tend to our melting mascara before exiting. We didn't want the media exploiting that image! We all walked out fighting the agony of the unknown.

I never turned back. I have often suffered through anguish of soul because I did not take the opportunity to hold him and beg for his return home. I have obsessed wondering; might he be alive today if I had? I may never know the answer, but I take comfort that God is in control.

CHAPTER 10

VINDICATION

*"All battles are fought by scared men
who'd rather be someplace else"*
—John Wayne

AUTHOR'S NOTES

The legacy Dad left behind is true to form of the many cherished Louis L'Amour western novels he read in his youth, as his "...story [is] of the just confronting the unjust, the right taking on the wrong, the strong serving the weak."[204]

The sound bites referencing the Hammond family before, during, and after the occupation included buzzwords like; 'welfare rancher,' 'terrorist,' 'arsonist,' and 'felon.'

On July 10, 2018, one year and six months after President Trump's inauguration and two years and five months after Dad's murder, Dwight and Steven Hammond were granted clemency (pardoned).[205] It is interesting to note the White House's drastic transition of tone toward its American ranching constituents. We read in the statement from the Press Secretary regarding the 2018 executive clemency for Dwight and Steven Hammond:

> *The Hammonds are devoted family men, respected contributors to their local community, and have widespread support from their neighbors, local law enforcement, and farmers and ranchers across the West. Justice is overdue for Dwight and Steven Hammond, both of whom are entirely deserving of these Grants of Executive Clemency.*[206]

Some attribute the Hammond clemency and the Associated Press's drastic change in tone solely to the January 20, 2017 White House shift from the Obama administration to the Trump administration. While everyone is free to their opinion, our family humbly asserts this budding of liberty to be the byproduct of the shocked American conscience. There was a national ebullition of fury the moment local, state, and federal agents orchestrated an ambush, killed my Father, and then cruelly incarcerated peaceful, law-abiding Americans.

The course of human events within the timestamp of the occupation and the Hammond pardon has shown the tree of liberty to have been successfully watered by the blood of my dad.[207]

As stated in the introduction, you become the jury—reviewing the many left-out details of his side for the first time. Was he the villain he was made out to be? Was the use deadly force truly warranted? You decide.

BEHIND THE NAME OF *ROBERT LAVOY*:

> Bright fame going to use the voice of reason to lead the way.
> "Robert" means bright fame from the Germanic name hrodebt meaning "Bright fame"
> "Voy" means go; in reference to a specific destination you are moving towards.
> In French La Voix (La Voa): the voice. Often used in the phase "the voice of reason"
> "Lavoie" is a surname of French origin, translated to mean 'the way'

CHAPTERS 11–21

DAD'S FUNDAMENTALS —BEFORE OREGON

*A deeper unfolding of the reasons for Dad's
association with the Bundy family
and his involvement
in the Malheur occupation.*

CHAPTER 11

BLURRING THE BOUNDARIES

"If the three powers maintain their mutual independence on each other, it may last long: but not so if either can assume the authorities of the other."
—**Thomas Jefferson**

After reading the pains associated with dad's murder and the details of the Hammond case, you might be asking yourself the same question that so many others have, "How can this even happen?"[208]

The earth, with all its majestic beauty and vast richness, was heretofore fashioned and given to mankind by the Creator. Dad believed the sole purpose for its creation was to be the place wherein all could have the opportunity to come to understand natural law set forth by *nature's God*, as it pertains to each individual's right to life, liberty, and the pursuit of happiness. Furthermore, he saw earth to be the place wherein mankind would have the opportunity to discover and hopefully choose obedience to laws that would produce an abundant life for *all* people.

The Creator saw to it that the earth was equipped with all the resources necessary for humanity's sustainment. Nature's God didn't stop there. The potential of the earth is to do much more than simply sustain life. There is within its matter the means to create luxury abundant living for *all* people. The unorganized matter just needs organization and to be properly governed. As the prophet and former President of the Church of Jesus Christ of Latter-day Saints said, Nature's God left "the world unfinished for man to work his skill upon. ...The electricity [was left in] the cloud, the oil in the earth. ...The rivers [were left] unbridged and the forests unfelled and the cities unbuilt. [Nature's God gave] to man the challenge of raw materials, not the ease of finished things. ...Pictures [are left] unpainted and the music unsung and the problems unsolved, that man might know the joys and glories of creation."[209]

Through time we have seen the cause and effect obedience to natural law brings. This obedience, by nature, causes the "unfinished things" of the world to beautifully bloom and prosper. The contrary is quite true as well. When individuals have sought to glut in the luxuries others produce without *"just compensation,"* then that which once was beautifully blooming begins to inevitably deteriorate.[210]

Despite the earth being a gift to all humanity, a person's life spent in pursuance of their choice (liberty) of creativity to bring about "finished," useful, and beautiful things indeed creates *private property*. This private property no other has right to without *just compensation*. When all people go about using their life and liberty to pursue their chosen form of happiness, by nature, *private property* becomes convoluted. This mess is what demands a need for governance. But when aggrandizing dispositions refuse to be tempered, refuse obedience to natural law, refuse respect for others' life, liberty, and private property, or refuse mastery of self, it becomes clear that not just any given governance will do. A specifically-engineered system becomes necessary to protect humanity against itself.

Remember nature's God left "the world unfinished for man to work his skill upon." This also applies to the search, discovery, development, and experimentation of systems of governance. There was no *user manual*, per se, with all the intricate details of how successful governance functions. Thus, the people's charge was and is to toil, search, and then develop. As with any system's beta, each system of governance calls for troubleshooting, maintenance of the good, and out with the bad.

Mankind's history has brought forth various systems of governance, most of which violate natural law. This tragic history is due to ignorance and/or tyrannical demagogue. Thus, we have the ongoing wrestle between those who wish to simply live enjoying their rights and those who wish to have dominion so as to increase in wealth through a systematic taking from others. Even in the beloved *'land of the free,'* people were and still are denied their right to life, liberty, and pursuit of happiness.

If we were to use simple adjectives to describe the latter domineering temperament, the words would include thief and robber. Let there be no mistake, systematic robbery has resulted in humanity's never-ending bloody dictum: this land is my land, *not yours*! Why is this, one might ask? The answer is simple. It is because all wealth comes from the earth. Remember, nature's God saw to it that earth was equipped with all the resources necessary for the entire human family to enjoy abundant living. It simply was the charge of humanity to use their life and liberty to pursue their happiness in organizing the earth's matter and create a system to protect everyone's life, liberty, and pursuit of happiness. Easy, right?

The various developed forms of governance through the years can all be categorized within the small list below. The five main categories include the following:[211]

1. **Monarchy:** control by one
2. **Anarchy:** control by none
3. **Oligarchy:** control by few (often those considered the elite)
4. **Democracy:** control by majority in a group
5. **Republic:** control by elected representatives.[212]

History says otherwise. Why? It is because the degree of obedience to natural law a people practice, in conjunction with the degree of maintenance to their system of government, unwaveringly determines the people's fate, for better or for worse. Natural law and the need for the systems maintenance applies to all nations, creeds, and ethnicities.

None are exempt from the consequences of neglect. Cicero said that such disobedience inevitably brings about the "worst penalties." It is impossible to read [the history of mankind] without horror. ...Every kind of death, every dreadful act was perpetrated. Fathers slew their children; some were dragged from alters, some were butchered at them...."[213]

The American founders made it their business to understand the cause and effects of humanity's history of brutal carnage. Their goal was to establish a system of governance that would avoid the continual horrific pendulum swing. In their search for answers they came across many great minds, one being John Locke. Locke was an English philosopher who died 83 years before the renowned American constitutional convention of 1787. It was Locke who described the origin of personal property to be the result of an individual mixing their labor (life/time plus liberty/choice) with unclaimed natural resource from the earth. Locke said, "Every man has a property in his own person. This nobody has a right to but himself."[214] Springboarding from Locke's enlightenment, a movement began that changed the world. It all started with a people willing to be true to natural law.

We hold these truths to be self-evident, that all men are created equal, that they are endowed by their Creator with certain unalienable Rights, that among these are Life, Liberty and the Pursuit of Happiness [property].[215]

To be clear as to why their government was organized, the very next sentence reads,

That to secure these Rights, Governments are instituted among Men....[216]

After such a declaration, a system of government was established with legislative, executive, and judicial separations of controls for the sole purpose of avoiding the violation of natural law as it pertains to the people's unalienable rights of life, liberty, and pursuit of happiness.[217]

John Adams boldly witnessed,

> We shall learn to prize the checks and balances of a free government, ...if we recollect the miseries of [history] which rose from their ignorance of them. The only balance [emphasis added] attempted against the ancient kings was a body of nobles; and the consequences were perpetual

> *altercations of rebellion and tyranny, and butcheries of thousands upon every revolution from one to another. When the kings were abolished, the aristocracies tyrannized; and then no balance [emphasis added] was attempted but between aristocracy and democracy. This, in nature of things, could be no balance [emphasis added] at all, and therefore the pendulum was forever on the swing.*[218]

The result of his observations was an unwavering confidence in his unflinching declarations of what would be the fate of the United States if proper balance between the system's controls was not narrowly defined in written contracts (constitutions) and maintained by its people (federalism).

> *Without…an effectual balance [emphasis added] between them [the divided governmental controls], …it must be destined to frequent unavoidable revolutions; if they are delayed a few years, they must come, in time.*[219]

I wonder if somewhere deep down Adams knew his prophetic words would come to pass in the country he toiled to safeguard against humanities fallen state.

> *If there is one certain truth to be collected from the history of all ages, it is this: That the people's rights and liberties, …can never be preserved without…separating the executive power from the legislative [emphasis added]. If the executive power, or any considerable part of it, is left in the hands either of an aristocratical or a democratical assembly, it will corrupt the legislature as necessarily as rust corrupts iron, or as arsenic poisons the human body; and when the legislature is corrupted the people are undone.*[220]

The shocking details found within the Hammond case seem to mirror John Adams prophetic foresight of what would become of a country whose people disregarded its sacred checks and balance of free government. If Adams was right, the heavy question left is this: Where is the hidden consolidation of control within the current legislative and executive branches of the American system? You may have even already ventured to the appendix to read the short history of the Bundy Standoff to discover more of the shocking abuses the people have suffered due to this very type of consolidation, not to mention the proven willingness to resort to murder to ensure that the "one great mission" is not frustrated. All these atrocities naturally cause more questions to arise.[221] How did this all happen?

CHAPTER 12

WHERE THE RUBBER MEETS THE ROAD

*"The accumulation of all powers,
legislative, executive, and judiciary, in the same hands,
whether of one, a few, or many, and whether hereditary, self-appointed,
or elective, may justly be pronounced the very definition of tyranny."*
—**James Madison**

Many nights I lay awake wondering how I was to begin to identify the cause of what happened to our family, to the Hammond and Bundy families? How was I going to help my children understand if I didn't fully understand? I thought about dad and how his choice was to study the Constitution and the language of the founders in their writings so that he might understand the original intent of the Constitution. My decision was to pray. Not surprising to me, my mind led me to turn to the words of the founders as well. I knew theirs were lives dedicated to study. For me, it felt right to use the findings from John Adams's life's work as a springboard to explore how the current executive branch might be merging its narrowly defined controls with the controls specific to the legislature. Remember, it was Adams who witnessed that "without...an effectual *balance* [emphasis added] between them [the divided governmental controls], ...it must be destined to frequent unavoidable revolutions." To do that we must understand the narrowly defined controls of both the executive and legislative branches of the U.S. Federal Government, or as Dad said, "The first thing [you need to do], if you're going to stand for freedom, is figure out where the line is, who's illegal and who's lawful."[222]

> The Constitution grants the executive a set of narrowly defined responsibilities. The intent was to avoid the setup of a monarch with wide blanketed controls.

The Executive Branch

The language defining the executive branch's specific controls is only about twenty percent of the Constitution and, strangely in today's world, it is the largest.

The most fundamental control delegated to the executive branch is to enforce the laws passed by the legislature-congress. The actual meaning of the word 'executive' is to 'carry out' or 'execute.' Article 2, Section 2 of the United States Constitution is where we can read the narrowly defined controls delegated to the executive branch of government.

A quick at glance list of the executive branch's controls are these:

1. Control to enforce law,
2. Control to veto laws,
3. Control to act as Commander-in-Chief,
4. Control to participate in diplomatic matters (treaties, only with the consent of two-thirds of the Senate),
5. Control to issue pardons (except in case of impeachment).

Furthermore, Article 4, Section 4 gives the executive some controls to protect the borders of the nation.

To provide the President with the support needed to govern effectively, the Executive Office of the President (EOP) was created in 1939 by President Franklin D. Roosevelt. The EOP responsibilities range from communicating the President's message to the American people to promoting trade interests abroad. Overseen by the White House Chief of Staff, the EOP has traditionally been home to many of the President's closest advisors.[223]

The executive office of the President includes the Office of Management and Budget, National Security Council, Council of Economic Advisers, Office of National Drug Control Policy, Office of Science and Technology Policy, and Council on Environmental Quality.[224]

Furthermore, the executive has what Article 2, Section 2 of the Constitution created: The Cabinet. The Cabinet's role is to advise the President on any subject he may require relating to the duties of each member's respective office. The Cabinet includes the President and Vice President of the United States and the heads of the fifteen executive departments:

1. Agriculture
2. Commerce
3. Defense
4. Education
5. Energy
6. Health and Human Services
7. Homeland Security
8. Housing and Urban Development
9. Interior
10. Labor
11. State
12. Transportation
13. Treasury
14. Veterans Affairs
15. The Attorney General (The Department of Justice)

Additionally, the Cabinet includes the White House Chief of Staff and heads of the Environmental Protection Agency, Office of Management and Budget, United States Trade Representative, United States Mission to the United Nations, and Small Business Administration.[225]

The fifteen executive departments answer directly to the President and were originally created by Congress. Under the fifteen executive departments are 411 agencies/bureaus/services/commissions/departments/administrations that dot the nation, functioning with countless employed individuals.[226]

You must be thinking, "Okay, that doesn't sound so bad. What is the big idea?"

Let's now move on to detailing the narrowly-defined controls granted to the legislative branch.

> "All legislative powers herein granted shall be vested in a Congress of the United States, which shall consist of a Senate and House of Representatives."
> **—United States Constitution,** *Article 1, Section 1*

Legislative Branch

The legislative branch is comprised of *elected officials* who are given control to author and organize law limited to a narrowly-defined scope outlined by the Constitution based upon the principle of limited government.[227] It is this law that the executive branch is to 'carry out' or 'execute.' For the purpose of this discussion, understand I'm only referring to law for federal jurisdictions. The same type of hierarchy system applies to state jurisdictions, but the states' constitutions and code books are named differently than those of the federal.

Aside from the United States Constitution trumping all, acts of Congress are the highest form of law that the executive branch enforces.

Next in the hierarchy, for federal jurisdictions, is an encyclopedic set of books known as the United States Code (USC). The USC contains all the various statutes passed by Congress. The Office of the Law Revision Counsel of the United States House of Representatives prepare and publish the United States Code, which is a consolidation and codification by subject matter of acts of Congress. The aim is to ensure new statutes mesh with existing ones. The USC is divided into 53 titles. The titles may be divided into subtitles, parts, subparts, chapters, and subchapters.

Next in hierarchy is the Code of Federal Regulations (CFR). The authors of this code are the 411 executive federal agencies that work under the 15 executive departments.[228] The CFR is the bureaucratic rulebook for implementing the laws set forth in the above-mentioned United States Code (USC).

Wait one minute!

According to John Adams's warnings, shouldn't we be worried that the Code of Federal Regulations (CFR) is authored law by the 411 *executive* federal agencies?[229] Adams said,

> *If there is one certain truth to be collected from the history of all ages, it is this: That the people's rights and liberties...can never be preserved without...separating the executive power from the legislative [emphasis added]. If the executive power, or any considerable part of it, is left in the hands either of an aristocratical or a democratical assembly, it will corrupt the legislature as necessarily as rust corrupts iron, or as arsenic poisons the human body; and when the legislature is corrupted the people are undone.*[230]

Witness of Adams's foresight, modern trends are showing that the 411 agencies, who shouldn't be writing law in the first place, are *not* staying within the boundaries set to avoid a circumvention of acts of Congress. By law, the United States Code (USC) and Code of Federal Regulations (CFR) are to write their code in a way that agrees with its authority—acts of Congress. There is a requirement for all of USC's or CFR's language to footnote its authority.

Even when a footnote is provided, the language is strategically organized to bypass the intent of the act of Congress. This willful guile fiat is very dangerous. Such has been a tactic used for years to grossly circumvent acts of Congress and simply violate the rule of law at the expense of life, liberty, and pursuit of happiness.[231]

> "If everything isn't black and white,
> I say, 'Why the hell not?'"
> **—John Wayne**

So, what does the Code of Federal Regulations (CFR) existence mean for us? It means we have more to vet and more agents to hold accountable. Remember that Thomas Jefferson humbly warned, "If once they [the governed] become inattentive to the public affairs, you and I, and Congress, and Assemblies, judges and governors shall all become wolves."[232] Boy, is that ever true. Jefferson understood the power behind accountability. Unfortunately, few have the grit, time, resources, and courage to audit CFR language in the court of law.

I have lived through the wretched results that this little to no accountability produces. We have seen governors become wolves. This is the *poison* of which John Adams prophesied. In the case of the Hammonds, Bundys, and ours, this poison manifested itself through a circumvention of acts of Congress through administrative law resulting in militarized rogue bureaucratic agents. As result, each of our cases experienced a form of loss of life, liberty, and the pursuit of happiness.

In layman terms, *unelected* agents who are *employed* within the 411 agencies working under the fifteen executive departments are *writing and enforcing administrative law*. Let there be no mistake, this is a breach of political boundaries. This is a consolidation of control between the legislative and executive branches of government.[233] It is unconstitutional. It is this type of governance that gives room for arbitrary authority, whimsically shifting left and right on policy. This is precisely what John Adams warned would bring sure revolution.[234] It is this type of consolidation of control under one head that many of the founders defined as tyranny.

This is where the rubber meets the road. This is fundamental to understanding the connections between the Hammond, Bundy, and Fincium cases. Realizing tyranny is only avoided with a limited federal government that has clear and concise separations of legislative, executive, and judicial controls explains the atrocities within the lengthy Hammond case, the lawlessness that took place before, during, and after the 2014 Bundy Standoff, and the dreadful blood-stained snow as result of the 2016 Oregon occupation.[235]

CHAPTER 13

ANOTHER WITNESS

*"In the mouth of two or three witnesses
shall every word be established."*
—**2 Corinthians 13:1**

I mentioned previously how the shocking details found within the Hammond case seem to mirror John Adams's prophetic foresight of what would become of a country whose people disregarded its sacred checks and balances of free government. You may have even already ventured to the appendix to read the short history of the Bundy Standoff to discover more of the shocking abuses the people have suffered due to this very type of consolidation.

We have already discussed the narrowly defined controls that the constitution grants the executive and legislative branches and pinpointed where a consolidation of control between the two branches are currently taking place.[236]

I now wish to illustrate once again for you the results of John Adams foresight, except this time it won't be the Hammond's story, or the Bundy's story, but our own.

After Dad was murdered, Mom was left to tend to all the loose ends. Unfortunately, there was no written will in order. I guess they thought there was still time. After all, Dad saw to it that his health was at its prime with his relentless daily maintenance to his body.

Despite having no will, Mom worried less about the ranch during the chaos of our politically-charged funeral since she still had four more months left on her winter range before needing to move the cattle. Furthermore, Arizona is a community property state. In a community property state, money earned by either spouse during marriage and all property bought with those earnings are considered community property that is owned equally by husband and wife. Likewise, debts incurred during marriage are generally debts of the couple.

In layman terms, what was his became all hers upon his passing. This is not to suggest that it was any different when Dad was living. While Dad was his own man, I witnessed him and Mom being partners in all they did.

After the funeral had come and gone, it was back to cow business as usual, only the main character in the pursuit was no longer living. Facing reality, Mom pressed forward only to find herself quickly blindsided. Just a few weeks after Dad's murder, she was rudely informed by the Bureau of Land Management (BLM) that she, as the widow of the LaVoy Finicum, had no right whatsoever to her forage and water property on her winter range.[237] She was told her choices were to immediately remove the cattle from her winter range or face very undesirable consequences.

Mom was no fool and knew her rights, thus, despite the BLM's ultimatum, her choice was to not remove the cattle. Of course, the BLM kept a detailed log of fines and fees.

Arbitrary Authority

That the BLM's demands were arbitrary must be understood. First, let me remind you, the forage and water on her winter range were her property, just as much as your car is your property. She holds deed to that property. She and Dad purchased it, and not from the BLM. The BLM claiming authority to deny her use of her winter range is a farce. Furthermore, removing the cattle at the drop of a hat is no small feat. Such an effort would require more than just pocket change. Most do not understand the implications associated with hauling hundreds of full-grown beasts to a new location equipped with enough water and feed to keep them alive. This, over a period of months, could have amounted in expenses that would easily put any middle-class family in definite financial ruin. Not to mention the time required to find the beasts.

When her time arrived, mom did move her cattle, but not to their typical summer range.[238] Unfortunately, she did not know the layout of the summer land well enough. Not knowing the location of the water was too much a risk, not to mention the difficulties an unknown rough terrain would present. What she was doing was picking her battles in wisdom because taking on the ranch alone, together with starting a major politically-charged wrongful death lawsuit was enough to worry about and manage.

During those summer months, Mom and her attorneys legally wrestled with the BLM to recognize her as legal rightful owner of her winter range.[239] Winter finally arrived and her pragmatic move was to comply with a new set of redlined BLM contractual agreements.[240] Yes, she decided to reenter the contractual working relationship with the BLM that her husband had removed himself from in 2015.[241]

Mom began the process of moving the cows back to her winter range. During the cattle drive, her mother-in-law arrived at the campsite to inform her that the BLM rejected the redlined contract and refused to accept the check. Furthermore, they firmly issued threats to arrest her and impound the cattle if she were to turn the cattle out onto her winter range.

Mom could not believe what she was hearing.[242] She was beyond frustrated, angry, and betrayed. She stayed out there with the cattle all that night. Not able to sleep, she looked into the night sky and got lost in the country stars. This brought a little comfort.[243] Sleep finally came. Early the next morning she decided to haul the cattle to Kanab, UT by semi. Ironically Mom's neighboring rancher received, within hours, verbal permission from their BLM range conservationist that Mom's cattle could graze on their range for the winter of 2016.

Why did the BLM sanction the use of the neighboring forage and water but threaten punishment if Mom used her own forage and water? The only logical explanation is that it seems they were making an example out of Mom. After all, it was her late husband who was a nonconformist to the practice of regional political philosophy.[244] While Dad had every right to end his contractual agreement with the BLM, it seemed the BLM agent's conduct after his murder was retaliation fueled by their belief of him being guilty of insubordination.[245] Their efforts to punish was just another attempt to legitimize their pretended edicts with the aim to intimidate any other ranchers contemplating the same course of action.

For fun, let's just pretend for a moment that the state of Arizona was not a community property state. If that were the case, then maybe the BLM's insensitive demands after Dad was killed could have held some legal weight. We know that is not the case. Arizona is a community property state, legally making Mom the owner of all that was in Dad's name.

Don't assume the BLM's agents were ignorant to the family's situation nor to Mom's legal right to her property. There is no way under the sun this could have been the case. Dad was well known. Even Loretta Lynch, who was the former Attorney General of the United States, knew who Dad was, as he, in a letter to her, explained the purpose for severing his contractual relationship with the BLM. Furthermore, the occupiers' efforts to stake a claim of adverse possession upon the refuge in Oregon was on national news. Their publicly-televised petition for a redress of grievance included the BLM as a recipient.[246]

Continuing on with mom's conflict with the BLM, it wasn't long before she and her attorneys found 4110.2-3 Transfer of Grazing Preference within the BLM's insanely thick rule book. In terms of her current case, this 4110.2-3 was a diamond in the rough. The language within this Code of Federal Regulation (CFR) clearly recognizes the transfer of ownership from Dad to Mom after his death, and yet the BLM still claimed she had no right to her forage and water property rights on her winter range. Despite the BLM's Code of Federal Regulation language stating that such a transfer of base property "will not affect the grazing preference ...for a period of two years after the transfer" the BLM issued threats in the form of administrative fees and trespass fines if she kept her cattle on the range, acting as if they were the owners of the property and the sole arbiters![247] Let's pretend to accept the BLM's regulatory law as the sole arbiter for just a moment, the question of concern then would be, why is it that the BLM can pick and choose which of the laws they are willing to abide by?[248]

I believe the BLM cognitively made this chess move assuming Mom would simply roll over and die a heartbroken poor widow. The BLM agents were not ignorant to what her removal from the land would do. Removing her from the land would impede her continual beneficial use of her forage and water property rights, thus setting in line a case for themselves to legally take her property under the guise of her non-use. You read about this same tactic being used against the Hammond family.

Yes, she was brokenhearted, but not dead. Mom is not one to just roll over and die. When things get really hard, and believe me, things at this point were *really* hard, she puts her head down and presses forward. After a long expensive court process fighting on this issue of ownership, the BLM's disposition strangely changed after almost two years of their inflicted firebrand. When it came time again for Mom to claim her winter forage and water property rights by moving the cattle to her winter range, in November of 2017, a meeting was called.

This time she was in the company of female BLM attorneys.[249] Mom couldn't help but notice their change in tone. She wondered who it was that pulled strings behind the scene. During the meeting, they negotiated a settlement agreement favorable to Mom in reference to the accrued fines and fees, which she gladly signed. Without it directly being said, she was also informed that the BLM was now adhering to its 4110.2-3 Transfer of Grazing Preference and that BLM now recognized her ownership. She could not believe what she was hearing. It was like someone had flipped a light switch. Her assumption was a higher up in the new Trump administration had some success at draining the swamp.[250] The future pardon of the Hammond cowboys gave rise to her speculation. It was from this point that the clock started ticking with respect to the two-year period granted to Mom, as stated in the 4110.2-3 CFR, as the time for a negotiation of new contracts.

Her cows were put on her winter range for the year of 2017 without any more fuss. This is how the transfer process should have been from the very beginning.

The BLM then called for an assessment of her winter range so as to document all the assets for the purpose of having what they called a complete case for the new contracts. It took a year for the BLM to finish the assessment and draft new contracts for Mom's review. Mom's attorneys and property right experts took a few months to review the drafted contracts. As of January 2019, Mom was able to sign a contract that for now keeps her forage and water property rights intact.

While it seems that Mom has entered into a season of smooth sailing with the BLM, I can't help but think of what Dad once said to me, "They [federal agencies] first come in soft, willing to help. But in time, dispositions shift to assuming more authority in an effort to gain increase and, as a result, they begin taking and controlling that which never was theirs to take and control." Over a span of many years, the same patterns have carved lesions into the Hammond and Bundy families, bringing forth, together with ours, three witnesses of grievous evidences within the court of law in just a short six-year span.[251] It would be foolish for our family to assume our case is exempt from the same patterns of human folly that the founders witnessed would be the people's fate if legislative and executive controls were ever to assume the controls of the other. When the time comes where the BLM starts to change disposition, and I believe it will, our job will become, as Dad said, "to claim our rights and tell them to go back to the confines of the rule of law. We must put the dragon back in its rightful box, the Constitution, which is the box that was created for it."

CHAPTER 14

REGIONAL GOVERNMENT

Rule by few!

There is always some form of governance in practice. While the American system was first established as a republic, the people have morphed it into functioning as something else.[252] As infuriating as it may be to some who implore the current American system to still be a healthy functioning republic, it must be realized that the once healthy republican system is now broken and currently functioning mainly as a democratic oligarchy—rule by few.

For review, remember the various developed forms of governance through the years can all be categorized within the small list below. The five main categories include the following:[253]

1. **Monarchy:** control by one.
2. **Anarchy:** control by none.
3. **Oligarchy:** control by few (often those considered the elite).
4. **Democracy:** control by majority in a group.
5. **Republic:** control by elected representatives.[254]

The horrific details within the stories of the Hammonds, Bundys, and ours, are the painful evidences that the current American system is functioning as a democratic oligarchy. But understanding the current system being ruled by a few is not enough if we wish to bring about positive change. We must also understand the political ideas and tactics used within this rule by few. In order to know how to fix something, we must first understand its mechanics.

We have already discussed the narrowly defined controls that the executive and legislative branches have been granted by the United States Constitution. We have pinpointed where a consolidation of control between the two branches are taking place and that is within the Code of Federal Regulations (CFR), which is administrative law authored and enforced by the executive branch. The next question I had in my discovery process was this: what methods were used to bring about this rule by few? A transition such as this doesn't just happen overnight. It is a slow process of planning and execution. It was not long before I was introduced to the ideology of regionalism.

> "Regional Government is where public officials from multiple units (jurisdictions) of government (schools, cities, counties, states, and federal government agencies, etc.) enter into contracts or otherwise to share control, functions, organization, and financing to address a problem (e.g. utilities) or a set of common problems (e.g. housing, transportation, environment, water etc.)."[255]

Regional government is a type of meritocracy, which is rule by expertise or merit. This type of rule falls under an oligarchy, rule by few. It was first formally introduced in the New World via a report called *Regional Factors in National Planning and Development*. This report is a 223-page document that was organized by the National Resources Committee upon the request of President Franklin D. Roosevelt. It was presented to him in December of 1935.[256] The report's preface is found on the first page in the letter to the President from the committee. It reads, "This report deals with important problems of planning and development which overlap *State lines* [emphasis added] or which require the use of combined Federal and State powers." The forward is found on the next page, wherein the title is, *The Problem* [emphasis added]. It is here where the authors of the report number what they feel are the top seven "urgent situations," the first being described as "The increasingly clear realization of the *inadequacy* [emphasis added] of single States to carry out all planning programs necessary for conserving our national resources..." Clearly, political boundaries were considered as a hindrance to the committee. Rather than state sovereignty and the right to private property ownership, the aim was to dissolve state boundaries and morph the nation's resources into one great whole. I don't know about you but that kind of reminds me of the philosophy found in *The Communist Manifesto*, wherein Karl Marx's theory is clearly an abolition of property in land and application of all rents of land to public purposes.[257]

A current detailed study of how the regionalisms introduced in the 1930s have negatively impacted the life, liberty, and pursuit of happiness of residents within each developed region would be a powerful tool proving there are dangers associated with centralized government. You have already read some of the recent devastating results from the regions within the states of Oregon, Nevada, and Arizona, including court discovery and rulings. If only time and whitespace would allow room to share the many unmentioned egregious details of suffering due to this centralized government within our nation. Because only a small part of these families' and states' histories are covered in this book. I am confident that such studies, if there ever are organized, would witness to the same as what Oregon, Nevada, and Arizona already currently testify of.

But maybe the fact that rural poverty in the West is greater than urban poverty in the West is enough to get someone questioning why that is.[258] If curiosity were to move any into research, it would not be long before they discovered the very thing the founders uncovered years ago, that "property is surely a right of mankind as real as liberty.... The moment the idea is admitted into society that property is not as sacred as the laws of God, and that there is not a force of law and public justice to protect it, anarchy and tyranny commence."²⁵⁹ Or maybe study would lead to the stories of the early Pilgrims witnessing of this same principle.

> *As the Pilgrims established their colony in America in 1620, their economic system was based upon a socialistic philosophy of communal property. It was a form of nonviolent communism. What they found was that they would starve to death under the concept, proving by their experience that work ceased and laziness ensued. Only when they set up private ownership were the Pilgrims able to begin to prosper. It was essential to their very survival. And of course, the repeated failure of successive communist "five-year economic plans" in the former Soviet Union and the near-starvation conditions that continually exist under communism are testimony of the fact that communism does not result in effective, productive efforts by those who suffer under it yoke.²⁶⁰*

It is sobering to see history negatively repeating itself. Just as the early Pilgrims, the rural people of the 21st century are starving. They are being choked by the results of putting into practice through the use of unconstitutional law, the principles of "nonviolent communism". As result they are forced to resort to federal welfare just to put food on the table and a roof over their heads. Whereas, if nationalist, socialistic, communist fiat would cease and desist and return to the confines of the American rule of law, these families who are regulated out of business could live, using their liberty to pursue their happiness and as result, prosper and contribute to their communities.

Fathers of Academic Regionalism

The authors of this 223-page report on regional government are the fathers of modern academic regionalism. It was their language that set the stage for an ever-emerging culture whose understanding of what a good system of government is to be contrary to that which really brings forth fruits of freedom and liberty. The ultimate fruits of regionalism are the formation of an empire, which never is in the favor of the people's freedom and liberty. The American nation never was intended to have an empire.

Whether or not if it truly was the intent of the authors of the 223-report to father a movement toward captivity, we will never know. All that can be done is draw meaning from the language used to communicate in the report. When read, the language conveys a frustration and contempt toward the United States political geographical boundaries. The words "frozen [progress due to] written ...constitutions and laws" was used to describe the separation of legislative, executive, and judicial controls within each jurisdiction.[261] There is no doubt there was a cognitive effort to compromise the integrity of the system of government the founders developed.

Below are a few of the suggested regions found within the 223-page report. It is no coincidence the suggested boundaries are influenced by the earth's *natural resources*. Why do you think that is?[262] Those authoring the 223-page report were not ignorant to the reality *"if one controls the earth's resources, then they control the people."*[263]

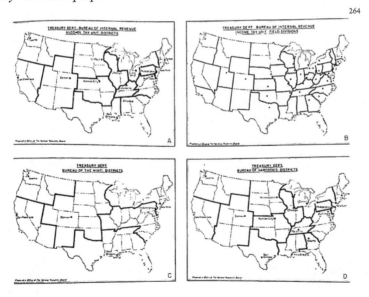

[264]

Experience has shown when a small group of people control the earth's resources by region (ignoring state social contracts), the desired result of freedom and liberty for *all* people is never the lasting outcome. Slavery, in some form or another, is always the result of regionalism.[265]

I wish to continue on with expressed sentiments within the 223-page regional factors study. It reads, "Regionalism envisages the Nation First, making the total national culture the final arbiter…"[266]

This idea contradicts state sovereignty and implies that the people have no right to representation that they vote on. The report goes on to read, "It is in this direction that Federal systems may find a solution for otherwise insoluble problems that arise out of the division of constitutional powers."[267]

Rather than doing as John Adams admonishes, to learn "to prize the checks and balances of a free government, … [and never forget] the miseries of [history], …which rose from their ignorance of [the importance of checks and balance]," the people seek to compromise the integrity of a system of government that would protect against frequent repeats of history's miseries."[268]

The report goes on to suggest that the "putting together of Federal powers into an unified program" is requisite and the only way for successful development.[269] This statement suggests the separation of controls with each political boundary was a mistake, assuming human nature to have mystically changed, therefore, no longer needing a system designed to protect humanity from aggrandizing opportunists. It goes on further, "Whenever State or Federal Government comes directly into contact with the realm of *natural resources* [emphasis added] the problem of regionalism tends to emerge."[270]

Why would this be a problem? Why not leave the things of the state to be managed and owned by the state? The intent never was for the federal government to own and control the nation's *natural resources*. If that were the case, the nation would be an empire, not the United States of America. The intent was for each state to have ownership and access to its *natural resources* so as to create industry for the people of the state.

Remember, sustainment of life and all wealth is derived from the earth's *natural resources*. It is not coincidence there continues to be cognitive efforts to "obtain sole management of the government" as a means to have control of the earth's *natural resources*. Such dispositions sees to it "that robbers fill…

judgement-seats—having usurped the power and authority of the land; laying aside the commandments of God, ...doing no justice unto the children of men; ...that they might get gain and glory of the world."[271]

The Center for Self Governance describes further the functions of regional government:

> *Regional government is an effort to address the challenges the interstate compact clause in the US Constitution poses to intergovernmental co-operation where a perceived common problem may exist. [Despite the mindset of those wishing to use regionalism], the division of constitutional powers between jurisdictions is inherent to the framework of the United States [to avoid the nation morphing into an empire. In the mind of those converted to the doctrine of regionalism, there is] conflict between jurisdictions, [which] limits cooperation between those jurisdictions. Regional Government is seen, by a growing number of public personnel through all levels of government, as the solution to this perceived problem.*
>
> *Regional Government is where public officials from multiple units (jurisdictions) of government (schools, cities, counties, states, and federal government agencies, etc.) enter into contracts or otherwise to share control, functions, organization, and financing to address a problem (e.g. utilities) or a set of common problems (e.g. housing, transportation, environment, water etc.) On agreement, the representatives of the member units will form a board that is recognized by the state or state encompassing the Regional Government.*
>
> *The newly formed Regional Government can be a non-profit corporation or a stand-alone jurisdiction. In some cases (and expanding), Regional Government is authorized by the State Government to legislate, tax, and assess. In most Regional Government, representatives are selected by the member unit of government. Representatives can be either an elected, proxy, or employee of the participating member unit.*
>
> *All 50 states have incorporated Regional Government into either the state constitution or state law. Most counties and municipalities, across the United States, have become or participate in municipal planning*

commissions, metropolitan planning organizations, regional planning agencies, council of governments, etc.[272]

For the Sake of Application

In the map below there is drawn five fictitious regions for the purpose of illustrating how organized regions breach political boundaries.

-(drawn by Thara Tenney)

Notice,

1. Region number one includes six states.
2. Region number two includes six states.
3. Region number three includes five states and that of another region.
4. Region number four includes six states and that of three regions.
5. Region number five includes 11 states and that of one region.

According to the function of regional government, there is regulatory law (CFR) governing each respective region for each separate department of the executive branch. This law is *'written and enforced'* by the agents who function under the executive branch.[273]

Any fair-minded person understanding Article 4, Section 4 of the Constitution in conjunction with the purpose of the Tenth Amendment is left exasperated. Why? Because the practice of regionalism will be the means whereby the United States will gradually transform into an empire. It was state sovereignty that was to be the way of safeguarding against this. Make no mistake, the practice of regionalism is chipping away state sovereignty.

Article IV, section four of the Constitution

Let's review Article 4, Section 4 of the Constitution: "The United States shall guarantee to every state in this Union a Republican Form of Government."[274]

Another way to define a republican form of government is "one in which the powers of sovereignty are vested in the people and are exercised by the people, either directly, or through representatives chosen by the people, to whom those powers are specially delegated."[275] While this definition is a vague comparative to the *many* elements of republicanism, it is good enough for the purpose of teaching how regionalism is a dangerous doctrine.

Regional government grossly violates each state's guarantee to a republican form of government. To illustrate, focus on the fictitious region number five on the map above. Think for a moment about the eleven different states and one region that are included within region five. The unelected agents who *'write and enforce'* law for region five are not *'chosen by the people'* through the democratic element of republicanism as Article 4, Section 4 of the United States Constitution guarantees each state. You see here that not only does regionalism grossly consolidate the legislative and executive controls but the people of these eleven different states do not get to vote on whom their representatives will be and thus there is no agent accountability. This is a recipe for disaster.

Dad tried to teach this to help people understand what the purpose was behind him ending his contractual relationship with the Bureau of Land Management. He said in one particular video,

> *Let's start by going back and laying down the intent of our founding fathers and the intent of the Constitution. Our founding fathers came out of tyranny and they were really concerned that this land be a land of freedom. So, they did several things. One of the first things they did when they laid out the Constitution, was to divide the powers into three branches. We all know what those are: the legislative, executive, and judicial.*
>
> *...The other thing they did to keep from having a centralization of power into a central government, which decreases the freedom of the individual. They limited the amount of landmass that the central power could control, called the federal government. Because if you can control the land, you can control the food production and you can control the people. Currently, the BLM or the federal government lays claim to one third of the landmass of the United States.*
>
> *...They say they own and control this. In this landmass, they claim to have what is called exclusive legislative ability. What they have done is combine all three branches of power [in a way where there is not power of recall]. In other words, we don't elect the [representatives who govern these mass lands]. They are not accountable to us. ...The founders knew that that was a potential of combining great power under one head. So they limited by the letter of the law what land the federal government could control. This is found in Article 1, Section 8, Clause 17.*[276]

Let's pretend for a moment the agents who see to the duties of the fictitious region five were elected by the people. The question then would be, what people, from what state, get to vote for the region's representatives? With this system, state sovereignty is completely dissolved! With this system no state can truly be guaranteed their republican form of government as Article 4, Section 4 of the Constitution decrees.

The Tenth Amendment

Let's now review the Tenth Amendment: "The powers not delegated to the United States by the Constitution, nor prohibited by it to the States, are reserved to the States respectively, or to the people."[277]

The founding fathers had good reason to pen the Tenth Amendment. Even the possibility of a good system transitioning into supporting big government was deeply feared. For this reason, the Tenth Amendment was written. Its language beautifully limits the controls delegated to the federal government, leaving the things of the states to be taken care of by the people of the states.

Please understand the 411 agencies, who *write and enforce* regulatory law (Code of Federal Regulations, CFR), do not function within the system the founders established. These executive agencies function within a system of government called regional government. When our representatives continually refuse to uphold the Constitution and refuse to be the necessary checks and balance to safeguard against centralized government and the results are painful loss of life, liberty, and pursuit of happiness as the Hammond, Bundy, and Finicum cases illustrate so clearly, what are a people to do?

How Has This Happened

If you are anything like me you must be asking yourself, how has this happened? What does the 411 executive agencies and its Code of Federal Regulations (CFR) mean for freedom and liberty if its practice is contrary to the laws that pertain the maintenance of freedom and liberty? How do we fix this so we might avoid the negative results of such governance?

When the root of a dangerous problem such as this is discovered, there is nothing more frustrating than not knowing how to effectively fix it. I say, don't despair. Know you are not alone. I have found that proper training is a must have, if successful results are really wanted. In my toil of looking for this, I have found resources that help, and you can too.[278]

Despite any questions of where to start in fixing the problems at hand, for now, it's enough to recognize that the modern use of regional governance demands from its people a heavier burden to maintain freedom's integrity. It means "the great American Experiment" George Washington spoke of is now exponentially more difficult.[279] While all is not yet lost for American freedom, wouldn't you, as the jury of this case, agree that the political pendulum is on its violent swing? Surely, my Dad's blood is witness of that. Again, I ask, was Dad the villain he was made out to be? Was the use deadly force truly warranted? You decide.

May the course of freedom's preservation not take more innocent lives is my prayer. It doesn't have to continue on this way, if we but truly learn what freedom and liberty are and begin our return to the principles of free government. If we do not, history tells there is no way of avoiding what the results will be.

CHAPTERS 15-20

THE GREAT AMERICAN EXPERIMENT

George Washington expressed in his first inaugural address, the "smiles of Heaven, can never be expected on a nation that disregards the eternal rules of order and right, which Heaven itself has ordained: And since the preservation of the sacred fire of liberty, and the destiny of the Republican model of Government, are justly considered as deeply, perhaps *as finally staked on the experiment entrusted to the hands of the American people.*"[280]

The previous section of "Dad's Fundamentals - Before Oregon" witnesses to the painful reality of our failing at this ongoing experiment. The collateral damage puts my stomach in knots. The heavy question remains: will we choose to continue to lose at this political tug of war?

CHAPTER 15

THE PUSH AND PULL BURDEN WE ALL FACE

Since the beginning of humanity, preserving the gift of life, liberty, and the pursuit of happiness has been burdened with an eternal, yet essential, tug of war. Grasping tentacles heretofore threatened these rights in beguiling ways. Pushing apathetic individuals into carnal delusions of false security, thus pulling freedoms asunder. This push and pull is the means by which, even the greatest people from all eras, are acted upon with the aim to influence an abandonment of that which is of greatest consequence. To assume such opposition does not exist in today's modern world is a damning delusion.

While it is imperative to realize this essential tug of war to be uniquely active in all aspects of life, the focus here is dedicated to the push and pull found within the world of politics. As this essential political tug of war process wades its course, with choice as the determining factor of what side wins, the preservation of life, liberty, and the pursuit of happiness continues to prove intensely difficult. Ironically, losing the three is extremely easy.

Why is it so easy to lose at this pull? Think of the metaphoric grasping tentacles tugging to win in your life. Allow the realization to swell within your mind and heart, the results if we continue to lose at this game of push and pull. We know the results; history has painfully revealed this. But I dare say, knowing about such results and personally feeling the sting are two entirely different things. My family's agony as a result of losing Dad the way we did is beyond the pen's ability to convey. Helping to prepare my father's dead body for viewing has forever burned a crater in my mind and heart. Be that as it may, I will forever be amazed by Dad's words he broadcast over the Utah wire just seven months before his life was taken. He said,

> [Long ago, on] Christmas eve and Christmas morning, there was a gentleman that I have great respect for called George Washington. He crossed the Delaware with his soldiers. He took on the British Hessians. He lost not one soldier to armed conflict. ...But he did lose two. Two died before they even got there. Two men frozen to death before they arrived there. The bloody foot tracks could be traced in the snow. Why is my life more valuable than their life? They gave their all. They didn't even get the chance to fire the musket. They died frozen. I am sure they had loved ones, mothers, fathers, and probably children. Their dreams were cut off, but they gave their all for this freedom. Why do we reap the fruits and rewards of their sacrifices and then when it comes down to this time [of needing to defend our rights] that we don't stand up? Will you be able to hold your head up? Will I be able to hold my head up when we meet together [in the next life with those who have gave their all]? If I don't stand, I can't. They gave everything and so many people have given everything. It is time to stand. I want anybody that hears this, please pull

your courage to the sticking point. Strengthen your resolve. Stiffen your back. Let's stand. It may cost you your life; that's okay. Just like I said to that cowboy, we all die. Die for something good. Let your children and posterity know where you stand. Don't disappoint your ancestors. This is the day and the time.[281]

Where do we begin our stand?

We must realize these metaphoric grasping tentacles are indeed pushing and pulling us. May we push aside the

> *psychological obstructions we all tend to erect in an attempt to shade our eyes from the glare of troublesome truths. [This] powerful tendency to obscure, distort, and fictionalize on behalf of a fabricated reality [is a] hindrance to self-understanding [that] is far more formidable than society's many diversionary temptations.... Those who fail [at] this [self-understanding] will never command the intuitions and insights requisite for real leadership.*[282]

Rather than accept failure, let's willingly choose to learn the tactics of these grasping tentacles. Ours can be a choice to toil to *know ourselves.*[283] Why? Because as we become aware, then appropriate strategy can aid success in this political push and pull. Such effort is a way to honor the toil and sacrifice of those who have given all.

Continue with me as I review a few of the themes these metaphoric grasping tentacles take on.

CHAPTER 16

ATROPHY TUG OF WAR

"Truth by nature is self-evident. As soon as you remove the cobwebs of ignorance that surround it, it shines clear."
—**Mahatma Gandhi**

Habit and Long Training

Dad was a creature of habit, right down to the clothing he wore. Ever since his adolescence, every day—with the exception of Sundays—he wore Wranglers, boots, a long-sleeve button-up, leather belt with a bull head buckle positioned on the left hip, and his keys hooked to a belt loop. While some people describe such custom as drag predictable, I call it the characteristic of being the same yesterday, today, and forever—order that can be trusted.

As far as accessories go, he was pretty simple, unless out on the range. It was then he wore his jingle spurs, handmade leather chaps, and on the left hip, his colt 45. No matter the occasion, with the exception of church, a cowboy hat was his go-to. I never knew until my mid-twenties that he kept hundred-dollar bills folded up in the brim. He referred to this hidden stash as *his boys* who'd rescue him and others in times of need.

Then there was his wedding ring. His workload often determined how it was worn. If not on his hand, it hung around his neck from a leather strip underneath his shirt. He also fashioned a black leather band watch on his left wrist. When not worn, his arm made people uncontrollably stare. I guess it's not every day you see a shockingly defined watch-shaped tan line.

Last, but certainly not least was what I call his man bag. This bag, while style varied over the years, was always black in color. This black man bag was notorious for weighing at least 50 pounds. He would carry that thing everywhere he went. He would even take it into sporting events and movie theaters, where people would look at him questioning, "What's the bag for, fella? We are here to be entertained, not work."

The old cliché "You can learn a lot about a woman by the contents of her purse" also applies to Dad's man bag. Anyone peering in would conclude that he was well-read. He used any down time to study, even if it was half time at a ball game. It wasn't until about a year before he was killed that he started venturing into using technology for his studies, giving the well-used man bag and his shoulder a rest.

Now you might be thinking, he must have been socially awkward hiding behind his books. In his mind, the case was quite contrary. While he was true to form of the phrase *work hard: play hard*, he just had no need for fanfare and yet, when he wanted to, he fit right in, no matter the audience.

He was good at interacting with others but doing so was not energizing to him. In the different seasons of his life where being the face was expected of him, he confessed to have often taken breaks in the one place he knew he couldn't be approached, a bathroom stall. While the idea is funny to some, this was his way of coping.

For him, that which was most energizing was a place of quiet deep thought. This was natural to him and that is what he often sought for. Dad once communicated how he loved silence, and so do I. For him it was during these quiet moments that he worked at internalizing his recent studies. This was important to him because he understood that a stable preservation of humanity's unalienable rights of life, liberty, and the pursuit of happiness greatly depended upon the intelligence of the people.

While every era has provided unique tug of wars to expand the minds of its people, Dad could see the acquisition of knowledge and wisdom faced great opposition in the 21st century. I see now this is why Dad helped facilitate healthy boundaries for electronics and entertainment. I am sure his motivation mirrored the sentiments of Ezra Taft Benson, a man Dad honored deeply. Benson prayed, "May it never come to pass that 'my people are destroyed for a lack of knowledge.'"[284]

As much of an advantage as having information at the fingertips is, Dad knew never in history has a people been so bombarded with content that is false, degrading, addictive, mind-numbing, time-wasting, and destructive. He often witnessed, truly our hearts are being sifted through as we prove who it is we serve by what our choice will be as to where to spend our time.

The Law of Atrophy

I grew up understanding that if I, when *pushed and pulled* into alluring content, do not choose proper balance between numbing the mind and disciplined growth, atrophy of my mind would become my fate. Atrophy is a gradual decline in effectiveness or vigor due to underuse or neglect. The idea that I'm either being dumbed down or progressing is sobering. This eternal law cannot be escaped.

Is it of any wonder that the laws of nature and of nature's God saw to it that even the anatomy of the body is bound by these same eternal laws? While Dad relentlessly sought to avoid atrophy on his mind, he did the same to spare his body of a gradual decline. The image of Dad exercising daily—with an exception of Sundays—in his '70s-style cutoff blue jean shorts, knee-high white socks, and a t-shirt was enough to forever mortify my teenage self. Despite his well-maintained physique, I cringed every time I saw his hairy legs. I swear his legs seemed as if they never saw the light of day. It was only during exercise that anyone would see him in a t-shirt and shorts, and boy were they short.[285]

Don't get me wrong, he never was a gym junkie. That just wasn't his style. He was a homebody and, thus, his morning regime was always in the living room before anyone got out of bed. He did a series of push-ups, sit-ups, bicep curls, and sometimes squats. He would always end his workout with an outdoor run. I remember once when I was a young adult visiting home suggesting in conversation how Dad really loved running. He responded to my assumption by boldly stating he did *not love* running. I was so dumbfounded that I was speechless. He didn't follow his statement with anything else. He just left me to my thoughts.

That moment of almost disbelief was another huge eye-opener into Dad's character. I thought to myself, "You mean all those years of early mornings, you choosing to exercise was not because you loved it?" I couldn't believe it. I am sure at that moment I looked like a deer in headlights. I marveled then at his willingness to choose a consistent uncomfortable practice to ensure his ability to have maximum effectiveness. From that point on, I resolved within myself to seek to do the same in all areas of my life that battle this push and pull of atrophy.

The Law of Maintenance

Dad taught me through example that to prolong effectiveness and vigor to whatever *matter* is experiencing atrophy, the unique laws of nature pertaining to that *matter* must be studied and applied.[286] This effort can be called *the law of maintenance*. This law is universal. No matter who we are, the body becomes prematurely sick and diseased if not properly maintained with healthy food, consistent exercise, and adequate amounts of sleep. No matter our age, relationships deteriorate if not properly maintained with meaningful time spent together, forgiveness, and repentance. No matter where we live, a garden is stricken with noxious weeds, drought, and pests if not properly maintained with the consistent plucking of weeds, strategic irrigation, and active pest control. No matter our denomination, spirituality darkens if not properly maintained with daily humble spiritual practices, weekly church attendance, and service. No matter our political system of governance, those in control of political switches seek to expand their control at the expense of others if not properly maintained with appropriate state and federal separations of controls, an active electorate educated on the reason for such separations, and a people loyal to the golden rule.

Every human is allotted the same 24 hours. The *great American political experiment* delicately hangs on the balance of choice.[287] Will the scale lean toward the maintenance of things that matter most, or will it be subservient to the disposition of 'eat, drink, and be merry for tomorrow we die?'[288] Thomas Jefferson said in a letter to Edward Everett in 1824, "The qualifications for self-government in society are not innate. They are the result of *habit and long training* [emphasis added]."

What is your choice?

CHAPTER 17

ATROPHY TUG OF WAR: PEOPLE AND THEIR SYSTEM OF GOVERNMENT

"...the burden should come upon all the people, that every man might bear his part."
—**Mosiah 29:34**

AUTHOR'S NOTES

I remember as a child lying on the living room floor listening to Dad read The Hobbit *to us kids. In my mind, I would take on the challenge of solving Bilbo Baggins's riddles, to no avail. Dad really enjoyed the works of J. R. R. Tolkien and, naturally, we kids followed suit.*

When the J. R. R. Tolkien movies came out in theater, Mom and Dad splurged and treated the entire family. This was a rare occasion as our family is so large.

After Dad's murder, my mind would often drift to memories like this, of him and us. Even before he was taken from us, I could never think of J. R. R. Tolkien's works without also thinking of Dad. Except now, it's different.

You must wonder how any of this correlates with the topic of 'atrophy tug of war' as it applies to people and the system of government' the Founders established?

Keep reading and you will begin to understand.

Classic narratives such as The Hobbit, The Lord of the Rings, Harry Potter, *and many others give a unique opportunity for the reader to develop a keen understanding into the complexities of social life. This happened for me as my perspective broadened into being able to see into the minds of characters as they experienced hardship and fulfillment. Whereas, in real life, only assumptions can be made into the why behind the state of others.*

While wrestling with the emotions of grief, anger, sadness, loneliness, frustration, and duty while being overwhelmed, lost, and exhausted after the loss of my Father, it was natural for me to identify, on an entire new level, with the characters from the books that we had come to know and love together. Frodo, the lead character from The Lord of the Rings, *and I, were now more alike than ever before.*

Frodo is a young carefree hobbit who was born and raised in the Shire. The Shire is a region of J. R. R. Tolkien's fictional Middle-earth. It's settled exclusively by Hobbits and known for its peaceful rolling hills of tall lush grass. The hobbits were quite alright remaining removed from the troublesome goings-on in the rest of Middle-earth. There was safety in the predictability their cultural customs of tea time before breakfast, brunch, lunch, dinner and finally supper. Any adventure out into the unknown was widely condemned. The safe Shire was all they needed.

Be that as it may, Frodo was the nephew of the Shire's nonconformist Bilbo Baggins whose life was anything but ordinary. His was the epitome of dangerous adventure as he, alongside wizards, elves, humans, and dwarves, took on the dark sides' goblins, trolls, and orcs. United, they pressed forward with what in time evolved into one cause, to preserve the life, liberty, and the pursuit of happiness for all of Middle-earth, despite their differing origins.

Notwithstanding, Bilbo's heart of gold that carried him through the years of his perilous stand, he grew old. Upon retirement from adventure, he bequeathed a curious ring to his young nephew Frodo. Unbeknownst to Frodo's young soul, this ring would be the driving force behind that which would change his destiny from his current carefree life in the Shire to that of one much like unto his beloved Bilbo. This endowment was the ring of power, which Frodo was destined to destroy. Such a quest would not be easy, for the whole of Middle-earth searched like ravages for this ring because it's owner would be given powers.

Frodo, the small unsuspecting creature, was seemingly not cut out for the task at hand to rid the world of the ring that corrupted any who laid hold of it, yet it was thrust upon him. The ring's opportunity for power caused even the very elect to tremble in want of it and act out in inhumane ways to gain possession of it, and yet innocent Frodo was its bearer. Its burden was heavy.

One day as it deeply weighed on him, he said to his trusted ally, Gandalf the Gray: "'I wish it need not have happened in my time,' said Frodo. 'So do I,' said Gandalf, 'and so do all who live to see such times. But that is not for them to decide. All we have to decide is what to do with the time that is given us.'"[289]

Prior to Dad's murder, I had been somewhat of an apathetic individual, much like unto innocent Frodo from the Shire. Mine was a life of maintaining the push and pull of church, family, and health. I guess I could have been stereotyped as your typical Christian, yoga pants, soccer mom.

While Frodo in the Shire and my direction in life prior to our shift was not completely unworthy, you could say we both had been pushed into a delusion of false security. We both understood there to be forces of evil out in the world. The illusion was earth's dark powers would never waste significant effort on us, for we were nobodies.

Just as Frodo's heart yearned to return to the Shire after tasting the sorrow and pains from piercing attacks, I too, deeply longed to return to my Shire. After Father's murder, I felt as if the evil of the world was out to devour our family, and Dad wasn't there in the flesh anymore to protect us. His murder was a huge blow and the pain was only amplified while witnessing countless people's hearts fail them for reasons we read of in 2 Timothy 3: 1-5:

> This know also, that in the last days perilous times shall come. For men shall be lovers of their own selves, covetous, boasters, proud, blasphemers, disobedient to parents, unthankful, unholy, without natural affection, trucebreakers, false accusers, incontinent, fierce, despisers of those that are good, traitors, heady, highminded, lovers of pleasures more than lovers of God; having a form of godliness, but denying the power thereof: from such turn away."

My Father's blood as the painful evidence to these things made my soul sick. There was no question, The People were losing the never-ending sick game of political tug of war and I wanted to know every ugly reason why, so I could do my part in fixing it. This was my point of no return. I had to fully understand.

Why, you ask, when the government is not upon my shoulders? I answer by saying it is not to assume omnipotence, but because something changed inside of me the day American agents murdered my Dad.

Yet, even after painful points of no return in our stories, a very real force sought to pull my fictional friend Frodo and I back into what once was our safe illusion. For Frodo, it was the Shire. My yearning was to return to the enjoyment my simple Christian, yoga-pants, soccer-mom life provided. That life was blissfully void of the undesirable pains that accompany political tug of war. Tried as I might, I was a changed person. So my duty became to press forward in search of further truth. This would be the foundation to the required work my new lifestyle habits would require.

Thus far, I have been blessed with an undeniable surety that Gandalf was right, that there are other forces at work in this world, besides the will of evil, and it is glorious to behold. I have also come to understand that all will stand before a crossroads, and too, must decide if they'll return to the Shire or press on in duty until the land is safe.

I quote a highly respected mentor of mine to convey what is in my heart about this topic of Atrophy Tug of War as it applies to people and the system of government the Founders established:

> My purpose today is to [share what I have learned]. I do it with great humility for two reasons. First, what I say could discourage some who are struggling in the midst of great adversity and feel their foundation of faith is crumbling. And second, I know that ever-greater tests lie before me before the end of life. Therefore, the prescription I offer you has yet to be proven in my own life through enduring to the end."[290]

The focus of my dear friend's sentiments was solely to encourage the sufferer through the type of deep personal adversity that tests belief in God, to remind all within reach of his witness that "if we have faith in Jesus Christ, the hardest as well as the easiest times in life can be a blessing." His humble sentiment can also apply to a person's wrestle to work toward proper balance in the push and pull maintenance process of family, church, and government.

Throughout time, humanity has wrestled with language to establish political boundaries for entrusted representatives in which to operate for the protection of life, liberty, and the pursuit of happiness. History has produced many social contracts forming different systems of government proving the preservation of these rights to be intensely difficult. Mournfully, experience has also shown that losing them at the hands of out-of-control people is shockingly easy.

In an effort to understand why this was, the Founders aggressively studied past and present human government of multiple cultures.[291] Their study unfolded before them patterns that always result in some form of anarchy, leading to tyranny.[292]

The Founders' study unfolded countless stories of chaos. Their findings were that this chaos was the result of the people's poorly established system of government. Each story had its fair share of aggrandizing opportunists who strategically laid in wait for the political pendulum to swing back under the guise of a different lipstick, creating a grossly false euphoria that those flipping the control switches of government were heroes. Some form of slavery was always the result.

Their study and enlightenment led to a heavy burden. Their burden was to organize a new system of government amid the pernicious patterns of human history. The hope was to diminish the forceful gravity effect behind the political pendulum they studied, to avoid continued blood and horror. Their goal was lasting peace and prosperity. They took it as their charge to develop a system of government to protect humanity against themselves. Their work was an effort to raise the bar of human government through federal and state separations of control outlined in social contracts known as constitutions. The integrity of the system hung on the balance of the people's willingness to maintain it, for atrophy in all its forms is always at play.

As stated previously, to achieve success at this political *push and pull* while not forgetting the laws I'd atrophy, the unique laws of nature that pertain to the Founders rise of the bar to the governmental system, must be studied and applied to avoid decline in effectiveness due to neglect. This is no trifle matter. Maintaining the integrity of the system truly is a matter of life or death, liberty or slavery, and the pursuit of property or oppression. Opting out of this maintenance process has and will continue to demand "blood and suffering to regain lost freedom."[293]

> *Perhaps this was the reason President George Washington expressed in his first inaugural address,*
>
>> the smiles of Heaven, can never be expected on a nation that disregards the eternal rules of order and right, which Heaven itself has ordained: And since the preservation of the sacred fire of liberty, and the destiny of the Republican model of Government, are justly considered as deeply, perhaps as finally staked on the experiment entrusted to the hands of the American people.[294]

The wise Benjamin Franklin, when exiting the Constitutional Convention was asked by a woman named Mrs. Powell, "Well, Doctor, what have we got, a republic or a monarchy?" Franklin responded with deep soberness, "a republic, if you can keep it."[295]

The American republican system of government, as a shared control between both the governed and governors, was divinely inspired. Jefferson admonished that all citizens must be involved, "holding everyone its delegated share of powers, and constituting truly a system of balance and checks for the government where every man is a share in the direction of his ward republic, ...and feel that he is a participator in the government of affairs, not merely at an election day in the year, but every day."[296]

Ancient leaders of a people who occupied North America before Jesus Christ's birth expressed the same concepts. Mosiah, who was a righteous King, counseled with his people at the end of his days;

> *Therefore, if it were possible that you could have just kings, who would establish the laws of God, and judge this people according to his commandments, yea, if you could have men for your Kings who would do even as my father Benjamin did for this people - I say until you if this could always be the case then it would be expedient that you should always have Kings to rule over you.*
>
> *Now I say unto you, that because all men are not just it is not expedient that ye should have a king or Kings to rule over you.*

For behold, how much iniquity doth one wicked King cause to be committed, yea, and what great destruction!

And now I desire that this inequality should be no more in this land, especially among this my people; but I desire that this land be a land of liberty, and every man may enjoy his rights and privileges alike… that the burden should come upon all the people, that every man might bear his part [emphasis added]."[297]

It is written of another North American pre-Christ military leader by the name of Moroni who developed what he called the Title of Liberty. He wrote upon it, "In memory of our God, our religion, and freedom, and our peace, our wives, and our children." He admonished the people to *covenant to actively maintain their rights and religion* [emphasis added].[298] It was said of Moroni, "if all men had been, and were, and ever would be, like unto Moroni, behold, the very powers of hell would have been shaken forever; yea, the devil would never have power over the hearts of the children of men."[299]

To modern men, God has said, the Constitution "should be *maintained* [emphasis added] for the rights and protection of all flesh."[300] Dad explained to me many times what he understood this to mean when he said,

When our politicians and courts fail to restrain this federal government to the strict confines of the law—remember they are specific and enumerated powers narrowly defined—then the individual states are to step up and restrain the federal government. Well, our states have failed to do that. They have failed to restrain them. What is the final recourse to uphold our Constitution, the law of the land, and the liberty of the people? It has to be the individual Americans. That is the last line of defense, the last recourse we have.[301]

Remember the mighty George Washington called the republican system of shared control "the great experiment entrusted to the hands of the American people." He did so because its success truly depends upon a citizenry who not only understand what freedom and liberty are but also a people who understand both federal and state social contracts (Constitutions) with a refined skill to appropriately wield civic authority with others in unity to ensure that the integrity of the social contracts is honored. Civic maintenance demands these things.

What does this maintenance process look like, some might ask? A friend of mine expressed once how it "is easy as 1-2-3."

1. Learn the system.
2. Create a community of keep the republic.[302]
3. Troubleshoot and fix."[303]

As straightforward as 1-2-3 sounds, it is the process of atrophy, in all its forms, that creates the elements of great difficulty. Remember, all things must have opposition to provide a means for agency, even the maintenance of systems of government.

The fruits from a lack of maintenance, whether it be in self or systems of government, allows atrophy to thrive and, as a result, produces all levels of captivity. We truly bring upon ourselves our own condemnation, whether that be personal or communal.

It's Your Choice

Choose to be actively engaged in the American *experiment* Washington spoke of. Choose to work toward being a powerful *keeper* of what was bequeathed to you. Hold your *Title of Liberty* in firm kindness. Choose to be on the path of *maintenance* of your rights.

Don't stand idly by. Don't be a contributor to the unavoidable suffering caused by individual and communal lack of maintenance and disobedience to natural law. No people are void of the possibility of repeating history. Read the mourning words of an ancient North American missionary:

> *And seeing the people in a state of such awful wickedness, and those Gadianton robbers filling the judgment-seats—having usurped the power and authority of the land; laying aside the commandments of God, and not in the least aright before him; doing no justice unto the children of men;*

Condemning the righteous because of their righteousness; letting the guilty and the wicked go unpunished because of their money; and moreover to be held in office at the head of government, to rule and do according to their wills, that they might get gain and glory of the world, and, moreover, that they might the more easily commit adultery, and steal, and kill, and do according to their own wills—

Now this great iniquity had come upon the Nephites, in the space of not many years; and when Nephi saw it, his heart was swollen with sorrow within his breast; and he did exclaim in the agony of his soul:

Oh, that I could have had my days in the days when my father Nephi first came out of the land of Jerusalem, that I could have joyed with him in the promised land; then were his people easy to be entreated, firm to keep the commandments of God, and slow to be led to do iniquity; and they were quick to hearken unto the words of the Lord—."[304]

Despite Agony's Heavy Load

While agony is a heavy load, truly, solace can be found from those who have ebbed and flowed through suffering, remaining loyal to a worthy cause greater than self. The witness of such persons is no evil will prevail over one who builds their foundation upon the rock of the Creator. There is strength found in hanging on to those who were heretofore found with faith, hope, and "fear[ed] not: [because it was known without a doubt] they that be with us are more than they that be with them."[305]

The words of the brave Patrick Henry, a Virginia house delegate of 1775, lives on to say, "for my part whatever anguish of spirit it might cost, I am willing to know the worst, and provide for it."[306] Or how the might of the beloved American independence leader John Adams still empowers as his passion rings from the dust saying, "yet through the gloom, I can see the rays of ravishing light and glory."[307]

Above all, Jesus Christ is the transcendent personage to have gone before, whose life is an inspiration to all who learn of Him. It is He who, in meek obedience, stood for the freedom and liberty of *all*.

> *He was the Great Jehovah of the Old Testament, the Messiah of the New. Under the direction of His Father, He was the creator of the earth. ...Though sinless, He was baptized to fulfill all righteousness. He "went about doing good,"[308] yet was despised for it. His gospel was a message of peace and goodwill. He entreated all to follow His example. He walked the roads of Palestine, healing the sick, causing the blind to see, and raising the dead. He taught the truths of eternity, the reality of our premortal existence, the purpose of our life on earth, and the potential for the sons and daughters of God in the life to come.*
>
> *He instituted the sacrament as a reminder of His great atoning sacrifice. He was arrested and condemned on spurious charges, convicted to satisfy a mob, and sentenced to die on Calvary's cross. He gave His life to atone for the sins of all mankind. His was a great vicarious gift in behalf of all who would ever live upon the earth."[309]*

Through Jesus Christ, the demands of justice and mercy are met. The deep sorrow associated with unrighteousness, that the pen cannot convey, has available the opportunity to be swallowed up and replaced with peace and healing.

Conclusion

The great human experiment is to see if people will choose to participate in the maintenance of their system of government to secure the safety of their rights. To increase the chances for success, the unique laws of nature that pertain to the Founders' governmental *raising of the bar*, must be studied and applied, for atrophy is always at play.

This is no trifle matter. The integrity of the system truly is a matter of life or death, liberty or slavery, and the pursuit of property or oppression. Opting out of this maintenance process will demand *blood and suffering to regain lost freedom*.

When troubled, may the passion and toil of those who have gone before always inspire, uplift, and urge posterity to press on in the stand for what is right. Unfortunately, there is no avoiding the anguish of spirit and gloom associated with kindly eradicating unrighteous dominion. The prayer is, may this constant wrestle never be the means by which well-meaning people become the very thing they say they oppose.

CHAPTER 18

PROPERTY TUG OF WAR

"Man can only derive life and enjoyment from a perpetual search and appropriation; that is, from a perpetual application of his faculties to objects, or from labor. This is the origin of property."
—**Frédéric Bastiat**

One summer when most of my time was spent shoveling trenches with Dad was the beginning of my understanding this. I was about fifteen years old at the time. We worked daily, from sunup to sundown. The blazing sun beat upon us both. Boy, did it feel good to lay my head down at night. I still marvel how Dad joyfully worked like a horse, while I screamed inside wanting rest.

One day specifically changed me forever. It was around midday, when we were both covered in sweat and dust. Our work was done in very close proximity as the long trench was only about three feet wide. I remember feeling so much frustration because in my adolescent mind it appeared that for every shovel of dirt I removed from the trench, that the same amount spilled back in the hole from the sides. Exasperated, I finally asked Dad, "Are my efforts making any difference?" He responded, "Absolutely, for every shovel you remove, that is one I don't have to."

After our brief exchange, we pressed on. This time my thoughts focused more on a deep desire to keep helping. A few hours later, in a different tone I asked Dad, "What keeps you going?" It was his two-word response that changed me forever. Looking at me, he paused and rested his elbow on top of the worn shovel handle and said with tender resolve, "*You* guys."

At that time, my adolescent intellect didn't have the language to express fully what Dad had profoundly communicated, but I knew what I felt—loved.

Now, a good twenty years later, I can somewhat concisely communicate what I had learned about Dad on that hot dirty day. "*You* guys," meaning his wife and children, were his *pursuit of happiness*. Dad understood the purpose of life to be a time to work toward obtaining the things of real value. To him those things were not the things of this world.

As imperfect as he was and, despite great difficulty, he never gave up seeking to valiantly use his life and liberty to pursue what he cherished most and deeply wanted as his, an eternal family with no empty saddles.

Property ownership is a process and has forms both tangible and intangible.

The language pursuit of happiness gives an opportunity to contemplate "property [as] the sum of, or the fruit of, [one's] life and liberty. [One] purchases [their] property, not with money, but with [their] life and liberty."[310] Moreover, "the purpose of life is to obtain the things of real value, things that bring true happiness. In other words, to be free to spend our life and liberty in the *pursuit of happiness*."[311]

Obtaining property is a process of choice that can bring happiness or unhappiness.

The bold term *pursuit of happiness* presupposes that not all are guaranteed to the state of happiness.[312] Such an idea is an interesting concept often convoluted by the 21st-century culture bred to *expect fairness*. In reality, to achieve the outcome of happiness, personal liberty must be used in obedience to natural law as it pertains to the matter of happiness. The byproduct of such pursuit becomes one's personal property, and that property either contributes to or subtracts from personal happiness. Thus, as long as humanity has a heartbeat (life) and choice (liberty) they are in *pursuit of happiness* (property).

> *Men are free according to the flesh, and all things are given them which are expedient unto man. And they are free to choose liberty and eternal life, through the great Mediator of all men, or to choose captivity and death, according to the captivity and power of the devil; for he seeketh that all men might be miserable like unto himself.*[313]

Thereby we see either liberty and eternal life or captivity and death become our property depending on what laws were enlisted with the use of our life and liberty. Truly, "life plus liberty equals the pursuit of happiness," which is one's property.[314]

Property is a 'self-evident' right requiring protection through the establishment of government.

> *Property, per se, has no rights; but the individual-the man [or woman]- has three great rights, equally sacred from arbitrary interference: the right to his life, the right to his liberty, the right to his property...The three rights are so bound together as to be essentially one right. To give him his life but deny him his liberty, is to take from him all that makes his life worth living. To give him his liberty but take from him the property, which is the fruit and badge of his liberty, is to still leave him a slave.*[315]

Life, "liberty, and property—this is man. It is of these three things that it may be said, apart from all demagogic subtlety, that they are anterior and superior to all human legislation."[316]

We must not forget that "governments were instituted among men, deriving their just powers from the consent of the governed" for the protection of humanity's trinity of unalienable rights against mankind's unrighteous dominion. Unfortunately, some have confused the founders' pursuit of happiness language to not include private property ownership.

The necessary protection to humanity's trinity of unalienable rights must be understood to include tangible private property ownership. Why? Because the result of this confusion has been and will continue to be the driving force behind a circumvention of life, liberty, and property through socialistic traditions espoused by educators, mass media, and, ultimately, a gratuitous legislator, the result being *slavery*.[317]

There is sagacity in the founders' phrase *pursuit of happiness*.

In America's divorce from tyranny, the founders highlighted three fundamental rights of mankind: life, liberty, and the pursuit of happiness. Understanding the sagacity of using the phrase *pursuit of happiness* rather than using the originally proposed word *property* is helpful to the effort of sifting through modern disguised agendas that *push and pull* at the protection of humanity's unalienable rights.

While we do understand, just as the founders, that property is so much more than tangible items, but also the results of our pursuit, we also must, in today's modern world, understand the founders' term *pursuit of happiness* to mean that tangible personal property ownership is a self-evident right of humanity needing to be secured through the establishment of government. While there are forms of property that can never be manipulated by mortal men, such as a person's state of being, the founders' intent was to ensure the protection of the *process* of and the *results* from humanity's *time* spent in creativity with the *earth's tangible natural resources*. In explaining the intent of the founders' phrase *pursuit of happiness* in this way, it can be considered synonymous with the phrase labor (with property being the result of labor). "Man can only derive life and enjoyment from a perpetual search and appropriation; that is, from a perpetual application of his faculties to objects, or from labor. This is the origin of property."[318]

CHAPTER 19

POWER TUG OF WAR

"Noah Webster recognized that language contained both the centrifugal and the centripetal forces working together. 'These changes are the necessary consequences of changes in customs…'"
—**Webster and Slater**

AUTHOR'S NOTE

Growing up Dad would always recite to us kids as we were off to bed, "Don't forget…," leaving the rest of the sentence to be filled by us. We would always enthusiastically finish his phrase by saying, "…to say your prayers."

"Let's take a knee," Dad would say at the beginning and end of each day, at meal time, before and after departure and arriving, as well as in moments of gratitude or sorrow. It would always be, "Let's take a knee." In those many moments, I got to hear his tender submissive voice in prayer to his Father in heaven. I learned through observation who it was that he worshiped. Witnessing his meekness when it came to his God was very interesting to observe, especially as I got older. This was because in all other contexts, Dad was the epitome of the phrase 'he's his own man'.

While he was strong, self-reliant, self-driven, healthy, smart, and never beguiled by silly ideas, he too knew where his power originated, and it wasn't from himself. Some of my last memories of him include him reciting Job 1:21, "Naked came I out of my mother's womb, and naked shall I return thither: the Lord gave, and the Lord hath taken away; blessed be the name of the Lord."

───────◆───────

The relentless pull to cause one to forget where power originates has forever been the cause of much chaos and oppression. The tug of war between falsehoods and the true source of power is real, worth exploring, and should not be dismissed.

When I take time to observe the beauty of this earth, I marvel at the immensity of earth and the cosmos. "The power that caused this earth to roll on its axis and regulate the planets in their diurnal and annual motions, is beyond [humankind]. Their revolutions and spheres are fixed by nature's God, and they are so beautifully arranged..."[319] It is curious to note the placement of humanity's home in the universe to be very concise. The third planet from the sun and if just a bit closer or farther, the result would be catastrophe, either by fire or ice, causing extinction to the human family. Earth is the only known planet equipped with an atmosphere holding free oxygen, oceans of water on its surface, and the ability to sustain life. The phenomenality springing from these few details does not begin to scratch the surface of the varieties of detailed beauty and life on planet earth, and yet the human is the most superb of all that occupies the planet. Humanity being superior to all else that inhabits earth serves "the premise that power *originates outside* of the [people], but *resides in* the [people]."[320]

Many names

Throughout time, power's origin has been given many names, some of which include, but are not limited to, Mother Nature, the Great Spirit, I Am, God, Jehovah, Allah, Messiah, Elohim, Savior, Nature's God, Father, and the Good Shepherd. The language found in the Declaration of Independence presupposes there is a creator and references 'the laws of nature and of nature's God' as the source of power's origin. Whatever your belief system may be, I think we all can conclude that there is a source where power originates and that a portion of that power resides in each person.

This source made earth so there might be a place prepared for all to have the opportunity to experience life, liberty, and their pursuit of happiness. Once the completion of humanity's stage was attained, life,[321] i.e. power, was then breathed into the first man and woman. They were given the charge to have joy in the journey of experiencing their given rights and to multiply and replenish the earth.

Confusion between the origin of power and control

It is safe to assume, at first going, that the process of pursuing joy is easy. But children grew into adults with personal ambitions lacking temperance. The story of Cain and Abel was one of sorrow. Theirs was the first of many testifying of the results of willfully breaking the golden rule. It was and still is *this type* that demands not just any given governance, but a specifically engineered system to protect humanity against itself. A system to protect everyone's life, liberty, and pursuit of happiness.

The system's functions are what began the distinction between those who govern and those who were governed. Within these two developed classes was bred confusion between the words *power* and *control*.[322]

Through time the meaning of the words *power* and *control* have been confused to mean one in the same when in reality they are not synonymous. When the two words are misconstrued "the relations between [governed] and the [governor] appear to be the same as those that exist between the clay and the potter."[323] Such a culture teaches the governed to become docile while the governors take "possession of omnipotence,"[324] truly assuming the disposition as if life, liberty, and the pursuit of happiness "are nothing but grist for the mill of the sagacity of lawgivers."[325]

The governmental system and those *controlling* it are not "a golden calf unless the people worship it and treat it as if it is superior and animate."[326] When a people have forgotten where *power* originates "the hour of despotism has struck"[327] causing a butterfly effect of chaos and/or slavery.

Opposition in all things

My perspective on the principle of opposition in all things and how it applies to the two developed classes of governed and governors with the associated confusion between *power* and *control* might be interesting to some. The Holy Bible informs us that "the great dragon was cast out [of heaven], that old serpent, called the Devil, and Satan, which deceiveth the whole world: he was cast out into the earth, and his angels were cast out with him."[328] I understand their sole purpose is to provide the opposition so that we might have the opportunity to practice choose between two ideas, one right and one wrong.

How does any of this apply to systems of governance and the distinction between *power* and *control*, one might ask. I asked the same question and was led to the words of a man whom I believe was a mouthpiece of God. He decreed, "one of Lucifer's primary strategies [to hedge up the progression of mortals] has been to restrict [liberty] through the power of earthly governments."[329] When the people do not understand their given power by their creator, it is easy for it to be manipulated by those with ill intent.

No wonder the origination of *power* is so easily forgotten because both the governed and governors "wrestle [between two ideas], not against flesh and blood, but against principalities, against powers, against the rulers of the darkness of the world, against spiritual wickedness in high places."[330] There are forces in motion whose aim is to cause confusion, to cause distraction, to cause us to forget. It has been my observation and experience that any who become lax will be beguiled and deceived by the souls who were 'cast out into the earth.' Not one person is exempt from this unseen opposition.

In going up against such a force, it seems it would behoove us to *learn of and remember power's true origin*. It does not come from humanity's limited intellect, one that is constantly assaulted by the guile of those 'cast out into the earth' with Satan. No. Power's origination is in the Creator of this world and none else.

Coming to know the origin of power to have stemmed from outside people, while also recognizing the portion of power that was *breathed into and resides in* each individual fosters a paradigm shift away from false omnipotence within human government. This gives room to foster a culture that mirrors the original intent of the Constitution.[331]

The language 'the laws of nature and of nature's God' beautifully invites all belief systems to the table of freedom's preservation

For the founders to express *power's* origin as *'the laws of nature and of nature's God'* was profound in that it invites atheists, Christians, agnostic, Buddhists, or Muslims—*all people*—to the table of freedom's preservation. This language is a homerun because no walk of life can deny the laws of nature on the pretense of personal belief. Most walks of life can relate to the effects of atrophy and the important role of maintenance. Anyone with a heartbeat, despite their beliefs, is somewhat acquainted with the fallen state of human nature. If we are not of the disposition to take part in the plunder of humanity's unalienable rights, our desire will be to put an end to such debauchery through a rigorous maintenance of the political boundaries established through federal and state constitutions.

Conclusion

Truly, we must see and always strive to remember: "power originates outside of the [people] but resides in the [people] as directed by 'the laws of nature and of nature's God.'" We each have great power within us to preserve or destroy. The heavy question remains, will we forget powers' origin and lose at this political tug of war?

The themes these grasping tentacles assume in this political tug of war can be many. The previous chapters have only begun to scratch at the surface. But maybe there is enough groundwork to inspire a deeper delve into 'knowing thyself' so to prime your contribution to be part of a winning pull.

CHAPTER 20

BEAUTIFUL YET FRIGHTENING DUTY

AUTHOR'S NOTE

After my Father's murder, my mind was filled with questions. How, in America, could a God-fearing, peaceful family man with no criminal record (or even a parking ticket) be shot in the back three times by authorities while his hands were up in surrender? I had been rudely awakened to the horrific state of our nation. If this could happen to my Father, it could happen to any of us.

For about a year, I traveled the nation with my mother. We told the true story about Dad to many people. While I was deeply grateful for all who graciously invited us into their communities to share our story, I was becoming angrier than I already had been. As result of my ongoing grieving, I lost an unhealthy 30 pounds and my beautiful long hair that Dad always said was a crown upon my head was literally falling out.

There were a few things that really troubled me, of which I will share only two. In our travels, we sometimes would be in the company of opportunists whose aim was to profit from our trauma. I sought to be gracious while experiencing silent disgust. Growing increasingly wary and suspicious was the result.

Something else that troubled me deeply was feeling as though I were unsuccessful. I unrealistically desired to move all into effective applied civics. While I believe the travesty of our family story always shocked the conscience, the desired results of igniting a massive movement of effective applied civics was not working. I felt like my efforts were having few results. Sometimes I felt as if I were a mere entertainer. I wondered, was I truly in a world of complacency.

While I could powerfully deliver our family story to help witness of the awful state our nation was in while simultaneously testifying of Jesus Christ, I could not confidently provide wise counsel concerning effective apply civics. Many would approach me and ask, "What should I do?" and I would always respond with the generic invitation to work toward becoming educated.

Through it all, the good Lord kept gently reminding me, "One cannot give that which they do not have." I wanted and needed to learn more. I yearned for real, meaningful relationships of trust. I needed mentors.

In response to my personal pleadings, my journey with the Center for Self Governance (CSG) began the summer of 2016, just a few months after my Father's murder. I enrolled in their level one class skeptical of the content. To my delight, I really enjoyed the class and was excited to progress and learn.

In the past, I had found knowledge and wisdom from personal study and from my father teaching us principles of liberty. Be that as it may, when Dad chose to go to Oregon in January of 2016 to stake a claim of adverse possession as part of their petition and redress of grievance, I found myself humbled by my ignorance regarding applied civics and government.

The rubric for the first CSG class asked the student to write how they were going to solve their chosen government issue. Ideas such as property rights and agent intimidation crossed my mind several times. As a victim in both of these areas, frustratingly, neither rang true as to what my core issue was. I was stuck on what my government issue should be for the required position paper.

I discovered why this was when seeking to draft an outline for my "governmental issue" paper. After some time, the blank word document witnessed of my ignorance. I could not connect the dots from the principles to the current American governmental system to a pragmatic solution. If I couldn't connect the dots in my mind, how was I to attempt writing a paper? All I knew was that there were serious issues that needed to be fixed. I just didn't know how to do it.

I wrestled with this for weeks, frustrated that I was not progressing to the next level. During another class, the instructor pointed out that the purpose of the position paper training exercise was to impress upon the mind of the student how they lack understanding of their system of government and, as such, to help the student see their efforts in ignorance cannot bring positive change. This made complete sense. It was then that I determined the focus of my paper should be me and my lack of understanding.

What is my issue? Exceedingly sorrowful, I recognized, it was me.[332]

The process of writing that position paper was one huge milestone in my process of healing and learning applied civics. It helped me turn my angry energy toward all those who participated in the murder of my father and away from all those who ignorantly ridiculed and unrighteously judged my family, toward the only person I have control of—myself.

> And why beholdest thou the mote that is in thy brother's eye, but considerest not the beam that is in thine own eye? Or how wilt thou say to thy brother, let me pull out the mote out of thine eye; and, behold, a beam is in thine own eye? Thou hypocrite, first cast out the beam out of thine own eye; and then shalt thou see clearly to cast out the mote out of thy brother's eye.[333]

A miracle allowed the admonitions of Jesus Christ that I have studied and pondered countless times throughout my life to enter my heart with a new glow.

Freedom of choice is so important with respect to both spiritual and temporal progression. Is it of any wonder, as previously mentioned, that the "primary strategies [of the contending force for good] has been to restrict... agency through the power of earthly governments?" Ezra Taft Benson, who served as the 15th United States Secretary of Agriculture for eight years and as an apostle for the Church of Jesus Christ of Latter-day Saints for 51 years, nine of which he was the 13th president of the Church, marveled while "look[ing] back in retrospect on almost six thousand years of human history, [recognizing] freedom's moments have been infrequent and exceptional."[334] The looming question is, why?

America's founders were scholar students of multiple methods of governance. These exceptional men marveled, just as Benson did, at the phenomenon of mankind's lack of cohorts where the people truly enjoyed freedom and liberty. Dad would say to those not quite sure of the *why* behind his personal stand, "I want my children to know what freedom is." He, like the founders, understood how the political pendulum of humanity's pattern relentlessly swung

> *from bondage to spiritual faith;*
> *from spiritual faith to great courage;*
> *from courage to liberty;*
> *from liberty to abundance;*
> *from abundance to selfishness;*
> *from selfishness to complacency;*
> *from complacency to dependency;*
> *from dependency back into bondage.*[335]

The American founders were deeply moved upon to take courage to find a way to rise above such odds. All unanimously felt it was high time people stood to be agents unto self, to work toward discovering a system of government that would provide a historical anomaly. Their aim was to create an ensign of freedom and liberty for all nations, resulting in a less dramatic swing of the pendulum.[336]

The founders, despite being foreordained for their great mission of establishing the American system, were not exempt from human follies. Notwithstanding their fallen state, they were

> *raised up by the Perfect Man to perform a great work. Foreordained were they, to lay the foundation of this republic, the Lord's base of operations in these latter days.*[337] *Blessed by the Almighty in their struggle for liberty and independence, the power of heaven rested on these founders as they drafted that great document for governing men, the Constitution of the United States. Like the Ten Commandments, the truths on which the Constitution was based were timeless; and also, as with the Decalogue, the hand of the Lord was in it. They fulfilled their mission well. From them [all] were endowed with a legacy of liberty—a constitutional republic.*[338]

Deep passion to discover a *superior* system of governance to those that had already been employed and failed rather than opt to take part in "lawful injustice" is a divine characteristic.

The great mind of Frederic Bastiat commented on the choice available when one approaches a crossroad such as this:

> *It is natural for men to rise against the injustice of which they are the victims. When, therefore, plunder is organized by law, for the profit of those who perpetrate it, all the plundered classes tend, either by peaceful or revolutionary means, to enter in some way into the manufacturing of laws. These classes, according to the degree of enlightenment at which they have arrived, may propose to themselves two very different ends, when they thus attempt the attainment of their political rights; either they may wish to put an end to lawful plunder, or they may desire to take part in it."*[339]

Dad found himself at such a crossroad after riding his horse at the 2014 Bundy Standoff. He went to support the family as they came face-to-face with heavily armed federal agents seeking to claim the Bundy family's property rights under the guise of what Bastiat described as plunder. Upon witnessing his fellow neighbors' rights being trampled on by the very government that was designed to protect such rights, Dad began a deep soul search. He wondered where he truly stood. He said in a radio interview a few months after his participation in the Bundy Standoff,

> *you don't begin to cross these lines without first having some serious introspection. You see the SWAT team [and must be firm on] who is the law breaker and the law abider. We knew they were the breaker both in letter and intent. The hidden intent was to have Bundy gone.*
>
> *...I have had a struggle within myself trying to be consistent with my belief. I am current on all my grazing fees—they're unconstitutional, but I'm current. There are mandatory terms and conditions we are to sign—I am in good standing. What I've been struggling with is how can*

> *I say I believe and continue to pay my grazing fees and sign my mandatory terms and conditions and be consistent with what I believe? I can't! I personally need to be consistent or sit down and be quiet.*
>
> *So, I'm announcing, I will no longer continue my relationship with the BLM [Bureau of Land Management]. Again, these are good people. I have had nothing but good experiences with my Range Cons [Range Conservationist or Rangeland Management Specialists]. I like them. But this is sole and separate.*[340]

The founders studied and personally encountered experiences much like unto the Bundy Standoff. Many people thank God that that day in 2014 didn't end in a horrific blood bath. The founders invested great effort into understanding exactly what it is that happens in human government that leads a people to dangerous points like the Bundy Standoff, where a people come head to head, one side seeking to plunder at gunpoint and the other side seeking to defend, even unto death, what is theirs. The motivation behind the founders' toil was so to gain enlightenment to aid their effort in establishing a system that would help prevent the political pendulum from continuing to swing to this dangerous point.

The American founders came to clearly understand they must put an end to systems that sustain a consolidation of legislative, executive, and judicial controls. The inspiration for their point of focus was history witnessing such a consolidation was always at the expense of the people's rights. Please realize the founders' legacy was a selfless life, dedicated to working toward developing a system that has concise federal and state separation of controls rather than using their intellect to selfishly glut in the perpetuation of that which would only serve self and produces chaos and slavery.

The Bundy family and my Dad understood the great importance of these federal and state separations of controls the founders developed within the American system. They recognized the deceptive tactic of the BLM using both my father and the Bundy's so called mandatory contractual agreements as a way to consolidate governmental controls. This consolidation of control and the dangers associated with such consolidation was the reason for their choice to discontinue their contractual relationship with the Bureau of Land Management.[341]

After long hours, weeks, months, and even years, those prepared to form "a more perfect union" found themselves, in the year 1787, meeting to amend the current flawed system of government, known as the Articles of Confederation. Rather than a slight change, a new social contract (constitution) was born with a new nation. Little did they know that this new constitution and new nation would stand the test of time and fulfill the measure of its creation and become the ensign of successful freedom, liberty, and prosperity to all other nations. Scripture reveals the Lord's decree as "it is not right that any man should be in bondage one to another… for this purpose [He]…established the Constitution of the land, by the hands of wise men whom [He]…raised up unto this very purpose."[342]

When studied, we discover that America has survived over 200 years under only one constitution. This is no small feat when comparing all other nations' histories, whose devastating pendulums swinging between anarchy and incorrect governance is still horrifically overwhelming. This swing, for some nations, is alarmingly fast in its shift. David Barton, an evangelical Christian, political activist, and author explained, "if you were 95 today and lived in Poland you would have suffered through seven revolutions and seven different constitutions. If you are a baby boomer in South Korea, you would have already lived through six constitutions." He went on to say, "Such possibilities seem like insanity but that is because we Americans are so use to safe security that we think it is ordinary when it is not."[343]

In retrospect, we must realize how freedom's moments have indeed been infrequent, even for America.[344] The scars of war cry from the dust. Father against son, brother against brother, neighbor against neighbor; leaving behind mothers and children mourning with the only choice to press forward alone to clean up the bloody mess only to find themselves subject to tyrants.[345]

The Process That Lead to Today's Freedom Moments

It is imperative to point out it was eleven long painful years prior to the crowning 1787 Constitutional Convention, that the colonists, through the 1776 Lee Resolution, declared sovereignty, claiming statehood. What followed next was the Declaration of Independence and the formation of their first government, the Articles of Confederation.

The process of pragmatic preparation to ensure a victorious independence was underway as the imminent powder keg kept heating. Upon the Lee Resolutions ratification, it already had been six years since the tragic Boston Massacre (1770), where the first shots fired upon civilians by their government took place. The battle of Lexington, which was known to be the fight to have officially started the war between the British government and its people, was a little over a year old before the colonies claimed sovereign statehood through the Lee Resolution. Contemplating the courage of the early patriots is humbling as they, for months, wrestled bloody battlefields against the greatest power on earth at the time, Great Britain, with few to no resources.

The God of the statesmen impressed upon their minds that to have any hope for victory against the world's greatest empire, foreign alliance had to be strategically leveraged because resources were scarce. Notwithstanding the great need, aid could not be received at the expense of territory in the New World. The states understood that declaring sovereignty while simultaneously pledging allegiance to an organized union of the states was paramount to working toward securing foreign alliance. This is what birthed the Articles of Confederation, the Nation's first Constitution. The union was to ward off opportunists of any foreign alliance seeking claim to territory in the New World.

For the early Americans to consider the possibility of aid coming at a price equating to foreign empires claiming territory in the New World, which would ultimately lead to the loss of their newly sovereign statehood, was profound. Sagacious it was for the early Americans to take strategic steps to avoid such a fate. This bloody fight was not waged to simply trade one landlord for another. The hope was that a union would help prevent losing territory. The idea was that taking on a union of sovereign states would prove more difficult than stand-alone sovereign states. Thomas Paine at the time preached, "It is not in numbers, but in unity, that our great strength lies; yet our present numbers are sufficient to repel the force of all the world."[346]

"If You Can Keep It"

Now let's fast forward to the day when 81-year-old Benjamin Franklin exited the 1787 constitutional convention, eleven painfully long years after the colonies declared their sovereignty. At that moment, he was briskly approached by a young woman, Mrs. Powell. She, despite the current culture denying her the right to have her voice heard at the ballot box, was intimately involved in being apprised of current government affairs. She asked, "Well, Doctor, what have we got, a republic or a monarchy?" Franklin responded with deep soberness, "A republic, Madam, if you can keep it."[347]

If you can keep it. What did he mean, *if you can keep it*? Might Franklin have understood liberty's preservation to be dependent upon *each individual* learning and obeying eternal law pertaining to correct governance? Perhaps Franklin recognized the sacredness of the people's freedom of choice in regard to systems of governance, even at the risk of ruin. Despite this risk of ruin, maybe he knew the other option of being coerced and forced never would produce fruits of true freedom. I am sure he understood the delicate process that preserving life, liberty and pursuit of happiness surely demands.[348]

He had to have understood the fragile yet necessary line that separates a people's right to organized in committees of safety when said rights are at risk.[349] Indeed, the hundreds of people gathering in 2014 at the Bundy Standoff, can be likened unto such committees of safety. The 2014 committee did preserve life, liberty, and property that day. Again, this last line of defense was tried in Burns, Oregon in 2016. Tragically that effort lost life, liberty, and property. This line of preservation is most delicate.

Just before the convention, Franklin gave a speech where he expressed, "When you assemble a number of men who have the advantage of their joint wisdom, you inevitably assemble with those men, all their prejudices, their passions, their errors of opinion, their local interests, and their selfish views."

The group was plagued with the question of "how to implement principles of popular majority rule while at the same time preserving stable governments that protect the rights and liberties of all citizens."[350] At that point, a perfect union seemed unattainable. It was only the current domestic bloody war that humbled the group enough to set aside pettiness so as to resolve on the "more perfect union."

The wise Franklin responded soberly to Mrs. Powell, not because he was displeased with the outcome of the convention; on the contrary, his heart must have been full. At last a people had organized a system of government that if rigorously maintained would provide for that which mankind had sought for over a span of six thousand years. Franklin's profound simple seven-word response to Mrs. Powell revealed his deep understanding of the risky yet necessary role freedom of choice must play for each generation. The looming question for Franklin, which still hangs today, was would the two groups in every society; governors (elected, appointed, and employed officials) and the governed (the people) win or lose at *the push and pull we all face*? Franklin so boldly expressed at the constitutional convention, "All history informs us, there has been in every state and kingdom a constant kind of warfare between the governing and the governed, the one striving to obtain more for its support, and the other to pay less."[351]

Franklin's Understanding of Governors in Every Era

For the governors, Franklin understood that "it is the nature and disposition of almost all men, as soon as they get a little authority… that they immediately begin to exercise unrighteous dominion."[352] Because he understood human natures' unchecked tendencies were that of patronizing, aggrandizing guile, the new system of government had interwoven within its mechanics a requirement of consistent appropriate maintenance to ward off such conduct. This was engineered to avoid compromise to the delicate line between preserving and losing freedom and liberty. The question is, in the case of governors of each new era, would they pull or be pushed in their personal tug of wars? Would they choose selfless refinement in their civic service or glut in selfish, patronizing, aggrandizing, guile for the benefit of their own gain?

Franklin's Understanding of the Governed in Every Era

In the case of the people (the governed), Franklin understood humanity's natural tendency was to selfishly seek the path of least resistance rather than welcome the exertion any *ascent* demands. The maintenance requirements of the new system would indeed call for a special liberty culture wherein everyday Americans (the governed) were found with uncompromising virtue, an ever-growing competence, and an unyielding righteous indignation burning within to fuel the long press forward. Franklin understood a people of this caliber would be the ones pressing for the accountability of the governors.

Franklin knew without such accountability consistently being peacefully enforced by the people (the governed), to keep aggrandizing governors in check using the Constitution as their guide, an inevitable colluding of governmental control would take place. The fallout of such oversight and sin of omission have left and will continue to leave a lasting sting to be felt not only by those guilty of such sins of omission, but also by innocent rising generations. Bastiat, in his book entitled *The Law*, called this path of least resistance "naked greed."[353]

> "It doesn't matter how it ends,
> it matters how you stand."
> **—LaVoy Finicum**

Whether this 'naked greed' is predominate in one or both classes, governors and governed, participation in it in any degree is violating the laws of nature and of nature's God. Assuming the consequences of perpetuating the plunder of humankind's unalienable rights in any way is foolishness. Yet, our culture persists in trying obedience to that which produces captivity. Why? Bastiat commented,

> *Man can only derive life and enjoyment from a perpetual search and appropriation; that is, from a perpetual application of his faculties to objects, or from labor. This is the origin of property. But also, he may live and enjoy, by seizing and appropriating the productions of the faculties of his fellow men. This is the origin of plunder. Now labor being in itself a pain, and man being naturally inclined to avoid pain, it follows, and history proves it, that wherever plunder is less burdensome than labor, it prevails;...when does plunder cease, then? When it becomes more burdensome and more dangerous than labor.[354]*

The Declaration of Independence mirrors Bastiat's thoughts on the burdens caused by plunder: "All experience hath shewn, that mankind are more disposed to suffer, while evils are sufferable, than to right themselves by abolishing the forms to which they are accustomed."[355] Despite these realities, Jefferson was firm in guarding the sacred right of choice even at the risk of potential ruin if the people choose obedience to the laws of oppression. He wrote in a letter of correspondence dated September 1820 (32 years after the Constitution's ratification),

> *I know no, start insertion, safe depository, of the ultimate powers of the society, but the people themselves: and if we think them not enlightened enough to exercise their control with a wholesome discretion, the remedy is, not to take it from them, but to inform their discretion by education. This is the true corrective of abuses of constitutional power.[356]*

Joseph Smith, the prophet of the restoration said, "teach them correct principles and they govern themselves."[357]

It is not happenstance that the resolve of so many great minds all concluded on the vital importance of choice. The people's opportunity to choose to take part in the process of effectively preserving life, liberty, and the pursuit of happiness, or to perpetuate captivity, is what has enabled this nation to be set up as a standard for all others. Choice is the only way despite the risk of ruin.

Such possibilities are *beautiful yet frightening* fathoms. What a blessing it is to be American!

Other nation's systems of governance echo the stories of barbarous tactics used to gain compliance of their citizens.[358] The reality of such ongoing horror in today's world must sink in your mind and heart. To mentally leave the safety of your American experience will give room for a new sense of gratitude to swell. Your privilege to be a beneficiary of America's divinely inspired system of government is a blessing. As unmaintained as the current American governmental system is, there are still great blessings enjoyed. What a privilege it is to live in the land where *choice* to apply your civic authority to preserve freedom and prosperity for your children is still available.

While many blessings from the toil of our American predecessors are still enjoyed, we must not forget our vital role in the process of maintaining freedom and liberty if we are going to win our era's political tug of war.

As cliché as it sounds, we are only able to reap what we sow. Thinking we can dodge the consequences of neglect is living in a lie. Make no mistake, negligence guarantees suffering. This is eternal law. The experiences of both the Bundy Standoff and Oregon occupation witness to this difficult reality. Once degrees of freedom are lost, it is "only by blood and suffering" that a regaining of freedom begins.[359] Why must we endure such a sting? It is because "when the wicked rule, the people mourn."[360]

Let us no more compromise the system's integrity through our negligence. Let us forever set aside aggrandizing and selfless tendencies. May the cognitive dissonance between the illusion of guaranteed freedom without being engaged in applied civics versus the unequivocal need for consistent applied civics as a way to maintain the systems integrity to safeguard life, liberty, and the pursuit of happiness be dissolved. May our efforts result in a softer sway of the political pendulum rather than its swift painful motion

> *from bondage to spiritual faith;*
> *from spiritual faith to great courage;*
> *from courage to liberty;*

from liberty to abundance;
from abundance to selfishness;
from selfishness to complacency;
from complacency to dependency;
from dependency back into bondage.[361]

"If you can keep it." Perhaps Franklin was attempting to convey to Mrs. Powell in the fewest words possible the opposition guaranteed to the duo of governors and governed, in trying to keep the republic. Perhaps this is the answer to the looming question of why "freedom's moments have been infrequent and exceptional."[362]

"A republic, ...*if* you can keep it."

CHAPTER 21

DAD'S CORE

CHAPTER 21

DAD'S CHOICE BETWEEN TWO CONTENDING FORCES

Are you a people watcher? I am. There never is a dull moment while observing the verbal and nonverbal expressions of others. It's not uncommon for me to get lost in thought wondering about their story and the condition of their heart. I wonder what it is that makes them tick, what gets them out of bed in the morning, what intent is behind their choices.

I always marveled when observing Dad. He appeared to never be idle. He seemed to always radiate a sense of joy. Maybe it was his high cheekbones that made him look like he had a constant slight smile. Whatever the cause, he was pleasant to sit in silence with. I remember often wondering if he truly was always laboring in deep thought. This nagged me enough to decide to pry. I honestly wondered if he ever rested. I admit, the nagging within stemmed from the desire to seek some type of justification for my mind wandering into idleness at times.

Finally, one day I organized my question phrased as a statement. I said to him, "It seems you are always deep in thought...." Surely an open-ended musing was less intrusive. Perhaps my employing such style in seeking to satisfy my inner irk was simply more comfortable for me. Never mind my motive, I remember him looking at me straight in the eye and simply responding so matter-of-factly, "That's because I am." The outward silence then ended with him and me returning to the company in our own thoughts.

In one of our quiet moments, Dad once expressed how his thoughts often drifted to Jesus Christ while out on the range. He loved the quiet peace he found in the country. There was no frenzied noise, no cell phone, no worries. He said many times it was easy for him, while out in the country, to get lost in the illusion that all was well. The familiar sounds and smells of his worn leather saddle, his beloved horse, dog, and cattle, the grass, sagebrush, and cedar, this all created a safe euphoria for him. He marveled at the cattle's meek purpose, which he believed was for them to live and die that people might have the choice to partake and live. He appreciated his mind recognizing witnesses of his Savior, Jesus Christ.

For Dad, his journey of discovering eternal truths started in his early adolescent years. As out of character as it sounds for a young boy to enjoy silence, he did. While a majority of his time was spent enjoying the outdoors, any time inside, not in conversation or play with his family, was spent experiencing the adventures found within the pages of the many Louis L'Amour western novels he read. "The thing about Louis L'Amour is that he really only tells one story, more or less, but in a hundred different ways. It's the story of the just confronting the unjust, the right taking on the wrong, the strong serving the weak."[363] There is no doubt these cowboy fiction stories nurtured Dad's drive to always be the one in aid of the less fortunate.

On one occasion, he stumbled upon an old well-used book with its cover and title page missing. Having read through the family library, he anticipated what adventures the nameless new read would bring. The untitled book was true to form in comparison to his typical go-to genre. While the formatting of the content was not conventional, its pages were full of tyrants, oppressive government, hate, war, carnage, hardship, brave heroes, faith, meekness, love, and deliverance. One crowning character was referenced countless times whose role in the story was to miraculously satisfy the demands of justice while giving a place for mercy. These pages witnessed again and again how this gift of mercy could be given to any tyrant as long as they possessed a broken heart and contrite spirit. This new concept of justice and mercy's relationship was unfamiliar to Dad as he was always out to protect the innocent against the perpetrator. Nevertheless, the concept spoke to his soul.

It wasn't until a time later that he discovered a little more about his new favorite read, which turned into a lifelong point of reference through his life's challenges. He discovered the book to be known as another testament of Jesus Christ and its title to be *The Book of Mormon*. Through diligent study with real intent to discover truth for himself, Dad uncovered the mystery in his mind as to what characteristic traits truly embody real heroes. At a young age, it was his choice to be baptized and by so doing became a proud, loyal, member of the Church of Jesus Christ of Latter-Day Saints.

As Dad continued reading, he came to understand how the dissension between liberty and captivity all started before this earth was. For members of the Church, the idea of there being a grand council in heaven before earth's creation is fundamental doctrine. The topic of discussion in this grand council was to decide upon a plan where the children of God would be ensured freedom of choice despite the risk of ruin that choice brings. Dad came to know his Creator as one who deeply wanted all to enjoy everything good, but also one who knew freedom of choice was the only way.

Dad knew he was the "master of his fate and captain of his soul."[364] God did not force him to get baptized. God did not force him to serve a Church mission. God did not force him to get married and then divorced. God did not force him to have children. God did not force him to pray. God did not force him to read. The act of forcing another is a characteristic trait of a tyrant and God is no tyrant. The freedom to opt in or out resonated with Dad as he was a man of his own.

I will never forget an experience I had with Dad in my rebellious adolescence. This event spearheaded my journey of beginning to also understand the powerful impact choice has on the disposition. While I can't remember the grievous thing I had done, the feelings I had during and after our exchange will never be forgotten. Rather than simply dictating what my fate would be, Dad kindly asked what I thought the consequence should be for my poor choices. I recall being taken aback. My child mind wondered why he would ask me. As I marveled, a greater degree of ownership began to burn in my heart. Ownership in the consequence, but more importantly, ownership of my poor choices with a deeper resolve to improve. My opportunity of choice fostered a special connection between us. There was a softening of my heart and a deeper feeling of respect and love. While I wasn't magically transfigured into perfection at that moment, my attitude was forever influenced for better as I was learning how to be a profitable agent unto myself. Dad knew freedom of choice was the only way for such progression.

I now know my little experience with him that day was requisite for me to, in time, gain greater understanding of this eternal law of choice. He knew that day, as I do now, that when individuals have choice in their process of learning from life's adversities, it has the force and effect of allowing them to really appreciate and enjoy the fruits of their choices. Dad really tried to live up to his belief that the purpose of his mortal life was to be a "probationary time, a time to repent and serve God."[365] He hoped to inspire his children to do the same.

Let's return to what Dad learned about the purpose of the Grand Council. The aim was to develop a system to provide a way for all to have the opportunity of choice during their process of progression on earth. The plan ensured a place for mercy for those who wished to repent of choices contrary to eternal law. It was because it was understood that "mercy could not take effect except it should destroy the works of justice. The work of justice could not be destroyed; if so, God would cease to be God" (Alma 42:13). For this reason, it had been made clear during the Grand Council how "mercy could not be brought about except an atonement should be made" (Alma 42:15). *Someone* had to pay the demands of justice.

Dad read about the two contending forces that came forward to offer their solution for the apparent justice and mercy dilemma. The first suggested that he be sent to earth. His plan was to destroy freedom of choice and simply force all back to heaven.[366] Then another came forward motivated by love, eager to do the will of the Father to allow freedom of choice and to assist in providing a way where the demands of justice could be satisfied while making room for mercy.[367]

If your initial feeling is surprise in pondering about this heavenly war between two ideas, one right and one wrong, take comfort in the fact that you are not alone. Dad too wondered why there was a war in heaven, of all places. While still developing in spiritual maturity, he was ambivalent about the idea of the two contending ideas. His study led him to others who asked the same questions as he, "Shall the children of God have untrampled agency to choose the course they should follow, whether good or evil, or shall they be coerced and forced to be obedient" during their mortal experience?[368]

He determined it was because the eternal progression of God's children was at stake, which, in his mind, was no trifling matter. He understood that one step in humanity's progression of becoming like God is the receiving of a body so to be tested and tried. The great test is to see if we will freely choose without coercion "liberty and eternal life through the great Mediator of all men, or to choose captivity and death, according to the captivity and power of the devil; for he seeketh that all men might be miserable like unto himself."[369] Dad came to know the Creator as one who honored choice in the process of progression.

When we each entered this world, perhaps the sentiments who remained in the before life were similar to Dr. Seuss's brilliant language in his famous work, *Oh, The Places You'll Go*. Dr. Seuss wrote,

> *Congratulations! Today is your day. You're off to Great Places! You're off and away! You have brains in your head. You have feet in your shoes. You can steer yourself any direction you choose. You're on your own. And you know what you know. And you are the guy who'll decide where to go.*"[370]

The Plan for Freedom of Choice was Chosen

A deep reverence was nurtured within Dad as he studied God's omniscience in choosing the latter of the two who stepped forward during what he had come to know as the Grand Council in heaven. As he got older, study of his Savior's role in providing an atonement became more frequent, meaningful, and sacred.

He marveled how Jesus Christ came to earth in the humblest circumstances, being born in a manger into a family who quickly became political refugees for many years. While his study was year-round, every Christmas Eve, Dad reverently read to us kids the witness Isaiah gave of Jesus: "For unto us a child is born, unto us a son is given: and the government shall be upon his shoulder: and his name shall be called Wonderful, Counsellor, The mighty God, The everlasting Father, The Prince of Peace."[371] As we got older, often we discussed how Christ obediently fulfilled His individual, unique purpose to gain a body, learn, and grow—line upon line—to prepare for His mission. We could not walk away from our discussions with Dad without feeling the magnitude of Christ's charge to atone for the sins of the world to satisfy the demands of justice and provide a place for mercy. His work has "had so profound an influence upon all who have lived and who will yet live upon the earth."[372]

In thinking about the two contending forces that came forward during the Grand Council, each side was understood to have had droves of people supporting either the side of freedom of choice or the side of compulsion. For those who campaigned before mortally for compulsion, the opportunity for a mortal body was denied as a result. The Holy Bible informs us what the fate was for these souls: "The great dragon was cast out [of heaven], that old serpent, called the Devil, and Satan, which deceiveth the whole world: he was cast out *into the earth*, and *his angels were cast out with him* [emphasis added]."[373]

Common sense told Dad, if there were those then who sided with the plan of compulsion,[374] who were denied a body and "cast out into the earth" to be the means wherewith mortal men and women would receive the necessary opposition so as to provide the opportunity for their choice between right and wrong, that explained why there are those now in mortality who sided with the idea of compulsion.[375] His logic told him, if there were those then who believed the crafty campaign of Lucifer, then why wouldn't there be those today in the flesh who would fall sway to the relentless *pull* of those "cast out into the earth" who press forward with the same compulsion campaign of old? Dad could see the real tug of war between the two contending forces: good versus bad, right versus wrong, light versus dark, God's plan versus Lucifer's plan.[376]

Dad grew to understand that Satan's agenda has had no deviation, its intent being to "destroy the souls of men" and claim the glory for himself.[377] Dad spoke as if he was all too familiar with the sting associated with the opposition Satan and his bodiless minions deliver. I remember once during an emotionally difficult time in my life, Dad powerfully witnessed that life is about getting back up again and again while growing in gratitude for the atonement of Jesus Christ.

This topic of freedom was no trivial matter during the Grand Council, just as much as it is not now. The consequence of captivity was not escaped then,[378] just as we have seen through mortality's history that captivity is never escaped when there's an adherence to law that perpetuates compulsion.

In Dad recognizing the gravity of this issue, true to form, he began a deep introspection, asking himself when it "was morally right to resist tyranny."[379] I marveled when I viewed his YouTube video where he shares with the world his real concerns on the matter. Just as he had shown me throughout my life, once again he was witnessing his intention to be on the right side no matter the cost, even if he stood alone.

I'm sure he never dreamed his fate would end dodging a hail of bullets. I believe, in that crowning moment, Dad possessed the same courage and faith as Shadrach, Meshach, and Abednego when they calmly expressed to the wicked King Nebuchadnezzar,

If it be so, our God whom we serve is able to deliver us from the burning fiery furnace, and he will deliver us out of thine hand, O king. But if not, be it known unto thee, O king, that we will not serve thy gods, nor worship the golden image which thou hast set up.[380]

The courage, faith, and peace to press forward in such moments could only have come from truly believing, just as the previously mentioned young

Helmuth Hubener did as he expressed, "My Father in Heaven knows that I have done nothing wrong."[381]

Patterns

For Dad, recognizing patterns within Satan's game of tug of war helped his personal discernment between right and wrong. It was interesting for him to see various games of pull simultaneously played wherein Satan and his angels worked their tactics to get people to lose their ground and cross that line in the sand. While the tactics of each were slightly different, the overall aim was the same.

He could see the first tactic targeted the individual, the strategy being to take one out at a time. Dr. Seuss brilliantly story tells of this tactic. He wrote:

> *I'm sorry to say so but, sadly, it's true that Bang-ups and Hang-ups can happen to you. You can get all hung up in a prickle-ly perch. And your gang will fly on. You'll be left in a Lurch. You'll come down from the Lurch with an unpleasant bump. And the chances are, then, that you'll be in a Slump.*
>
> *You can get so confused that you'll start in to race down long wiggled roads at a break-necking pace and grind on for miles cross weirdish wild space, headed, I fear, toward a most useless place. On and on you will hike, And I know you'll hike far and face up to your problems whatever they are.*
>
> *You'll get mixed up, of course, as you already know. So be sure when you step. Step with care and great tact and remember that Life's a Great Balancing Act. Just never forget to be dexterous and deft. And never mix up your right foot with your left.*[382]

While each individual wrestles with the "places they'll go," the simultaneously worked tactic attacks the people's systems of governance. Remember, "one of Lucifer's primary strategies [to hedge up the progression of mortals] has been to restrict [liberty] through the power of earthly governments."[383] The intent of this tactic is for a broader effect of misguidance.

Whatever the strategy, individual or communal, the intent is to push apathetic individuals into carnal delusions of false security, thus pulling their freedoms asunder, causing bondage and suffering.

Dad's Legacy

In my observing Dad, I know he saw tribulation as an opportunity to practice meek humility. I witnessed his choice to be a journey of continued refinement and loyalty to his God. What made him tick was the opportunity to witness that the current war of ideas is no new thing to humanity, no matter the name given to the contending forces. The love of God is what got him out of bed with purpose in his step. To me, it seemed he had obtained something that was beyond this fallen world in that it only mattered to him if his God was smiling.

Dad's relentless admonition to all and the legacy he left behind was for us to do as he had; learn of the two forces and then choose who it is you will to serve and to do it will all your heart, might, mind, and soul, "relying wholly upon the merits of him who is mighty to save."[384] He entreated all to have "ears to hear", "eyes to see", and to treat life experiences as sacred tutorials.[385]

EPILOGUE

DAD'S DAY IN COURT

Our family currently has great momentum working with the same legal team that helped bring about the 2016 Oregon occupation acquittals and the 2018 Nevada Bundy mistrial. Our legal team's work uncovered both agent and bureau acts of misconduct that had been going unchecked for decades. Let's be clear, the influence of these very agents and bureaus, who have begun to be exposed, strongly influenced the orchestration of Dad's murder. The details gathered by deposition and subpoena in the Oregon and Nevada trials are crowning jewels for the our case.

We move forward in faith and hope that our efforts will contribute to a better America. Thus, the civil complaint, demand for jury trial in the district of Oregon was filed January 25th, 2018.[386]

The defendants include,

United State of America: FBI, BLM, Daniel P. Love, Salvatore Lauro, Harry Mason Reid, Greg T. Bretzing, W. Joseph Astarita.

The State of Oregon: Katherine Brown, Ronald Lee Wyden.

Harney County: David M. Ward, Steven E. Grasty and The Center for Biological Diversity.

Unfortunately, due to the 2019 government shutdown resulting from the dispute regarding President Trump's mission to build the U.S.-Mexico border wall, our case was delayed.[387] What does this mean? It means our case will take longer than anticipated.[388]

Be that as it may, we very much look forward to the discovery process. While we understand each deposition and subpoena will demand time, toil, faith, hope, and, yes, more money, we look forward to holding out-of-control government agents, bureau agents, and organizations accountable.

When the time is right, my hope is to print a second edition with details of this process and outcome of the trial. For now, it is enough to know the process has begun.

Until then, the family, in deep gratitude, offers heartfelt *appreciation* to all who have offered support in this difficult journey. Thank *you*! Thank you for the purchase of this book, as doing so helps finance our civil case.

Every little bit helps. May God bless this great land we call America!

APPENDICES

APPENDIX A

TIMELINE OF EVENTS

4/12/2014	Dad participated in the Nevada Bundy Standoff. He rides his horse with the cowboys.[389]
4/14/2014	Dad calls the *Glenn Beck Radio Program* to counter Beck's narrative about Bundy Standoff.[390]
5/2015	Dad actively campaigns in the local ranching community to help others cancel their contractual agreement with the Bureau of Land Management (BLM). *St. George News* reported this.[391]
6/25/2015	Dad publicly announces on the *Bryan Hyde HD* radio show his cancelation of the contractual relationship he had with the Bureau of Land Management (BLM).[392]
7/2015	Dad turned his cows out on his winter allotment Tuckup about ten weeks before the BLM's scheduled date would have granted permission. Due to his previous contractual agreement with the BLM, he had not been able to graze on this allotment for six years. Dad turned his cows in early so the cows could eat the grass before the sun killed it and so the cows could drink the water in the reservoir before the sun dried it up.[393]

8/4/2015	The local range conservationists noticed Dad's cattle on the above described "restricted" allotment and wrote a letter to Dad informing him he would be fined and the he better get the cattle off the allotment Tuckup. Of course, Dad did not remove his cattle, as he claimed to be the owner of the forage and water rights.[394]
8/7/2015	The BLM took Dad's water from his only water tank without permission. They did not replace it.[395]
6/15 – 8/15	The BLM removed Dad's name and registered cattle brand from his winter allotment permit called Tuckup (Oct. 15 - May 15) but left his name on the deed. Agents then started verbal intimidation suggesting something bad would happen if they saw Dad's cattle brand out on any of his allotments (Tuckup, Hog, and Cannan).
9/10/2015	Dad received a tip from someone who would know that his water tank had been sabotaged by BLM agents.[396] It was indeed sabotaged.
10/14/2015	Dad shares his outrage about the Hammond case on his *YouTube* channel.[397]
1/1/2016	Dad decides to travel to Oregon to rally with others to show respect and support to the Hammond family before the Hammond father and son, once again, were admitted into prison to serve a second time for the same erroneous charges.
1/2/2016	Dad decides to join the Bundy brothers and a few others to occupy the Malheur National Wildlife Refuge to participate in a "legitimate political protest, using the lawful principles and rights pertaining to setting up and attempting an adverse possession claim" as a way to reclaim the land that had been unlawfully taken by the different bureaus functioning under fifteen executive departments.[398]

1/4/2016	Shawna Cox, one of the occupiers, read their redress of grievance to the *Associated Press*. This was also the day the Hammond father and son reported to prison for a second time.[399]
1/8/2016	Finicum family and friends caravanned from homes in Arizona, Utah, and Idaho for a scheduled mid-morning press conference. The aim in journeying to Oregon was to facilitate a shift in the occupation's current public relations, but most importantly to bring Dad home.
1/8 – 1/15	Mom and Dad's foster children were taken out of the home. They were told to get in line with the government's demands and that then maybe they would be granted the opportunity to foster again. They had been providing therapeutic foster care for over fifteen years and were highly respected in their field.
1/15/2016	The occupiers renamed the Malheur National Wildlife Refuge, The Harney County Resource Center and changed the sign at the entrance. Doing so is part of the requirements for attempting an adverse possession claim.[400]
1/20/2016	Six days before Dad's life was taken, Kate Brown, the governor of Oregon, delivered two letters. One of the letters was to President Obama and the other to U.S. Attorney General Loretta Lynch and FBI director James Comey. In her correspondence Governor Brown label lynched the occupiers, calling them "armed radicals" and requested "swift resolution."[401] You can find the letters in the appendix.
1/23/2016	Two ranchers signed a letter addressed to the U.S. Solicitor General with the purpose of ending their contractual agreement with the BLM.[402]
1/26/2016	Just hours before the ambush, Oregon Senator Ron Wyden likened the occupation unto a spreading virus that needed action.[403]

1/26/2016	Oregon State Police (OSP) and the Federal Bureau of Investigation (FBI) ambushed the occupiers on U.S. 395 as they were heading to a community meeting in the neighboring county. Dad was murdered and the others were taken into custody.[404]
1/26/2016	The Bundy boys and others were taken to prison.
2/5/2016	The funeral service for Robert LaVoy Finicum was hosted at the Church of Jesus Christ Kanab, Utah Kaibab Stake Center.
2/6/2016	LaVoy was buried at the Finicum Family Cemetery
2/2016	Mom and her attorneys were in a constant dispute with the BLM over her being the legal and rightful owner of Tuckup, as Arizona is a community property state, not to mention CFR 4110.2-3 Transfer of Grazing Preference. In terms of her current case, the language in CFR 4110.2-3 clearly recognizes the transfer of grazing preference and yet the BLM denied her her forage and water property rights for months.[405]
3/2016	A grand jury indicts 26 people on felony charges of conspiracy to impede federal employees from doing their work at the refuge through intimidation, threats or force, and other charges, including possession of firearms in a federal facility. Those indicted were Ammon Bundy, his brother Ryan Bundy, Jon Ritzheimer, Ryan Payne, Brian Cavalier, Shawna Cox, Jason Patrick, Dylan Anderson, Sean Anderson and his wife, Sandra Anderson, David Fry, Jeff Banta, Wesley Kjar, Corey Lequieu, Jason Blomgren, Darryl Thorn, Geoffrey Stanek, Travis Cox, Eric Flores, Joseph O'Shaughnessy, Duane Ehmer, Kenneth Medenbach, Blaine Cooper, Neil Wampler, Pete Santilli, and Jake Ryan.[406]
5/8/2016	11 of the 26 plead guilty to conspiracy—Ryan Payne, Jon Ritzheimer, Brian Cavalier, Blaine Cooper, Joseph

O'Shaughnessy, Wesley Kjar, Corey Lequieu, Jason Blomgren, Geoffrey Stanek, Travis Cox, and Eric Flores. They all await sentencing. Recommended sentences range from home detention to up to 12 years in prison. Payne, O'Shaughnessy, Ritzheimer and Flores later tried to withdraw their pleas. The judge denied Payne's and O'Shaughnessy's requests.[407]

7/4/2016   Mom moved cows from their winter allotment Tuckup to a feedlot Dad's father provided, wherein she was forced to provide daily feed and water while still maintaining payments on their loans for the allotments. She was paying for a forage and water property that she was fined for using and eventually denied use of. Thus, she had to buy additional feed and water to keep the cattle alive, which is very expensive. Kind people helped by donating feed.

10/13/2016   Mom began the process of moving the cows back to her winter allotment Tuckup. She signed the contracts and provided a check to the BLM that covered all their farce fees and fines. During the cattle drive, her mother-in-law arrived at the campsite to inform her that the BLM had refused to accept the check and issued threats to arrest her and impound the cattle if she were to turn the cattle out onto her winter allotment Tuckup.

10/14/2016   Mom hauled her cattle to Kanab, Utah by semi, where Mom's neighboring rancher received, within hours, verbal permission from her BLM range conservationist that Mom's cattle could graze on her allotment.

10/27/2016   The first group of defendants who did not take a plea deal were acquitted: Ammon Bundy, Ryan Bundy, Shawna Cox, David Fry, Neil Wampler, Jeff Banta and Kenneth Medenbach of conspiracy, weapons and theft charges at the end of a five-week trial.[408] Hard lesson learned; never take a plea deal.

10/27/2016	After they were declared not guilty, Ammon Bundy's lawyer, Marcus Mumford, stood before the judge and argued that his client should be released from custody immediately and allowed to walk out of the courtroom a free man. The judge declined and Mumford was tackled and tasered in the courtroom by the U.S. Marshals.[409]
1/20/2017	President Trump takes the oath of office as the President of the United States.
1/23/2017	Shortly after Dad's murder, the presiding FBI special agent in charge of the Portland Oregon FBI, Greg T. Bretzing, retired from the FBI. He now is the new director of global security and special projects for the Lake Oswego-based Greenbrier Companies. Greenbrier transports uranium for the federal government. Could Greenbrier recruitment of former top FBI agents, the transport of uranium, and the ongoing Clinton foundation uranium conspiracy be connected? Only time will tell.[410]
3/3/2017	After approaching the Senate President more than once, Arizona Senator Sylvia Allen insisted on a hearing regarding the death of LaVoy Finicum and the continued negative fallout the family suffered due to his political stand. The results of the hearing were a more educated legislature, relationship building, a reissuance of the Finicum foster license, and the road by the Finicum home being named after LaVoy Finicum.[411]
5/9/2017	President Trump fired his FBI director James Comey who was the bureau's 7th director. President Trump is only the second president to ever do this. Deputy Director Andrew McCabe began serving as acting director.[412]
6/2017	Special FBI agent W. Joseph Astarita was indicted by a grand jury. He is accused of counts of obstruction of justice. The claim

is he was trying to cover up the firing of gunshots during the January 2016 ambush on U.S. 395.[413]

10/16 – 6/16 Our family sought to employ Marcus Mumford as our attorney for our wrongful death case. Mumford first accepts but then discovers there were some powerful individuals seeking to destroy his ability to practice law. He had to pick between two evils and voluntarily agreed to no longer practice law in the state of Oregon so as to preserve his ability to practice law in the state of Utah.[414]

6/7/2017 President Trump announced who he had selected to be his new FBI director: Christopher A. Wray.[415]

8/2017 Dan Love, who once led law enforcement for the BLM's Nevada—(Love ran the militarized NV Bund Standoff)—and Utah state offices, was fired not long after an Aug. 24 report from the Interior's Office of Inspector General (OIG) faulting him a second time for official misconduct, according to a memo circulated Friday by Deputy Secretary of the Interior David Bernhardt.[416]

10/2017 Mom had an appointment with the BLM where their disposition changed completely. Her Tuckup winter allotment was restored and fines forgiven to almost nothing. Might this be due to the new administration and its agents' efforts to clean the swamp, we will never know.

10/13/2017 Mom took cows to Tuckup for winter allotment.

11/27/2017 A very telling memo was released from the lead investigator, Larry Wooten, who had been the lead case agent and investigator for the U.S. Bureau of Land Management (BLM) after the tense NV Bundy Standoff. Wooten assessed how federal officers handled the 2014 armed standoff with Nevada rancher Cliven Bundy and accused agents of far-reaching misconduct,

	recklessness, and unrestrained antipathy toward the family. The memo was an 18-page document.[417]
12/20/2017	A U.S. judge declares mistrial for the NV Bundy case for the 2014 Bundy Standoff.[418]
12/20/2017	The Bundy boys and others were released from prison after almost two years of being treated as if they were guilty before they were granted an opportunity to prove their innocence. They suffered many forms of cruel and unusual punishment, one of which was solitary confinement for months.[419]
1/25/2018	Our family filed the civil complaint, demanded for jury trial in the district of Oregon for the murder of Dad.
3/16/2018	Attorney General Jeff Sessions fired former FBI Deputy Director Andrew McCabe for lack of candor.[420]
7/10/2018	President Trump granted Dwight and Steven Hammond clemency (pardoned) and they were sent home free men. This took place only one year and six months after President Trump took office and two years and five months after Dad's murder.[421]
8/10/2018	A federal jury delivered not-guilty verdicts in the trial of FBI agent W. Joseph Astarita, who was accused of obstruction of justice the day Dad was murdered in January 2016. The verdict "plays into the narrative that there's some kind of government coverup," although the alleged cover up wasn't proven in court by prosecutors. The presiding juror said, "it's possible someone is lying, I don't know which side, or who, or it could be both. There are still two unattributed shots, and I feel like we're never going to know for sure who took them. It's not my job to know who shot, …. It's my job to find out if these facts were proven beyond a reasonable doubt, and they weren't."[422]

10/25/2018   FBI agent W. Joseph Astarita and several colleagues on the bureau's elite Hostage Rescue Team were put under investigation for alleged "lack of candor" in their statements after Dad's murder in January 2016. The federal agents are the subject of an ongoing administrative investigation and review by the U.S. Department of Justice's Office of the Inspector General.[423]

1/3/2019   As result of the government shutdown caused by the dispute over President Trump's mission to build the U.S.-Mexico border wall, our wrongful death case was delayed.[424]

1/28/2019   The Bureau of Land Management (BLM) reissued the grazing permits to the Hammond Ranch.

APPENDIX B

ADDITIONAL MATERIALS

Chapter 2: Laying Him to Rest

OFFICIAL FAMILY STATEMENT AFTER THE MURDER OF LAVOY, 1-29-2016.

A forever thank you to Todd Macfarlane for ministering to us by helping to write this statement in our time of greatest need.

We know that there are always at least two sides to every story. We also know and recognize that the FBI and law enforcement agencies involved will do everything in their power to make it appear as if the needless death of our husband, father, grandfather, brother, and son, LaVoy Finicum, was justified.

Like almost everyone else, we were not there, so we don't know exactly what happened. Like most others, we have no choice but to rely on other sources of information. One of those sources of information is the account of Victoria Sharp. Another piece of information is the video recently released by the FBI, along with the FBI's chosen narrative of what happened. In response to this information, we would like to make a few observations.

The first observation is that, from what we understand, the occupation was on track toward a peaceful resolution. LaVoy and those he was with were en route to a public meeting in an adjoining county when they were stopped in something far different than a "routine traffic stop," as has been portrayed by the media. Unfortunately, the powers that be were not interested in being patient enough for the occupation to come to a peaceful end. Some had called for LaVoy and those he was with to simply be gunned down, just as he was, with no due process. Oregon Governor, Kate Brown, was putting pressure on the FBI to end it sooner rather than later. The Harney County Sheriff's Department, working in conjunction with the FBI, tried to do everything they could to emphasize how disruptive the occupation was to the local community, when in reality it appears to have been their own reaction that was causing most of the disruption. And it was the FBI that chose to escalate the situation to force a confrontation and violent ending.

With respect to the actual facts and circumstances surrounding LaVoy's death, the video really speaks for itself. People will interpret it according to their own views. As the FBI's own narrative stated, LaVoy was not wielding a firearm or any other weapon when he was killed. His hands were obviously in the air. Knowing LaVoy, it is our view that he was moving away from the vehicle in an attempt to draw any hostility or violence away from the others. Unfortunately, we don't know what he was saying, and what was being said to him. He appears to have been gesturing or trying to keep his balance while moving in the deep snow. Although he may have been animated, he does not appear to have been threatening or posing any real threat or danger to anyone. The FBI claims that LaVoy had a loaded firearm in an inside pocket of his coat. After re-reviewing the extended video, at this point we are not accepting at face value the FBI's statement that LaVoy was actually armed. But even if he was, as far as we can see, that firearm posed no more danger to anyone than it would have if he had stayed in the vehicle, with his hands on the steering wheel. Contrary to what has been stated by some sources, LaVoy was not "charging" anyone. He appears to have been shot in the back, with his hands in the air.

It is our understanding that according to applicable law, the use of deadly force is justified only if there is a genuine threat of death or serious bodily injury. It is our understanding and position that deadly force should only be used as a last resort. In LaVoy's case, it appears that they were determined to go straight to the last resort. It is our understanding that the U.S. Supreme Court and Ninth Circuit Court of appeals have ruled as follows:

> *The reasonableness of [officers'] actions depends both on whether the officers were in danger at the precise moment that they used force and on whether [the officers'] own reckless or deliberate conduct during the seizure unreasonably created the need to use such force.*
>
> *[W]here an officer intentionally or recklessly provokes a violent confrontation . . . he may be held liable for his otherwise defensive use of deadly force.*[425]

Although officers may claim self-defense, they may still be liable for using excessive force if their reckless and unconstitutional actions create the need to use excessive force.

It is our understanding that, in addition to shooting LaVoy multiple times, after he was left lying harmlessly on the ground, the officers also fired upon his truck and the passengers in it, putting them all at risk, despite the fact that they were posing no threat to anyone. The video clearly shows one of the windows being blown out. It has been gut-wrenching for our family to view the video of LaVoy being shot and then left to lie in the snow while a whole army of so-called "public servants" terrorized the others. We can only hope their families never have to watch such a thing. We will be interested to inspect the vehicle. We will also be interested to see the autopsy report.

At this point we will await the outcome of any investigation, but based on the information currently available to us, we do *not* believe that LaVoy's shooting was justified. We, likewise, can't see any justification for the force and risk of serious injury or death that was exerted against the others in the truck, who posed no threat.

We know that, under such circumstances, law enforcement typically makes every attempt to cast such shooting victims in the worst possible light. In that regard, we also want to observe and emphasize that LaVoy had a squeaky-clean record and had never had so much as a speeding ticket. In addition to raising his own eleven children, he had also been entrusted with the care of at least fifty foster children over the course of approximately ten years.

On January 7, 2016, LaVoy issued an official statement from the Malheur Wildlife Refuge. Among other things, the statement said, "We want to clarify that we share any and all concerns about safety for everyone involved, including ourselves, our families, the public, and law enforcement officers. All lives are important to us. Ultimately, we want everyone involved to be able to return safely to their homes and families."

We are deeply troubled and saddened that our governments do not share the same concern for human life. We are deeply troubled that our governments would view whatever was happening at the Malheur Wildlife Refuge to be worth spilling blood over. We are deeply troubled and saddened that our governments have come to place so little value on life, liberty, property, and the pursuit of happiness.

We love LaVoy as our husband, father, grandfather, brother, and son. He was a hero to us. We believe he died as a patriotic martyr. Regardless of any and all differing opinions, we know that he died standing for a cause *he* believed in.

LaVoy's funeral will be held in Kanab, Utah on Friday, February 5, 2016. We take comfort in our faith and our belief that LaVoy is now in a better place. May our dear Lord bless and receive him into that realm. We sincerely appreciate all the thoughts and prayers that have been sent our way. We pray for those who chose to take LaVoy's life. We desire justice and genuine accountability for what happened, but we pray for them.

And finally, we thank God for this country and what it is supposed to stand for. We pray for this country, and that God will please bless, help, and forgive us all.

LYRICS OF THE DAUGHTERS FREEDOM'S CRY SONG

Are you, are you going to agree?
Our freedoms are waning, and we'll lose our liberty.
Slipping one by one until there's nothing left to see.
Are you, are you willing to stand with me?

Are you, are you just going to let it be?
The ranchers are first, but brother next it may be me.
We all stand together, or we'll hang separately.
Are you, are you going to the tree?

Are you, are you willing to be free?
It won't get any easier to regain lost liberty.
Strange things are happening in this
Land that once was free!

So, brother, I ask you,
are you, are you going to stand by me?
—Finicum Daughters[426]

LYRICS TO THE BALLAD OF LAVOY FINICUM: COWBOY STAND FOR FREEDOM SONG

He was a man who loved to walk the land,
Turn his cheek but also take a stand.
His conviction, he followed what he felt was right.
There is no telling what time will bring.
You can live for nothing or everything
But when the push comes to shove
Tell me will you fight?

Chorus
I'm only talking about a cowboy's stand for freedom.
I just talking about a name carved in a stone.
A friend and brother to anyone.
He is riding off into the setting sun.
Ride on cowboy, he's heading home.

Well, there's almost right and there's nearly wrong
As you live your life from rise to dawn.

And then it's over and the moment's gone.
You can testify to the things unseen
But the world is blind, can't see a thing
All you can do is try to be human being.

Chorus

I know not what course of man may take
I can't see that far down the road
But as for me and my
Make no mistake
The weight of justice is a heavy load
And I'm living back home

He left his home to go and take a stand
His voice rang out across a deafened land
And in the end it was bullet that exposed a lie
A truth remembered is a battle won
And though his murder cannot be undone
It rings out like an echo thunderin' across the night.

Here is to all the cowboys stand for freedom
Why do we watch them from afar with hearts of stone?
His is riding off into the setting sun
The thoughts of many from the voice of one.
Well, drive on cowboy, your work is done.

Well Godspeed cowboy, we will carry on.
—**Jordan Page**[427]

FUNERAL PRESS CONFERENCE, THARA AND TIERRA-BELLE SPEAKING—FEBRUARY 5, 2016

A forever thank you to Cherilyn Bacon Eagar, Board of Governors Phyllis Schlafly Eagles, for ministering to us by helping to write this script in our time of greatest need.

We thank you for coming from far and wide to join us this day in mourning the loss of our father, Robert LaVoy Finicum. Through this tragedy we find hope and peace as we build a stronger family unit of forgiveness, love, and loyalty.

Our family is united to press forward with our father's message that he fervently taught all of us: "Only virtuous people are capable of freedom."

These past few weeks our family has watched as the world called LaVoy Finicum many names; but we are here today to let you know what we call him. We call him *Daddy*, and we are grateful that our faith teaches us that we will live together forever with our daddy someday.

Our daddy taught us time tested principles. He taught us to be honest and kind and to always have hope. He taught us by example of self-discipline and daily diligence how to conduct our lives. As his children, we have learned so much about faith, respect, and love from him. We were not done learning from his wisdom, and we will miss hearing those inspiring words from his mouth.

Our daddy was an honest man and he believed passionately in the rule of law. He was an inspiring teacher. Many believed that, while on the refuge in Oregon, he spent his time covered up under a blue tarp defending that outpost at gunpoint. That is a false narrative. I was there.

True to form, "Tarpman" spent his days in Oregon meeting with people, befriending them, helping them and teaching them the principle that our leaders have abandoned.[428] Many were grateful he had come because he was giving them hope. They saw him differently from how the media characterized him, and some have even joined us here today.

For many years, Western-states ranchers have respected our father for his leadership in their long struggle to defend their property against federal overreach. He boldly took the stance that it was the federal government, not the ranchers, that had violated the law, as found in Article 1, Section 8, Clause 17.

In the tradition of Patrick Henry, liberty was worth more than life. Our father's teachings are preserved on his website onecowboystandforfreedom.com. We urge everyone to learn more about what our daddy believed.

Throughout history, a few courageous people have stood alone and held uncommon views. Cicero, Joan of Arc, Sir Thomas More, and the founders of the American Republic. They all had one thing in common: they were mocked, ridiculed, and called extremists. Today's defenders of the U.S. Constitution are now called "Domestic Terrorists." A Reuters headline from a few days ago read, "U.S. Finds ways to toughen fight against domestic extremists."

But isn't it interesting to note that yesterday's extremists typically become tomorrow's heroes? Robert LaVoy Finicum was and is our hero.

Our father read and studied that founding document. He sincerely believed that he was following the rule of law, and that it was the federal government that was violating it. And we agree with him. We also agree with Thomas Jefferson who once said, "When governments fear the people, there is liberty. When the people fear the government, there is tyranny." But few remember the rest of that famous quote: "The strongest reason for the people to retain the right to keep and bear arms is, as a last resort, to protect themselves against tyranny in government."

Whether or not you believe our father did the right thing, we now step forward to publicly ask: Who are we as Americans? Who are we as human beings? Do we now believe that mere words justify the use of deadly force? Do we believe that peaceful actions justify the use of deadly force? Do we believe that two hands up in surrender justifies the use of deadly force? And do we believe that following the rule of law—the U.S. Constitution—warrants the use of deadly force? If we do, then where is liberty?

Today, many questions are being asked and many questions are left unanswered about our father's wrongful death. We don't want the media bias. We don't want the FBI bias. We want the truth. And so today we celebrate our father's life. But going forward, we call for a private, independent investigation to find out exactly what happened to our daddy in an ambush on that lonely, desolate stretch of highway in the dead of winter in eastern Oregon.

We are grateful to all who have come to honor Robert LaVoy Finicum today. We will greatly miss our daddy. And we look forward to answering more of your questions as soon as we receive more answers to ours. Thank you again for coming here to be with us today.

Chapter 3: Murder Mayhem

JANUARY 4TH, 2016, SHAWNA COX READS THE REDRESS OF GRIEVANCE, WHICH WAS THE FUEL BEHIND THE OREGON OCCUPATION.

We the People, united individuals of these states united:

Coalition of Western States

Pacific Patriot Network

Bundy family and supporters

Oregon Oath Keepers

Idaho Three Percent

Central Oregon Constitutional Guard

Oregon Tactical

Oregon Bearded Bastards

Liberty Watch Washington

Nevada Committee for Full Statehood

Rural Heritage Preservation Project

Liberty for All

there are more names that I do not have listed here…

Notice to agent and notice to principal, notice to principal is notice to agent:

Sheriff David Ward

Commissioner Dan Nichols

Commissioner Pete Reynolds

Justice of the Peace Donna Thomas

District Attorney Tim Colehane

Attorney General Ellen Rosenblum

Governor Kate Brown

Dear Sirs,

After extensive research on the Hammond case, we the people of these states united have reason to believe that Dwight and Steven Hammond were not afforded their rights to due process as protected under the United States Constitution. We have principled evidence that Dwight and Steve Hammond committed no crime in the act of performing the prescribed burn and backfire, that the US government does not have authority to enforce territorial law under Article 4 within the of State Oregon, and the County of Harney and State of Oregon failed to protect the Hammond's rights as guaranteed by the U.S. Constitution, USC 42.1986, 18.242, 18.121, 42.1983, 42.1985.

We hold compelling evidence that the U.S. government abused the federal courts systems, situating the Hammond family into duress under an effort to force the Hammonds to sell their Sten Mountain property to a federal agency. We have substantial evidence that the U.S. Attorney's office exploited an act of Congress, imposing cruel and unusual punishment upon residents of Harney County. We hold substantial evidence that inside the borders of Harney County, the U.S. government is acting outside the authority enumerated in the Constitution of the United States. We secure evidence that the U.S. attorney's office independently prepared the indictment against Dwight and Steven Hammond and that the Grand Jury did not properly assemble or investigate before the indictment. We have no evidence that the Grand Jury participated in the indictment altogether. We have sure evidence that the U.S. Congress does not have authority to legislate minimum sentences requiring Dwight and Steven Hammond to serve five years in a federal prison penitentiary. We hold confirming video evidence of federal agents exhibiting a culture of intimidation toward individuals and businesses within the borders of Harney County—that federal agents, by fire, destroyed private property and that the Hammond family is being denied the same protection of the laws that are enjoyed by federal agents. We have supporting evidence that Judge Hogan controlled the narrative and did not allow full disclosure in the courtroom. We have additional evidence that Dwight and Steven Hammond were sentenced for something different than what they were found guilty of. We hold sound evidence that Dwight and Steven Hammond are victims of cruel and unusual punishment and the U.S. Justice Department is violating the 8th Amendment. We hold sure evidence that Dwight and Steven Hammond are being subject for the same offense, twice put in jeopardy, including that the 9th Circuit District Court of Appeals is in violation of the 5th Amendment. We have obtained appalling evidence that the U.S. Attorney's Office threatened the Hammond family with early detention and further punishment if the Hammonds family continued to communicate with a certain individual. This evidence foundationally speaks against the U.S. attorney's office and their gross effort to infringe upon the Hammond's rights to free exercise of speech, the 1st Amendment, the U.S. Constitution 18.242.

In a commitment to expose the truth and administrate justice, we the people of these states united insist that we immediately assemble an independent evidentiary hearing board, call witnesses, and investigate each of these allegations publicly, and that Harney County Board of Commissions and the Sheriff's Department enforce the conclusion of the evidentiary hearing board in support of the U.S. Constitution. We further insist that the Hammond family be protected from reporting to federal prison until all allegations can be determined.

We need not remind you of your lawful duty to act on these matters as insisted, or of the consequences if you knowingly neglected your duty, UCS 18.22382, 18.2071, 18.2076, 42.1983, 42.1985, 42, 1986. In light of the information presented, we require your thoughtful response within five days of the date of this notice. If we do not receive your response within five days, we will have no choice but to understand that you do not wish to do your duty and are content in acting in negligence to your obligation to defend the rights and liberties of the people.

Therefore, govern yourselves accordingly.

Respectfully,

We the people, United individuals of these states united.

We had tens of thousands of people put their names to this across the United States, including Hawaii. All 50 states.[429]

THE FAMILY'S STATEMENT IN RESPONSE TO MARCH 8TH, 2016, BEND, OREGON'S NEWS CONFERENCE REGARDING THE INVESTIGATION OF LAVOY'S DEATH

A forever thank you to Cherilyn Bacon Eagar, Board of Governors Phyllis Schlafly Eagles, for ministering to us by helping write this statement in our time of greatest need.

The news conference held earlier today in Bend, Oregon to release the report of the investigation regarding my husband's death was to be expected. No surprises. The purpose of that announcement was for the state and federal agencies to continue to lay the foundation for their legal case. However, they have brought forth selective evidence. As in all such situations, there is another side to the story.

We will provide a more thorough analysis of a follow-up news conference tomorrow and will be taking questions at that time. According to an AP (Associated Press) wire from Portland, Oregon, "officials investigating the death of Robert LaVoy Finicum are ready to release results of the fatal shooting during a January 26th traffic stop while trying to arrest the rancher and others involved in the take-over of an Oregon wildlife refuge." However, the FBI video shows this was not a typical traffic stop. It was an ambush, involving a roadblock on a blind curve along a lonely stretch of highway—a Deadman's blockade or kill stop, which is illegal.

The AP continues, "the FBI said Finicum was shot after reaching for a gun." We reject that statement. The FBI's aerial video was of poor quality, edited and provided no audio. Our family asserts that he was shot with both hands up and he was not reaching for anything at the time of the first shot. He was walking with his hands in the air, a symbol of surrender. When he reached down to his left he was reaching to the pain of having been shot. I can hardly believe that a team of qualified law enforcement officers could look at the facts of this case and say that no criminal laws were violated. How could they have reached this decision in the face of evidence that clearly shows intent to kill my husband?

We have talked with an independent investigator who has stated that the video provides a setup assassination. We have many people, including my lawyers who have tried to prepare me for this. Be strong, accept this with peace, but I do not think anything could prepare me to accept what is so clearly a finding that challenges the Constitution my husband died defending. I know that under the Constitution the men who shot my husband to death while he was surrendering are entitled to due process of law. But they are not entitled to walk free and not have to face the same legal process that is a barrier to you or to me. They shot my husband, and they left him lying in a snow bank with no medical assistance, no charges, no arraignments, no preliminary hearing, no indictment, no trial by a jury; and should they just walk free? It's just not right.

The consolation I have had is from thousands of Americans who have seen and know the truth and believe as I do that my husband was murdered intentionally and deliberately with malice. My lawyer has assured me that we will seek justice in a different court, under different circumstances and I look forward to the day when these men do face a jury that is unbiased enough to return a fair verdict.

After the funeral, rallies spontaneously began to organize in many states. The organizers counted possibly as many as a thousand rallies that took place throughout the country in every state but Rhode Island. It has been asked how this movement got such momentum so quickly. When Americans heard the details of this story and how these American patriots, who have no criminal record and who have stood on the same interpretation of the U.S. Constitution as Justice Scalia, have been treated, the actions of law enforcement and the FBI have shocked the conscience. Our Supreme Court has set as the standard guideline for practices of law, enforcements that are unacceptable to our society as those that shock the conscience. A deadman's blockade with the intent to kill shocks the conscience. Shooting to kill with both hands up shocks the conscience. Violating the 8th amendment of cruel and unusual punishment by placing Americans with no criminal record, who are apparently guilty of defending the U.S. Constitution and protesting the overreach of federal authorities, into solitary confinement and then removing their Constitutional right to bear arms are two examples of how elected and appointed officials in our courts system, legislative body, and law enforcement are violating the rule of law. The Supreme Court has referred to solitary confinement as being torture that drives victims violently insane. The court has recognized that solitary confinement tortures our human brain and diminishes our God-given strength to overcome obstacles. Solitary confinement is a form of torture that often drives the incarcerated mad. Last year a Supreme Court Justice wrote a concurring opinion that described the history of solitary confinement saying, "the practice bears a peculiar mark of infamy in its ability to shatter the minds and spirits of their prisoners."

Who are we?

We are outraged that men and women who have no criminal records and who posed no threat during the protest in Oregon are being treated as mere animals. The American people are outraged at this inhumanity, this brutality, this barbarism by the courts and law enforcement. It has created a new American awakening from both left and right. It shocks our conscience and that is why around a thousand rallies spontaneously organized in support of my assassinated husband and these patriots who are being held as political prisoners.

Again, my lawyer has assured me that we will seek justice in a different court under different circumstances and we will be commenting on the FBI and the Deschutes County press release tomorrow after we review their findings.

Thank you so very much for coming.

Chapter 4: Lords of the Message

GOVERNOR KATE BROWN LETTER TO PRESIDENT OBAMA

KATE BROWN
Governor

January 20, 2016

The Honorable Barack Obama
President of the United States
The White House
1600 Pennsylvania Avenue, N.W.
Washington, DC 20500

Mr. President:

On January 19, 2016, I spoke with Deputy Assistant to the President and Director of Intergovernmental Affairs Jerry Abramson to share my concerns with the handling of the occupation of the Malheur National Wildlife Refuge by armed radicals. Today I spoke with James Comey, Director of the Federal Bureau of Investigation. I followed up on these conversations by sending the enclosed letter.

During my conversations, I conveyed the harm that is being done to the citizens of Harney County by the occupation, and the necessity that this unlawful occupation end peacefully and without further delay from federal law enforcement.

On behalf of all Oregonians, I appreciate your consideration of our desire to see this situation come to a close, and I thank you for your timely attention to this matter.

Sincerely,

Governor Kate Brown

KB/HM/sb

254 STATE CAPITOL, SALEM OR 97301-4047 (503) 378-3111 FAX (503) 378-8970
WWW.GOVERNOR.OREGON.GOV

GOVERNOR KATE BROWN LETTER TO U.S. DEPARTMENT OF JUSTICE ATTORNEY GENERAL LORETTA LYNCH AND FBI DIRECTOR JAMES COMEY

January 20, 2016

KATE BROWN
Governor

The Honorable Loretta E. Lynch
U.S. Department of Justice
950 Pennsylvania Avenue, NW
Washington, DC 20530-0001

The Honorable James B. Comey
FBI Headquarters
935 Pennsylvania Avenue, NW
Washington, DC 20535-0001

Madam Attorney General and Director Comey:

Earlier today I spoke with Mr. Comey to share my issues with the handling of the occupation of the Malheur National Wildlife Refuge by armed radicals.

The citizens of Harney County are resilient and diverse and include members of the Burns-Paiute Tribe. Like most Oregonians, those from Harney County have a history of resolving difficult issues through a collaborative approach. They have worked hard through the years to develop the Malheur Refuge Comprehensive Conservation Plan, the Harney County Wetlands Initiative, the Harney County Restoration Collaborative, the Harney County Wildfire Collaborative, and SageCon. It is for this work that they should be recognized, and yet the national focus has instead been fixed on outsiders seeking to exploit and manipulate a local matter for their own agenda.

As you are both aware, for more than two weeks now, these radicals have been allowed to stay unlawfully in the refuge approximately 30 miles to the south of Burns, Oregon, in Harney County. While it is easy to assume that an occupation in such a remote location does not threaten public safety and does not harm any victims, that perception is far from accurate.

Even before the events of January 2, 2016, the local community was put under strain by the presence of outsiders who made unrealistic demands and began harassing law enforcement and their family members. While all were prepared for a tense but lawful protest on January 2 in the town, few were prepared for what would follow.

The unlawful seizure of the refuge by criminals seeking to advance a misguided agenda is in and of itself a strain. What adds to the tensions felt by the community is the reality that multiple "supporters" of these individuals have joined, staying in local motels in the City of Burns, and the criminals on the refuge are allowed to travel on and off the premises with little fear of law

254 STATE CAPITOL, SALEM OR 97301-4047 (503) 378-3111 FAX (503) 378-8970
WWW.GOVERNOR.OREGON.GOV

The Honorable Loretta E. Lynch
The Honorable James B. Comey
January 20, 2016
Page 2

enforcement contact or interaction. The residents of Harney County are being intimated in their own hometown by armed criminals who appear to be seeking occasions for confrontation. The harm being done to the innocent men, women and children in Harney County is real and manifest. With each passing day, tensions increase exponentially.

In addition to the federal agents deployed in town, the Oregon State Police and counties and cities from around the state are continuing to deploy additional officers to enhance local patrol and community safety. The reality is that this is not a sustainable law enforcement model for any extended period of time.

Because this occupation has occurred on federal land, it is appropriate that the FBI and other federal law enforcement entities are the leaders on any response to it, and we appreciate the recognition of their responsibility in this situation. They asked state officials, including me, to limit our public comments, which I have done, with considerable difficulty.

However, for the citizens of Harney County and indeed all Oregonians, I must insist on a swift resolution to this matter. Efforts to negotiate have not been successful, and now it is unclear what steps, if any, federal authorities might take to bring this untenable situation to an end and restore normalcy to this community.

I request on behalf of my fellow Oregonians that you instruct your agencies to end the unlawful occupation of the Malheur National Wildlife Refuge as safely and quickly as possible.

Sincerely,

Governor Kate Brown

KB/HM/sb

WHISTLEBLOWER LARRY WOOTEN MEMO

Larry "Clint" Wooten

From: Larry C. Wooten
Special Agent
U.S. Department of Interior, Bureau of Land Management
1387 S. Vinnell Way, Boise, ID 83709
Office Phone ████████ Gov't Cell Phone: ████████,
Email: ████████
Personal Cell Phone ████████ Personal Email ████████

To: Andrew D. Goldsmith
Associate Deputy Attorney General
National Criminal Discovery Coordinator
Email: ████████

Subject: Disclosure and Complaint Narrative in Regard to Bureau of Land Management Law Enforcement Supervisory Misconduct and Associated Cover-ups as well as Potential Unethical Actions, Malfeasance and Misfeasance by United States Attorney's Office Prosecutors from the District of Nevada, (Las Vegas) in Reference to the Cliven Bundy Investigation

Reference: DI-17-2830, MA-17-2863, LM14015035, District of Nevada Case 2:16-cr-00046-GMN-PAL (United States of America v. Cliven Bundy, et al)

Issue: As a U.S. Department of Interior (DOI), Bureau of Land Management (BLM), Office of Law Enforcement and Security (OLES) Special Agent (SA) and Case Agent/Lead Investigator for the Cliven Bundy/2014 Gold Butte Trespass Cattle Impound Case out of the District of Nevada in Las Vegas (Case 2:16-cr-00046-GMN-PAL-United States of America v. Cliven Bundy, et al), I routinely observed, and the investigation revealed a widespread pattern of bad judgment, lack of discipline, incredible bias, unprofessionalism and misconduct, as well as likely policy, ethical, and legal violations among senior and supervisory staff at the BLM's Office of Law Enforcement and Security. The investigation indicated that these issues amongst law enforcement supervisors in our agency made a mockery of our position of special trust and confidence, portrayed extreme unprofessional bias, adversely affected our agency's mission and likely the trial regarding Cliven Bundy and his alleged co-conspirators and ignored the letter and intent of the law. The issues I uncovered in my opinion also likely put our agency and specific law enforcement supervisors in potential legal, civil, and administrative jeopardy.

When I discovered these issues, I promptly reported them to my supervisor (a BLM Assistant Special Agent-in-Charge, but also my subordinate co-case agent). Often, I realized that my supervisor was already aware of the issues, participated in, or instigated the misconduct himself, was present when the issues were reported to both of us, or was the reporting party himself. When I reported these issues, my supervisor seemed generally unsurprised and uninterested and was dismissive, and seemed unconcerned.

I tried to respectfully and discretely urge and influence my supervision to stop the misconduct themselves, correct and/or further report the issues as appropriate and remind other employees that their use of electronic communications was likely subject to Federal Records Protections, the case Litigation Hold, the Freedom of Information Act (FOIA) and Case/Trial Discovery. I also tried to convey to my supervisor that the openly made statements and actions could also potentially could be considered bias, used in witness impeachment and considered exculpatory and subject to trial discovery.

As the Case Agent and Lead Investigator for the DOI/BLM (for approximately 2 years and 10 months), I found myself in an unusual situation. I was specifically asked to lead a comprehensive, professional, thorough, unbiased and independent investigation into the largest and most expansive and important investigation ever within the Department of Interior. Instead of having a normal investigative team and chain of command, a BLM Assistant Special Agent-in-Charge (ASAC) decided to act as a subordinate co-case agent, but also as my supervisor. Agent's senior to me acted as my helpers. I was basically the paper work, organizational and research guy. I did all the stuff that the senior and supervisory agents didn't want to do, but they called me the "Case Agent" and "Lead Investigator." They often publicly recognized and thanked me, and nominated me for many awards, but their lack of effort and dependability led to numerous case issues. During this timeframe, my supervisor (but subordinate), a BLM ASAC specifically wanted and had the responsibility of liaison and coordinator for interaction with higher agency officials, cooperating/assisting agencies and with the U.S. Attorney's Office. Although the BLM ASAC was generally uninterested in the mundane day to day work, he specifically took on assignments that were potentially questionable and damaging (such as document shredding research, discovery email search documentation and as the affiant for the Dave Bundy iPad Search Warrant) and attended coordination and staff meetings. Sometimes, I felt like he wanted to steer the investigation away from misconduct discovery by refusing to get case assistance, dismissing my concerns and participating in the misconduct himself. In February of 2017, it became clear to me that keeping quite became an unofficial condition of my future employment with the BLM, future awards, promotions, and a good future job reference.

The longer the investigation went on, the more extremely unprofessional, familiar, racy, vulgar and bias filled actions, open comments, and inappropriate electronic communications I was made aware of, or I personally witnessed. In my opinion, these issues would likely undermine the investigation, cast considerable doubt on the professionalism of our agency and be possibly used to claim investigator bias/unprofessionalism and to impeach and undermine key witness credibility. The ridiculousness of the conduct, unprofessional amateurish carnival atmosphere, openly made statements, and electronic communications tended to mitigate the defendant's culpability and cast a shadow of doubt of inexcusable bias, unprofessionalism and embarrassment on our agency. These actions and comments were in my opinion offensive in a professional federal law enforcement work environment and were a clear violation of professional workplace norms, our code of conduct, policy, and possibly even law. The misconduct caused considerable disruption in our workplace, was discriminatory, harassing and showed clear prejudice against the defendants, their supporters and Mormons. Often times this misconduct centered on being sexually inappropriate, profanity, appearance/body shaming and likely violated privacy and civil rights.

Many times, these open unprofessional and disrespectful comments and name calling (often by law enforcement supervisors who are potential witnesses and investigative team supervisors) reminded me of middle school. At any given time, you could hear subjects of this investigation openly referred to as "ret*rds," "r*d-necks," "Overweight woman with the big jowls," "d*uche bags," "tractor-face," "idiots," "in-br*d," etc., etc. Also, it was common to receive or have electronic communications reported to me during the course of the investigation in which senior investigators and law enforcement supervisors (some are potential witnesses and investigative team members) specifically made fun of suspects and referenced "Cliven Bundy felony...just kind of rolls off the tongue, doesn't it?," di1dos, western themed g@y bars, odors of sweat, playing chess with menstru*ting women, Cliven Bundy sh1tthing on cold stainless steel, personal lubricant and Ryan Bundy holding a giant pen1s (on April 12, 2014). Extremely bias and degrading fliers were also openly displayed and passed around the office, a booking photo of Cliven Bundy was (and is) inappropriately, openly, prominently and proudly displayed in the office of a potential trial witness and my supervisor and an altered and degrading suspect photos were put in an office presentation by my supervisor. Additionally, this investigation also indicated that former BLM SAC Dan Love sent photographs of his own feces and his girl-friend's vag1na to coworkers and subordinates. It was also reported by another BLM SAC that former BLM SAC Dan Love told him that there is no way he gets more pu$$y than him. Furthermore, I became aware of potentially captured comments in which our own law enforcement officers allegedly bragged about roughing up Dave Bundy, grinding his face into the ground, and Dave Bundy having little bits of gravel stuck in his face (from April 6, 2014). On two occasions, I also overheard a BLM SAC tell a BLM ASAC that another/other BLM employee(s) and potential trial witnesses didn't properly turn in the required discovery material (likely exculpatory evidence). My supervisor even instigated the unprofessional monitoring of jail calls between defendants and their wives, without prosecutor or FBI consent, for the apparent purpose of making fun of post arrest telephone calls between Idaho defendants/FBI targets (not subjects of BLM's investigation). Thankfully, AUSA Steven Myhre stopped this issue. I even had a BLM ASAC tell me that he tried to report the misconduct, but no one listened to him. I had my own supervisor tell me that former BLM SAC Dan Love is the BLM OLES "Directors boy" and they indicated they were going to hide and protect him. The BLM OLES Chief of the Office of Professional Responsibility/Internal Affairs indicated to me the former BLM OLES Director protected former BLM SAC Love and shut the Office of Professional Responsibility out when misconduct allegations were reported about Love and that the former BLM OLES Director personally (inappropriately) investigated misconduct allegations about Love. Another former BLM ASAC indicated to me that former BLM SAC Love was a liability to our agency and the Cliven Bundy Case. I was even told of threats of physical harm that this former BLM SAC made to his subordinate employee and his family.

4

Also, more and more it was becoming apparent that the numerous statements made by potential trial witnesses and victims (even by good officers under duress), could potentially cast an unfavorable light on the BLM. (See openly available video/audio footage titled "The Bundy Trial 2017 Leaked Fed Body Cam Evidence," or a video posted on You Tube titled "Leaked Body Cams from the Bundy Ranch!" published by Gavin Seim.) Some of these statements included the following: "Jack-up Hage" (Wayne Hage Jr.), "Are you fucXXXX people stupid or what," "Fat dude, right behind the tree has a long gun," "MotherFuXXXX, you come find me and you're gonna have hell to pay," "FatAsX slid down," "Pretty much a shoot first, ask questions later," "No gun there. He's just holding his back standing like a sissy," "She must not be married," "Shoot his fucXXXX dog first," "We gotta have fucXXXX fire discipline," and "I'm recording by the way guys, so…" Additional Note: *In this timeframe, a key witness deactivated his body camera.* Further Note: *It became clear to me a serious public and professional image problem had developed within the BLM Office of Law Enforcement and Security. I felt I needed to work to correct this and mitigate the damage it no doubt had already done.*

This carnival, inappropriate and childish behavior didn't stop with the directed bias and degradation of subjects of investigations. The childish misconduct extended to citizens, cooperators from other agencies and even our own employees. BLM Law Enforcement Supervisors also openly talked about and gossiped about private employee personnel matters such as medical conditions (to include mental illness), work performance, marriage issues, religion, punishments, internal investigations and derogatory opinions of higher level BLM supervisors. Some of these open comments centered on Blow JObs, Ma$terbation in the office closet, Addiction to P0rn, a Disgusting Butt Crack, a "Weak Sister," high self-opinions, crying and scared women, "Leather Face," "Mormons (little Mormon Girl)," "he has mental problems and that he had some sort of mental breakdown," "PTSD," etc., etc., etc.

Additionally, it should be noted that there was a "religious test" of sorts. On two occasions, I was asked "You're not a Mormon are you" and I was told "I bet you think I am going to hell, don't you." (I can explain these and other related incidents later.)

The investigation also indicated that on multiple occasions, former BLM Special Agent-in-Charge (SAC) Love specifically and purposely ignored U.S. Attorney's Office and BLM civilian management direction and intent as well as Nevada State Official recommendations in order to command the most intrusive, oppressive, large scale, and militaristic trespass cattle impound possible. Additionally, this investigation also indicated excessive use of force, civil rights and policy violations. The investigation indicated that there was little doubt there was an improper cover-up in virtually every matter that a particular BLM SAC participated in, or oversaw and that the BLM SAC was immune from discipline and the consequences of his actions. (I can further explain these issues later. These instances are widely documented.)

As the investigation went on, it became clear to me that my supervisor wasn't keeping the U.S. Attorney's Office up to date on substantive and exculpatory case findings and unacceptable bias indications. Therefore, I personally informed Acting United States Attorney Steven Myhre and Assistant United States Attorney (AUSA) Nadia Ahmed, as well as Federal Bureau of Investigation (FBI) Special Agent Joel Willis by telephone of these issues. When I did, my supervisor in my opinion deceptively acted ignorant and surprised. As the case continued, it became clear to me that once again, my supervisor failed to inform the U.S. Attorney's Office Prosecution Team about exculpatory key witness statements. Note: *During this investigation, my supervisor would also deceptively indicate to the Prosecution Team that no one else was in the room when he was on speakerphone. Thereby, allowing potential trial witnesses and his friends to inappropriately hear the contents of the discussion.*

My supervisor even took photographs in the secure command post area of the Las Vegas FBI Headquarters and even after he was told that no photographs were allowed, he recklessly emailed out photographs of the "Arrest Tracking Wall" in which Eric Parker and Cliven Bundy had "X's" through their face and body (indicating prejudice and bias). Thereby, making this electronic communication subject to Federal Records Protections, the Litigation Hold, Discovery, and the FOIA.

On February 16, 2017, I personally informed then AUSA (First Assistant and Lead Prosecutor) Steven Myhre of those specific comments (which I had previously disclosed to, and discussed with my supervisor) and reminded Special Assistant United States Attorney (SAUSA) Erin Creegan about an email chain by a particular BLM SAC in reference to the Arrest of David Bundy on April 6, 2014, in which prior to Dave Bundy's arrest, the BLM SAC and others were told not to make any arrests. When I asked Mr. Myhre if the former BLM SAC's statements like "Go out there and kick Cliven Bundy in the mouth (or teeth) and take his cattle" and "I need you to get the troops fired up to go get those cows and not take any crap from anyone" would be exculpatory or if we would have to inform the defense counsel, he said something like "we do now," or "it is now."

On February 18, 2017, I was removed from my position as the Case Agent/Lead Investigator for the Cliven Bundy/Gold Butte Nevada Case by my supervisor despite my recently documented and awarded hard work and excellent and often praised performance. Additionally, a BLM ASAC (my supervisor, but also my co-case agent) violated my privacy and conduced a search of my individually occupied secured office and secured safe within that office. During this search, the BLM ASAC without notification or permission seized the Cliven Bundy/Gold Butte Nevada Investigative "hard copy" Case File, notes (to include specific notes on issues I uncovered during the 2014 Gold Butte Nevada Trespass Cattle Impound and "lessons learned") and several computer hard drives that contained case material, collected emails, text messages, instant messages, and other information. Following this seizure outside of my presence and without my permission, the BLM ASAC didn't provide any property receipt documentation (DI-105/Form 9260-43) or other chain of custody documentation (reasonably needed for trial) on what was seized. The BLM ASAC also directed me to turn over all my personal case related notes on my personal calendars and aggressively questioned me to determine if I had ever audio recorded him or a BLM SAC. I was also aggressively questioned about who I had told about the case related issues and other severe issues uncovered in reference to the case and Dan Love (see Congressional

Subpoena by former Congressman Jason Chaffetz and the February 14, 2017, letter that Congressman Jason Chaffetz and Congressman Blake Farenthold sent the U.S. Department of Interior's Deputy Inspector General, Ms. Mary L. Kendall regarding Dan Love allegedly directing the deletion of official documents). Also after this, I believe I overheard part of a conversation in an open office space where my supervisor was speaking to a BLM SAC as they discussed getting access to my government email account. Note: *The personal notes that I was directed to turn in and the items seized from my office and safe wasn't for discovery, because I was transferring to another agency, because I was the subject of an investigation, or because my supervisor simply needed to reference a file. These items were taken because they contained significant evidence of misconduct and items that would potentially embarrass BLM Law Enforcement Supervision.* Additional Note: *The BLM ASAC also ordered me not to contact the U.S. Attorney's Office, even on my own time and with my personal phone. Later, when I repeatedly asked to speak with the BLM OLES Director, my requests went unanswered until April 26, 2017. The BLM ASAC simply told me it is clear no one wants to speak with me and that no one is going to apologize to me.* Further Note: *In this same secured individual office space and safe, I kept copies of my important personal documents such as medical records, military records, family personal papers, computer passwords, personal property serial numbers, etc., as a precaution in case for some reason my house is destroyed and personal papers are lost/destroyed. It was clear to me the BLM ASAC didn't know what he seized and when I told him about my personal papers, the BLM ASAC just told me "no one is interested in your medical records." It is unknown what unrelated case materials, notes, and personal documents were actually taken and it is impossible for me, any misconduct investigator, or any attorney to prove to a court or Congress what case information was taken. I still haven't heard back what (if any) personal items were in the seized materials and I don't know where the seized materials are being stored. It should be noted that I am missing personal medical physical results that I previously has stored in my office. Additionally, I believe if the BLM ASAC found my accidently seized medical records, instead of giving them back to me, he would shred them just like I have seen him shred other items from an agent that he didn't like.* (I can elaborate on this.)

Please Note: *This seized case related material (to include the hard drives) contains evidence that directly relates to a BLM SAC's heavy handedness during the 2014 Gold Butte Nevada Trespass Cattle Impound, the BLM SAC ignoring U.S. Attorney's Office and higher level BLM direction, documentation of the BLM SAC's alleged gross supervisory misconduct, potential misconduct and violation of rights issues during the 2014 Gold Butte Nevada Trespass Cattle Impound, as well as potential emails that were possibly identified and captured before they could have been deleted (as identified as an issue in the Office of Inspector General Report and possibly concerning a Congressional subpoena). I believe this information would likely be considered substantive exculpatory/jencks material in reference to the Cliven Bundy Nevada Series of Trials and would be greatly discrediting and embarrassing, as well as possibly indicate liability on the BLM and the BLM SAC.*

I am convinced that I was removed to prevent the ethical and proper further disclosure of the severe misconduct, failure to correct and report, and cover-ups by BLM OLES supervision. My supervisor told me that AUSA Steven Myhre "furiously demanded" that I be removed from the case and mentioned something about us (the BLM, specifically my supervisor) not turning over (or disclosing) discovery related material (which is true), issues I had with the BLM not following its own enabling statute (which is true, I can elaborate on that later), and a personal issue they thought I had with former BLM SAC Dan Love. Note: *Prior to taking the assignment as Bundy/Gold Butte Investigation Case Agent/Lead Investigator for the BLM/DOI, I didn't know and had never spoken to former BLM SAC Dan Love. I was new to the agency and I was also specifically directed to lead an unbiased, professional, and independent investigation, which I tried to do, despite supervisory misconduct. Time after time, I was told of former BLM SAC Love's misconduct. I was told by BLM Law Enforcement Supervisors that he had a Kill Book" as a trophy and in essence bragged about getting three individuals in Utah to commit suicide (see Operation Cerberus Action out of Blanding, Utah and the death of Dr. Redd), the "Failure Rock," Directing Subordinates to Erase Official Government Files in order to impede the efforts of rival civilian BLM employees in preparation for the "Burning Man" Special Event, unlawfully removing evidence, bragging about the number of OIG and internal investigations on him and indicating that he is untouchable, encouraging subordinates not to cooperate with internal and OIG investigations, his harassment of a female Native American subordinate employee where Mr. Love allegedly had a doll that he referred to by the employees name and called her his drunk little Indian, etc., etc., etc. (I can further explain these many issues.)*

Following this, I became convinced that my supervisor failed to properly disclose substantive and exculpatory case and witness bias related issues to the U.S. Attorney's Office. Also, after speaking with the BLM OLES Chief of the Office of Professional Responsibility/Internal Affairs and two former BLM ASAC's, I became convinced that the previous BLM OLES Director Salvatore Lauro not only allowed former BLM SAC Dan Love complete autonomy and discretion, but also likely provided no oversight and even contributed to an atmosphere of cover-ups, harassment and retaliation for anyone that questioned or reported former BLM SAC Dan Love's misconduct.

In time, I also became convinced (based on my supervisor and Mr. Myhre's statements) that although the U.S. Attorney's Office was generally aware of former BLM SAC Dan Love's misconduct and likely civil rights and excessive force issues, the lead prosecutor (currently the Acting Nevada United States Attorney) Steven Myhre adopted an attitude of "don't ask, don't tell," in reference to BLM Law Enforcement Supervisory Misconduct that was of a substantive, exculpatory and incredible biased nature. Not only did Mr. Myhre in my opinion not want to know or seek out evidence favorable to the accused, he and my supervisor discouraged the reporting of such issues and even likely covered up the misconduct. Furthermore, when I did report the misconduct, ethical, professional, and legal issues, I also became a victim of whistleblower retaliation.

Additionally, AUSA Steven Myhre adopted a few troubling policies in reference to this case. When we became aware that Dave Bundy's seized iPad likely contained remarks from BLM Law Enforcement Officers that is potentially evidence of civil rights violations and excessive use of force, Mr. Myhre and my supervisor not only apparently failed initiate the appropriate follow-on actions, Mr. Myhre apparently failed to notify the

Defense Counsel and also decided not to return the iPad back to Dave Bundy, even though the iPad wasn't going to be searched pursuant to a search warrant or used as evidence in trial and Dave Bundy claimed he needed the iPad for his business. Mr. Myhre also adopted a policy of not giving a jury the option or ability to convict on lesser offenses and instead relied on a hard to prove, complicated prosecution theory in order to achieve maximum punishments (which has generally failed to this point). Also, the government relied on factually incorrect talking points and on (or about) February 15, 2017, misrepresented the case facts about government snipers during trial (it is unknown if this misrepresentation was on purpose or accidental, I can explain this in detail). Note: *The investigation indicated that there was at least one school trained Federal Sniper equipped with a scoped/magnified optic bolt action precision rifle, another Federal Officer equipped with a scoped/magnified optic large frame (308 caliber) AR style rifle, and many officers that utilized magnified optics with long range graduated reticles (out to 1,000 meters-approximately 500 meters on issued rifles depending on environmental conditions) on standard law enforcement issued AR (223 caliber/5.56mm) and that often officers were in "over watch" positions. Additionally, the investigation also indicated the possibility that the FBI and the Las Vegas Metropolitan Police Department had law enforcement snipers/designated marksmen on hand for possible deployment.*

The reporting of these severe issues and associated cover-ups are a last resort. I tried continually to respectfully and discretely influence my chain of command to do the right thing and I made every effort to make sure the Prosecution Team had the information they needed and were accurate in their talking points. I just wanted the misconduct to stop, the necessary and required actions be taken and I wanted to be sure these issues wouldn't create a fatal error in the case and further undermine our agency's mission. I also needed to be convinced that I was correct. If I was wrong, or errors were simply mistakes or simple errors in professional judgement or discretion, I didn't want to create more problems or embarrass anyone. However, my personal experience and investigation indicated that not only did my management fail to correct and report the misconduct, they made every effort to cover it up, dismiss the concerns, discourage its reporting and retaliate against the reporting party. I also tried to make sure that despite my supervisor's failings, the Prosecution Team had the most accurate information in terms of case facts, Discovery, and witness liability.

The Whistleblower Retaliation and agency wrongdoing is being investigated by the U.S. Office of Special Counsel and is also being looked at by the House Committee on Natural Resources (Subcommittee on Oversight & Investigations) and the House Oversight and Government Reform Committee (Subcommittee on the Interior, Energy, and the Environment). Additionally, a formal complaint has been filed with my agency in reference to the religious, sexually vulgar, and the other workplace harassment. Furthermore, there have been several investigations by the DOI Office of Inspector General (OIG) that at least in part contributed to the recent firing of BLM Special Agent-in-Charge Dan Love (which I wasn't a part of).

I ask that your office ensure that Acting United States Attorney Steven Myhre and the rest of the Cliven Bundy/Gold Butte Nevada Prosecution and Investigative Team is conducting the prosecution in an ethical, appropriate, and professional matter. I also specifically ask that your office provide oversight to Mr. Myhre and his team regarding the affirmative responsibility to seek out evidence favorable to the accused, not to discourage the reporting of case issues and suspected misconduct, to report/act on suspected civil rights violations and not to retaliate against an agent that does his required duty. I also ask that your office ensure that the Prosecution Team is free of bias and has ethically and correctly turned over exculpatory evidence to the Defense. I ask that as appropriate, prosecution team bias (by Mr. Myhre and possibly by AUSA Daniel Schiess) and factually incorrect talking points (by AUSA Nadia Ahmed and Mr. Myhre) be disclosed and corrected. Note: *Mr. Myhre previously referred to the defendants as a cult and Mr. Schiess said let's get these "shall we say Deplorables." I was also asked "You're not a Mormon are you." (I can explain these and similar issues in detail.)*

I don't make this complaint lightly. I do this with a heavy heart and I hope that at least in some ways I am mistaken. However, I know that is extremely unlikely. When we speak I can identify subjects, witnesses, and the location of evidence and corroborating information.

I believe this case closely mirrors the circumstances of former Alaska Senator Ted Stevens trial. As you may notice from the trials and several defense cross-examinations, very little of the impeachment and exculpatory issues were brought up by the defense. I believe this is most likely because the defense counsel was unethically not made aware of them and the severe issues were covered up. Additionally, I believe I can easily show that both my supervision and possibly Mr. Myhre entered into an unethical agreement to remove me from being the lead investigator and case agent for the BLM/DOI due to my objection to, and disclosure of outrageous misconduct, the belief that my testimony under oath would embarrass supervisory law enforcement officials in our agency and negatively affect the prosecution, my insistence that my supervisor stop his individual misconduct, correct the misconduct of other employees and report the misconduct as appropriate (for counseling, correction, discipline and the possible required internal investigations) and my belief that my agency is violating the letter and intent of the law.

In regard to prosecution team misconduct, I believe some of it may be attributable to simple mistakes and simple poor judgement. However, I believe it is unlikely (if my supervisor's statements to me are true) that Mr. Myhre wasn't himself acting unethically and inappropriately. Prior to the last few weeks of the investigation, I held Mr. Myhre in the highest of regards. He is an extremely hard worker and very intelligent. However, I feel that his judgement is likely clouded by extreme personal and religious bias and a desire to win the case at all costs. I feel he is likely willing to ignore and fail to report exculpatory material, extreme bias and act unethically and possibly deceptively to win.

All in all, it is my assessment and the investigation showed that the 2014 Gold Butte Trespass Cattle Impound was in part a punitive and ego driven expedition by a Senior BLM Law Enforcement Supervisor (former BLM Special Agent-in-Charge Dan Love) that was only in part focused on the intent of the associated Federal Court Orders and the mission of our agency (to sustain the health, diversity, and productivity of America's public lands for the multiple use and enjoyment of present and future generations). My investigation also indicated that the involved officers and protestors were themselves pawns in what was almost a great American tragedy on April 12, 2014, in which law enforcement officers (Federal, State, and Local), protestors, and the motoring public were caught in the danger area. This investigation also indicated, the primary reasons for the escalation was due to the recklessness, lack of oversight, and arrogance of a BLM Special Agent-in-Charge and the recklessness, failure to adhere to Federal Court Orders and lack of recognition of the Federal Government in matters related to land management within Nevada, by Rancher Cliven Bundy.

The investigation further indicated that the BLM SAC's peers didn't likely attempt to properly influence or counsel the BLM SAC into more appropriate courses of action and conduct or were unsuccessful in their attempts. The investigation indicated that it was likely that the BLM SAC's peers failed to report the BLM SAC's unethical/unprofessional actions, misconduct, and potential crimes up the chain of command and/or to the appropriate authorities, or that the chain of command simply ignored and dismissed these reports. The investigation further indicated when individuals did report issues with the BLM SAC, the reports were likely ignored or marginalized by higher BLM OLES officials. The investigation also indicated that former BLM OLES Director Salvatore Lauro likely gave the former BLM SAC complete autonomy and discretion without oversight or supervision. The investigation further indicated that it was unlikely that the BLM OLES Director wasn't aware of the BLM SAC's unethical/unprofessional actions, poor decisions, misconduct, and potential crimes. My investigation and personal observations in the investigation further revealed a likely unethical/unlawful "cover-up" of this BLM SAC's actions, by very senior law enforcement management within BLM OLES. This investigation indicated that on numerous occasions, senior BLM OLES management broke their own policies and overlooked ethical, professional, and conduct violations and likely provided cover and protection for the BLM SAC and any activity or operation this BLM SAC was associated with. My investigation further indicated that the BLM's civilian leadership didn't condone and/or was likely unaware of the BLM SAC's actions and the associated cover-ups, at least until it was too late.

During the investigation, I also came to believe that the case prosecution team at United States Attorney's Office out of Las Vegas in the District of Nevada wasn't being kept up to date on important investigative findings about the BLM SAC's likely alleged misconduct. I also came to believe that discovery related and possibly relevant and substantive trial, impeachment, and biased related and/or exculpatory information wasn't likely turned over to, or properly disclosed to the prosecution team by my supervisor.

I also came to believe there were such serious case findings that an outside investigation was warranted on several issues to include misconduct, ethics/code of conduct issues, use of force issues (to include civil rights violations), non-adherence to law, and the loss/destruction of, or purposeful non-recording of key evidentiary items (Unknown Items 1 & 2, Video/Audio, April 6, 2014, April 9, 2014, April 12, 2014-the most important and critical times in the operation). I believe these issues would shock the conscious of the public and greatly embarrass our agency if they were disclosed.

Ultimately, I believe I was removed from my position as Case Agent/Lead Investigator for the Cliven Bundy/Gold Butte, Nevada Investigation because my management and possibly the prosecution team believed I would properly disclose these embarrassing and substantive issues on the stand and under oath at trial (if I was asked), because my supervision believed I had contacted others about this misconduct (Congress, possibly the defense and press) and possibly audio recorded them, because I had uncovered, reported, and objected to suspected violations of law, ethics directives, policy, and the code of conduct, and because I was critical of the misconduct of a particular BLM SAC. This is despite having already testified in Federal Grand Jury and being on the trial witness list.

The purpose of this narrative is not to take up for or defend the actions of the subjects of this investigation. To get an idea of the relevant historical facts, conduct of the subjects of the investigation and contributing factors, you may consider familiarizing yourself with the 2014 Gold Butte Timeline (which I authored) and the uncovered facts of this investigation. The investigation revealed that many of the subjects likely knowingly and willingly ignored, obstructed, and/or attempted to unlawfully thwart the associated Federal Court Orders through their specific actions and veiled threats, and that many of the subjects also likely violated several laws. This investigation also showed that subjects of the investigation in part adopted an aggressive and bully type strategy that ultimately led to the shutdown of I-15, where many armed followers of Cliven Bundy brandished and pointed weapons at Federal Officers and Agents in the Toquop Wash near Bunkerville, Nevada, on April 12, 2014, in a dangerous, high risk, high profile national incident. This investigation further indicated that instead of Cliven Bundy properly using the court system or other avenues to properly address his grievances, he chose an illegal, uncivilized, and dangerous strategy in which a tragedy was narrowly and thankfully avoided.

Additionally, it should be noted that I was also personally subjected to Whistleblowing Discouragement, Retaliation, and Intimidation. Threatening and questionable behaviors included the following: Invasion of Privacy, Search and Seizure, Harassment, Intimidation, Bullying, Blacklisting, Religious "tests," and Rude and Condescending Language. Simply put, I believe I was expected to keep quiet as a condition of my continued employment, any future promotions, future awards, or a favorable recommendation to another employer.

During the course of the investigation, I determined that any disagreement with the BLM SAC, or any reporting of his many likely embarrassing, unethical/unprofessional actions and misconduct was thought to be career destroying. Time and time again, I came to believe that the BLM SAC's subordinates and peers were afraid to correct him or properly report his misconduct (despite a duty to act) out of fear for their own jobs and reputation.

Sometimes, I felt these issues (described in depth below) were reported to me by senior BLM OLES management and line Rangers/Agents/employees because they personally didn't like a particular BLM SAC (although, some of these same people seemed to flatter, buddy up to, openly like, and protect the BLM SAC). Sometimes, I thought BLM OLES management wanted to talk about these actions because they thought these blatant inappropriate acts by a BLM SAC and others were funny. Sometimes, I thought the reporting parties wanted the misconduct corrected and the truth to come to light, but they were afraid/unwilling to report and correct the misconduct themselves. Sometimes, I thought the reporting parties just wanted to get the issues off their chest. Sometimes, I thought supervisors wanted to report the misconduct to me, so they could later say they did report it (since I was the Case Agent/Lead Investigator). Therefore, in their mind limit their liability to correct and report the misconduct and issues. However, it was confusing that at the same time, I thought some of these reporting parties (particularly in management) sought deniability and didn't want to go "on the record." These same reporting/witnessing parties in most cases apparently refused to correct the misconduct and further report it to higher level supervision, the Office of Inspector General, and the U.S. Attorney's Office (as required/necessary) and even discouraged me from further reporting and correcting the issues. When I did try to correct and further report the issues as I believed appropriate and necessary, these same supervisors (who were reporting/witnessing parties) acted confused and unaware. Ultimately, I became an outcast and was retaliated against.

I also feel there are likely a great many other issues that even I am not aware of, that were likely disclosed or known to my supervisor, at least two other BLM SACs, the former BLM SAC's subordinates, and the former BLM OLES Director. In addition to the witnesses I identify, I would also recommend interviews with the BLM OLES Chief of the Office of Professional Responsibility/Internal Affairs and I would recommend reviews of my chain of command's emails and text messages.

Unfortunately, I also believe that the U.S. Attorney's Office Prosecution Team may have adopted an inappropriate under the table/unofficial policy of "preferred ignorance" in regard to the likely gross misconduct on the part of senior management from the BLM Office of Law Enforcement and Security and Discovery/Exculpatory related trial issues.

What indicated to me there was likely deception and a failure to act on the part of my supervision was the actions, comments, and questions of senior BLM Law Enforcement Officials, comments by the BLM's Chief of the Office of Professional Responsibility (Internal Affairs), and the pretrial Giglio/Henthorn Review.

Additionally, actions, comments, and questions by the U.S. Attorney's Office Lead Prosecutor, the strategy to deny the Dave Bundy iPad evidence from coming to light, the direction by a BLM ASAC for me not to speak with any member of the Prosecution Team, and factually deceptive/incorrect talking points (snipers, Bundy property, Bundy cattle overall health, etc.), indicated to me the Prosecution Team wanted to possibly and purposefully remain ignorant of some of the case facts and possibly use unethical legal tricks to prevent the appropriate release of substantive/exculpatory and bias/impeachment material. I believe that it is more likely than not, that there was not only a lack of due diligence by the Prosecution Team in identifying and locating exculpatory material, but there was also a desire to purposely stay ignorant (which my chain of command was happy to go along with) of some of the issues and likely an inappropriate strategy to not disclose substantive material to the Defense Counsel and initiate any necessary civil rights related or internal investigations. Furthermore, I was surprised about the lack of

Defense Counsel questions about critical vulnerabilities in the case that should have been disclosed to the Defense in a timely manner. It is my belief that the Defense Counsel was simply ignorant of these issues.

Also, please keep in mind that I am not an "Internal Affairs," "Inspector General," or "Office of Professional Responsibility Investigator." Therefore, I couldn't, and can't independently conduct investigations into government law enforcement personnel. Additionally, I haven't been formally trained on internal investigations. Therefore, my perception, the opinions I offer, and the fact pattern that I found relevant was gained from my experience as a regular line investigator and former uniformed patrol and Field Training Officer (FTO).

Each, and every time I came across any potential criminal, ethical, or policy related issue, in the course of my duties as the DOI/BLM Case Agent/Lead Investigator for the Gold Butte/Cliven Bundy Nevada Investigation, I reported the issues up my chain of command with the intent to run an independent and unbiased, professional investigation, as I was instructed. Later, I determined my chain of command was likely already aware of many of these issues and were likely not reporting those issues to the prosecution team and higher headquarters. Later, I also was informed by the BLM Office of Professional Responsibility (OPR) Chief that any issues that had anything to do with a particular favored BLM SAC, the BLM OLES Director looked at himself instead of OPR. The OPR Chief told me he was shut out of those types of inquiries. I noted in the pre-trial Giglio/Henthorn Review that this appeared to be accurate. I also noted that these types of issues I discovered apparently weren't properly investigated as required. The bad joke I heard around the office was that the BLM SAC knew where the BLM OLES Director had buried the pr0stitutes body and that is why the BLM OLES Director protects him.

I know good people make mistakes, are sometimes immature and use bad judgement. I do it all the time. I am not addressing simple issues here. However, some simple issues are included to indicate a wide spread pattern, openly condoned prohibited/unprofessional conduct and an inappropriate familiar and carnival atmosphere. Additionally, the refusal to correct these simple issues and conduct discrepancies, harassment, and ultimately cover-ups and retaliation are indicated and explained throughout this document.

Since I wasn't a supervisor and since I was one of the most junior criminal investigators in our agency, I tried to positively influence those above me by my example and discrete one on one mentoring and urging. I simply wanted the offensive and case/agency destructive conduct to stop, to correct the record where appropriate, and inform those who we had a duty to inform of the potential wrong-doing. I attempted to positively influence my management in the most respectful and least visible way possible. In order to accomplish this, I adopted a praise in public and counsel in private approach. When that failed to work for the long term, I had to become more "matter of fact" (but always respectful), when that failed to work I resorted to documenting the instances and discussions. Later, I resorted to official government email to make a permanent record of the issues. When this failed to deter the offensive conduct or instigate appropriate action by my supervision, I had to notify others and identify witnesses. I respected and stayed within my chain of command until I was expressly forbidden from contacting the U.S. Attorney's Office and my requests to speak with the BLM OLES Director went unanswered.

Simply put, as a law enforcement officer, I can't allow injustices and cover-ups to go unreported or half-truths and skewed narratives go unopposed. I have learned that when conduct of this sort isn't corrected, then by default it is condoned, and it becomes unofficial policy. When I determined there were severe issues that hurt more than just me, and I determined that my supervision apparently lacked the character to correct the situation, I knew that duty fell to me. I still felt I could accomplish this duty without embarrassing my supervision, bringing shame on our agency, or creating a fatal flaw in our investigation.

Initially, I felt I could simply mentor and properly influence my supervision to do the right thing. Time and time again, I urged my supervision to correct actions and counsel individuals who participate in conduct damaging to our agency and possibly destructive to the integrity of our case or future investigations. I attempted to urge my supervision to report certain information to senior BLM management and the U.S. Attorney's Office. Note: *Evidence of some of this offensive conduct is potentially available through Freedom of Information Act (FOIA) requests and subject to a Litigation Hold, may be considered Exculpatory Material in trial discovery process, and may be subject to federal records protections. Additionally, in many instances, I can provide evidence, identify the location of evidence and identify witnesses.*

Ultimately, in addition to discovering crimes likely committed by those targeted in the investigation, I found that likely a BLM Special Agent-in-Charge recklessly and against advisement from the U.S. Attorney's Office and apparent direction from the BLM Deputy Director set in motion a chain of events that nearly resulted in an American tragedy and mass loss of life. Additionally, I determined that reckless and unprofessional conduct within BLM Law Enforcement supervisory staff was apparently widespread, widely known and even likely "covered up." I also found that in virtually every case, BLM senior law enforcement management knew of the suspected issues with this BLM SAC, but were either too afraid of retaliation, or lacked the character to report and/or correct the suspected issues.

Note: *This entire document was constructed without the aid of my original notes due to their seizure by a BLM Assistant Special Agent-in-Charge outside of my presence and without my knowledge or permission. Additionally, I was aggressively questioned regarding the belief that I may have audio recorded BLM OLES management regarding their answers concerning this and other issues. All dates, times, and quotes are approximate and made to the best of my ability and memory. I'm sure there are more noteworthy items that I can't recall at the time I constructed this document.* Also Note: *The other likely report worthy items were seized from me on February 18, 2017, and are believed to be in the possession of a BLM ASAC. I recommend these items be safeguarded and reviewed.*

As the case agent/lead investigator for the DOI in the Cliven Bundy investigation out of the District of Nevada, I became aware of a great number of instances when senior BLM OLES leadership were likely involved in **Gross Mismanagement** and **Abuse of Authority** (which may have posed a substantial and specific threat to employee and public safety as well as wrongfully denied the public Constitutionally protected rights). The BLM OLES leadership and others may have also violated **Merit System Principles** (Fair/Equitable Treatment, High Standards of Conduct, Failing to Manage Employee Performance by Failing to Address Poor Performance and Unprofessional Conduct, Potential Unjust Political Influence, and Whistleblower Retaliation), **Prohibited Personnel Practices** (Retaliation Against Whistleblowers, Retaliation Against Employees that Exercise Their Rights, Violation of Rules that Support the Merit System Principles, Enforcement of Policies (unwritten) that Don't Allow Whistleblowing), **Ethics Rules** (Putting Forth an Honest Effort in the Performance of Duties, the Obligation to Disclose Waste, Fraud, Abuse, and Corruption, Endeavoring to Avoid Any Action that Creates the Appearance that there is a Violation of the Law, and Standards of Ethical Conduct for Employees), **BLM OLES Code of Conduct** (Faithfully Striving to Abide by all Laws, Rules, Regulations, and Customs Governing the Performance of Duties, Potentially Violating Laws and Regulations in a Unique Position of High Pubic Trust and Integrity of Profession and Confidence of the Public, Peers, Supervisors, and Society in General, Knowingly Committing Acts in the Conduct of Official Business and/or in Personal Life that Subjects the Department of Interior to Public Censure and/or Adverse Criticism, Conducting all Investigations and Law Enforcement Functions Impartially and Thoroughly and Reporting the Results Thereof Fully, Objectively, and Accurately, and Potentially Using Greater Force than Necessary in Accomplishing the Mission of the Department), **BLM Values** (To serve with honesty, integrity, accountability, respect, courage and commitment to make a difference), **BLM Guiding Principles** (to respect, value, and support our employees. To pursue excellence in business practices, improve accountability to our stake holders and deliver better service to our customers), **BLM OLES General Order 38** (Internal Affairs Investigations), **Departmental and Agency Policies** (BLM Director Neil Kornze Policy on Equal Opportunity and the Prevention of Harassment dated January 19, 2016, DOI Secretary Sally Jewell Policy on Promoting an Ethical Culture dated June 15, 2016, DOI Secretary Sally Jewell Policy on Equal Opportunity in the Workplace dated September 14, 2016, DOI Deputy Secretary of Interior Michael Connor Policy on Workplace Conduct dated October 4, 2016, DOI Secretary Ryan Zinke Policy on Strengthening the Department's Ethical Culture dated March 2, 2017, DOI Secretary Ryan Zinke Policy on Harassment dated April 12, 2017, Memorandum dated December 12, 2013, from Acting DOI Deputy Assistant Secretary for Human Capital and Diversity Mary F. Pletcher titled "The Whistleblower Protection Enhancement Act of 2012 and Non-Disclosure Policies, Forms, Agreements, and Acknowledgements, Email Guidance by Deputy Secretary of Interior David Bernhardt titled "Month One Message," dated August 1, 2017, Email Guidance by Deputy Secretary of Interior David Bernhardt titled "Month Two Message," dated September 22, 2017, BLM Acting Deputy Director of Operations John Ruhs guidance contained in an Email titled "Thank You for Making a Difference," dated September 29, 2017, which referenced BLM Values and Guiding Principles, BLM/DOI Email and Computer Ethical Rules of Behavior, BLM "Zero Tolerance" Policy Regarding Inappropriate Use of the Internet, 18 USC 1663 Protection of Public Records and Documents, 18 USC 4 Misprison of a Felony, 18 USC 1519 Destruction, Alteration, or Falsification of Records in Federal Investigations, 18 USC 241 Conspiracy Against Rights, 18 USC 242 Deprivation of Rights Under Color of Law, 43 USC 1733 (c) (1) Federal Land Policy Management Act, 43 USC 315 (a) Taylor Grazing Act, 5 USC 2302 Whistleblower Protections-Prohibited Personnel Practices/Whistleblower Protection/Enhancement Acts, 5 CFR 2635 Gifts Between Employees, 5 USC 7211 Employees Rights to Petition Congress, and Public Law 112-199 of November 27, 2012.

Additionally, the BLM Criminal Investigator/Special Agent Position Description (LE140) in part states the following: "Comprehensive and professional knowledge of the laws, rules, and regulations which govern the protection of public lands under jurisdiction of the Bureau of land Management, and their applicability on a national basis,"(under Factor 1, Knowledge Required by the Position), "Knowledge of the various methods, procedures, and techniques applicable to complex investigations and other law enforcement activities required in the protection of natural resources on public land. The applicable methods, procedures, and techniques selected require a high degree of judgement that recognizes sensitivity to the violations, as alleged, discretion in the manner that evidence and facts are developed, and an awareness of all ramifications of a criminal investigation. The incumbent must have the ability to establish the interrelationship of facts and evidence and to present findings in reports that are clear, concise, accurate, and timely submitted for appropriate review and action." (under Factor 1, Knowledge Required by the Position), "Comprehensive knowledge of current and present court decisions, criminal rules of evidence, constitutional law, and court procedures to be followed in criminal matters, formal hearings and administrative matters in order to apply court and constitutional requirements during the conduct of an investigation and to effectively testify on behalf of the Government." (under Factor 1, Knowledge Required by the Position), "great discretion must be taken to avoid entrapment of suspects and to protect the integrity of the investigation" (under Factor 4, Complexity), and "The incumbent must be able to safely utilize firearms...." (Factor 8, Physical Demands)

Please also note the potential Constitutional issues regarding "religious tests," search and seizure, and speech/assembly protections.

Please further note the following Rules of Criminal Procedure/Evidence: Memorandum of Department Prosecutors dated January 4, 2010, from David W. Ogden to the Deputy Attorney General, Rule 16, 18 USC 3500-the Jencks Act, the Brady Rule, Giglio, U.S. Attorney's Manuel 9-5.001 Policy Regarding Disclosure of Exculpatory and Impeachment Information, 9-5.100 Policy Regarding the Disclosure to Prosecutors of Potential Impeachment Information Concerning Law Enforcement Agency Witnesses, American Bar Association Standards 3-1.2 The Function of the Prosecutor, 3-2.8 Relations with the Courts and Bar, 3-3.1 Conflict of Interest, 3-3.11 Disclosure of Evidence by the Prosecutor, 3-5.6 Presentation of Evidence, and 3-6.2 Information Relevant to Sentencing.

Case Details: 2-year/10-month case, approximately 570 DOI Exhibits/Follow-on Turn-in Items, approximately 508 DOI Identified Individuals-19 Defendants

Chapter 5: A Force to be Reckoned With

DETAILS OF FBI AND BLM COLORADO EVENT ENCOUNTER

Picture of the envelope that our Colorado event host, Barbara Hulet, received in response to her freedom of information request (FOIA) after she found out agents were asking to be deputized to raid her event she hosted for the Finicum family. Barbara sent this photo to the family when she disclosed what was happening.

Below is a copy of the letter that was found in the above envelope.

July 22, 2016

Via Email and U.S. Mail
Barbara Hulet
Olathe, CO 81425
E-mail:

Dear Ms. Hulet,

I write on behalf of the City of Delta in response to your Request for Inspection/Copying of Records, received by this office at 4:20 p.m. on July 20, 2016.

Enclosed please find documentation responsive to your request. The privileged portions have been redacted as permitted by Colorado law. On the grounds that further disclosure would be contrary to the public interest, and pursuant to the Colorado Criminal Justice Act and/or the Colorado Open Records Act, access is hereby denied to other records, if any, related to (1) investigations, intelligence information, or security procedures of any sheriff, district attorney, or police department or (2) contained within an investigatory file compiled for any other law enforcement purpose. *See* C.R.S. § 24-72-305(5); C.R.S. § 24-72-204(2)(a)(I).

Respectively,
/s/
Jolene E. Nelson
Court Clerk

Below is a copy of what the above letter said they enclosed.

From: **David Torgler** <david@cityofdelta.net>
Date: Tue, Jun 28, 2016 at 3:07 PM
Subject:
To: Bill Raley <billr@cityofdelta.net>, Christopher Ryan <chrisr@cityofdelta.net>, Ed Sisson <ed@cityofdelta.net>, "Gerald E. Roberts" <gerald@cityofdelta.net>, Ron Austin <rona@cityofdelta.net>, Charles Kettle <charles@cityofdelta.net>, Tod Dezeeuw <tod@cityofdelta.net>, Glen Black <glen@cityofdelta.net>, Steve Glammeyer <steve@cityofdelta.net>, Wilma Erven <wilma@cityofdelta.net>

To all:

Please be advised that the Delta PD was informed that there will be a group of sovereign citizens meeting at the Fireside Restaurant located in Delta on Wednesday July 6th, 2016 at 1830 hours. They will be here doing a fundraiser for the sovereign citizen who was shot and killed in the Oregon standoff. It has been reported that among the people attending will be the sovereign citizens' wife who was shot and killed.

David Torgler

City Manager
City of Delta
360 Main Street
Delta, Colorado 81416

Below is a copy of the letter that I wrote with the help of President and Co-founder of Center for Self Governance Mark Herr in response to the out-of-control agents in Colorado. It was delivered to both my mother's and my state and district representatives. I did not receive any contact from my representatives, but my mom did, which produced a good outcome.

A forever thank you to Mark Herr, president and co-founder of Center for Self Governance and co-author of Speaking the Language of Liberty, for ministering to us by helping to draft this letter in our time of greatest need.

Subject: My mother and I are seeking your advice and support.

Dear ...,

OVERVIEW OF ISSUE

My father, Lavoy Finicum, was shot and killed by Oregon State agents, in co-ordination with federal agents, on January 26, 2016. My mother, Jeanette, and I have been invited to speak at events around the country to give a voice to our father's death. Since then, the FBI, BLM, and Oregon agents are practicing irresponsible tactics of intimidation and libel with the assumed goal to silence my mother's and my right of free speech.

They have libelously labeled us as an irresponsible group known as "Sovereign Citizens." And they have sought to be deputized and raid an event, held for us, outside of their jurisdictions.

My mother and I are seeking to remedy these irresponsible actions through your advice and support. We sincerely desire and seek a relationship process that includes rebuilding trust between us and our governors.

THE HISTORY OF THE ISSUE

A meeting took place roughly around June 20– 28, 2016 involving the FBI, BLM, Oregon State and Delta County agents. We do not know who organized the meeting in Grand Junction, Mesa County, CO but it has been assumed the FBI, BLM and Oregon officials led the meeting.

Delta County Sheriff Fred McKee and Charles Kettle who is the Delta, CO interim police chief attended the meeting. Barbara Hulet (organizer of the event for my mother and me) along with other individuals met with Sheriff McKee and Chief Kettle to confirm the meeting and their attendance. The sheriff and chief of police were very concerned about not disclosing any names of the agents who were there or any other details such as who organized the meeting, why it was organized, when the exact date and location was, etc.

They didn't disclose how the agents were asked permission to conduct a raid on the symposium that was being held at the Delta Fireside Inn, 820 Highway 92 in Delta, Delta County, CO scheduled for July 6th, 2016. Fortunately, the Delta Sheriff Fred McKee and Charles Kettle, the interim chief of police did not give them permission to raid the event. They expressed how many people in the event would be carrying a firearm on their person and how they had a right to do so. Barbara thanked the sheriff and expressed how there were children at this event, (including my children and Barbara Hulet's daughter).

Barbara Hulet found a memo labeling all those who attended the July 6th symposium as "Sovereign Citizens." This memo was sent out to the Delta City Council, Interim city police, and all department heads. She filed an open records request on July 20, 2016 to get a copy of that memo (see attached). This memo was dated June 28, 2016, eight days before the event that I, Thara Tenney, spoke at. It specifically stated how my father, LaVoy Finicum was labeled as a "Sovereign Citizen" and how his wife, Jeanette Finicum, would be in attendance. There is no evidence my father was a member of or made any public declaration of support for "Sovereign Citizens." He always instructed us to be responsible citizens with a responsible government.

On August 2nd, Rosemary Anderson, Bev Watts, and Barbara Hulet (individuals who helped organize the July 6th symposium I spoke at that the FBI wanted to raid) went to the City of Delta's council meeting. They read the memo into the public record. They mentioned how they were libeled as very dangerous people, Rosemary talked of the power in words and read from the FBI's website how they are defining "Sovereign Citizen." Bev Watts spoke of how they don't belong to or support any such groups. When Rosemary, Donna, and Barbara Hulet went in to get the minutes on Friday August 12, 2016, they found how they did not transcribe their words.[430]

When Barbara Hulet, Rosemary, and Donna Biliko spoke face-to-face with Charles Kettle, the interim police chief on August 11, 2016 about the memo, he said he told the city manager David Torgler to send out the memo and that he (Charles Kettle) is taking full responsibility for the memo, despite the fact that he says David Torgler, the city manager, is his boss. In speaking with Charles Kettle (police chief), he expressed he did not fully understand the meaning of being libeled sovereign citizens. Rosemary told him he needed to write a letter to the editor apologizing and Chief Kettle said he would have to have that approved by his boss Mr. David Torgler, city manager, whose name is on the memo. The apology has not taken place as of September 1, 2016.

The local Delta County Independent published an article talking about these three women contesting the libel against them by this memo. The article was published one day before they spoke with Charles Kettle, the interim police chief on August 11, 2016.[431]

WHO IS INFLICTED BY THE INTIMIDATION AND LIBEL

> Colorado citizens; Barbara Hulet, Donna Biliko, Rosemary Anderson, David Justice, Bev Watts and Betty Oglesby.

- Colorado county government agents Sheriff Fred McKee and Police Chief Charles Kettle.
- Arizona citizen Jeanette Finicum, the wife of LaVoy Finicum.
- Utah citizen Thara Tenney, the oldest daughter of LaVoy Finicum.

This irresponsible intimidation and libel is both unacceptable and bordering on harmful. And it needs to stop.

MY DECLARATION

I, Thara Tenney, the oldest daughter of LaVoy Finicum, was the main speaker at this symposium. My speech is titled "Habits of the Heart; a Perpetuation of Freedom." In this speech, I talk of my father, LaVoy Finicum, who he truly was, what enabled him to be a powerful voice for freedom, what got him to Oregon, what he was accomplishing in Oregon, and I end with an invitation for others to do their due diligence to maintain our republic as responsible citizens.

I am a citizen following the law within the boundaries of a republican form of government. I reject any form of government where the governed or the governors misuse government irresponsibly. I reject soundly forms of government supported by any governed who claim they are without law and who consider themselves sovereign and without government. I reject soundly forms of government supported by any governor who claim that the governed are subject to all laws, regardless of abuse and irresponsible application and who, subsequently, take advantage of the governed's ignorance and irresponsible reactions.

EXAMPLES OF IRRESPONSIBLE GOVERNORS

- **Baltimore** — Mayor "Let it burn"
- **Ferguson** — Governor, 48 hours before support
- **Burns** — FBI lying about firing my father

I CALL FOR A FRESH, NEW ERA OF PRO-RESPONSIBLE GOVERNMENT BY BOTH THE GOVERNED AND THE GOVERNORS!

It is very clear how the governed are sensing this modern irresponsibility and are reacting the best they know how. I say stop abusing their ignorance, stop abusing their trust, stop the intimidation and the slander!

The *government* (it) is being misused by irresponsible governors to intimidate and slander me and my mother, as we are being followed by them, having our reputation and character libeled and slandered by them and intimidating citizens and governors of other states. My children were put in harm's way as the FBI sought the blessing from the local sheriff to raid our event.

We will continue to remain steadfast! We will continue sharing our account of my mother's husband's and my father's voice. We refuse to have his voice buried along with his body! We claim our right to freedom of speech, free from intimidation by those entrusted with the reins of our government.

MY FATHER'S SUPPORT OF "PRO-RESPONSIBLE GOVERNMENT" (VISIT HIS YOUTUBE CHANNEL - LAVOY FINICUM)

"We are not just a bunch of wannabe anarchist… who don't believe in government… contrary… I believe in the government… I believe in the federal government… we need the federal government… in the proper place…"

"I believe in government. I believe in the Federal government. We need the federal government. How else are we going to protect our country? I believe in the proper relationship between the states and the federal government and the counties"

WHAT YOU CAN DO FOR US

> - We would like to know any unknown details about the CO event meeting of FBI, BLM, Oregon State, and Delta County agents (i.e. such as who organized the meeting, who was in attendance, and how any such irresponsible governors are going to be held accountable, e.g. IRS targeting conservative groups, etc.).
> - We would like an inquiry into what criteria was used to link my mother, any aforementioned Colorado citizens and myself to an abhorrent group known as "Sovereign Citizens."
> - We would like to know whether we are on a list linking us to this irresponsible group. And, if so, where is the list? What is the criteria for placement on the list? What is the process for removal (i.e. you would handle that, we would sue, etc.)?

> We would like you to ask the House Speaker and Senate President Pro Tempore for a Joint Citizen's commission to study and recommend clearly-defined boundaries of what is and is not 'domestic' and/or so-called 'right-wing' extremism in relation to the abhorrent group known as 'Sovereign Citizens.'

> We would like an inquiry into the Department of Justice's criteria for labeling 'domestic,' 'home grown,' and so-called 'right-wing' extremists, intergovernmental coordination for interdicting those labeled as 'domestic,' 'home-grown,' and so-called 'right wing' extremists and what remedies or appeals exist for those governed who find themselves labeled as such.

> We would like a face-to-face meeting with you to discuss our situation and ways to move forward in building the disintegrating trust between the governed and those who are governing. Be assured our request is sincere and it is our hope to find ways to rebuild and bridge the gap that exists. Our pain is palpable but our resolve to improve the future is concrete. We would like to do this together.

MY DECLARATION

I call for an end to irresponsible governors using intimidation and borderline libelous slander that is injuring me, Thara Tenney and my mother, Jeanette Finicum, and hindering and restricting our freedom of speech.

I will forever support my father's view of pro-responsible government and I intend to continue to promote his view of pro-responsible government nationwide.

I declare and pledge my allegiance and responsibility to support, keep, and maintain a pro-responsible government—The United States of America.

Yours Affectionately – With Humility and Resolve,

Chapter 7: History of Hammond Ranching Family

THE DEVELOPMENT OF DAD'S CATTLE BRAND

As a young boy, Dad dreamed of becoming a cattle rancher. In his young mind the first step to seeing this come to fruition was the creation of his cattle brand.

During school he began his creative flow on the cover of his note book. It wasn't long before he settled on the perfect brand that included the main letters of his name LaVoy. He added the bar as he believed every serious rancher must have a bar in his brand.

Starting from a very young age he used this symbol as a key signature to his identity.

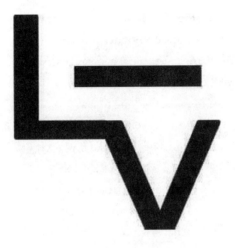

Chapter 9: My Time at Ground Zero

MY SOCIAL MEDIA POST JUST DAYS AFTER MY EXPERIENCE AT GROUND ZERO, POSTED JANUARY 13TH, 2016.

My name is Thara Lynn Tenney. LaVoy Finicum, the man this divided nation is calling a terrorist or #tarpman is my father.[432] I do not waste any energy in being angry at the pretentious slander directed toward my father, my family, or the Bundy family but rather find it quite humorous because such statements are so far from reality that one cannot help chuckle.

On January 7th, 2016, I packed my bags and caravanned with other family members to the Malheur National Wildlife Refuge in Burns, Oregon. Five of my siblings were able to make the long trek at this time. When we arrived, it was midmorning. We parked our vehicle by the refuge buildings. The day was beautiful that I almost found a need to take my jacket off. The grounds were quiet. The individuals there were busy in a meeting. Our father was notified his daughters had arrived and out he came from his meeting with open arms and teary eyes. This says a million words coming from a 'tuff-as-nails' cowboy. We daughters always have had the power to melt his heart. We all cheerfully embraced and said our hellos after which he gave us a tour of the refuge. He then returned to his meeting to prepare for the upcoming press conference scheduled for 11 a.m.. While we waited for the time to pass, the kids played in the snow, found bird tracks there, and enjoyed sliding down the packed icy driveway. Not at any point did I worry for the safety of my children. There was such a feeling of peace with a buzz of energy.

Just before the press conference, we all gathered in a circle. The audience included five of my siblings, one son-in-law, six of LaVoy's grandchildren, LaVoy's parents, LaVoy's brother, and other key figures in this peaceful protest. Some words of sentiment were communicated with great emotion and then LaVoy offered a word of prayer. We then started the walk up the hill to the press. Halfway up the hill, reporters began snapping away their cameras. After the press conference we walked back down the hill talking and laughing.

Most of us ate beans for lunch while LaVoy busily welcomed local community members who had traveled the 35 minutes out of city center Burns to the refuge to see for themselves what the spirit and atmosphere was like at the refuge. I witnessed cowboys bringing truckloads of supplies and expressing their sentiments. I could see it in these cowboys' eyes and hear it in their voice the desire for counsel and encouragement on how they too can face the tyranny they have suffered.

In the kitchen, also known as the mess hall, there was a buzz of energy. There were a few women running the place. One of these fine ladies is from my husband's hometown of Prescott, AZ. She had been there since the beginning. All the food had been donated by local members of Harney County and individuals of neighboring counties as well. There was an abundance for which everyone was in awe and most grateful.

I am grateful that I traveled to Burns, Oregon to experience the atmosphere of the refuge myself. I do not regret taking my children. There was no danger. Before traveling to Oregon, I fell on my knees and pleaded with the Lord and told Him that I had decided to travel to the refuge and that if I was going to be in harm's way to please make it known to me. I then proceeded with my preparations to leave and was filled with peace and assurance that my decision to go was good.

Being there I could not help but feel a sense of calm despite all the uncertainties of a peaceful protest. I hope all you readers can gain some insight from my experience and maybe even consider doing as I have and go and experience it for yourself.

Chapter 10: Vindication

THE HAMMOND FAMILY RELEASED STATEMENTS AFTER DWIGHT AND STEVEN WERE PARDONED

For Immediate Release

Contact:
Morgan Philpot,
Hammond Family Attorney
Phone: 801.891-4499
morgan@jmphilpotlaw.com

Statement from Hammond Family
On President Trump's Pardon of Dwight and Steven

Tuesday July 10, 2018--Diamond, OR. - Today, President Trump issued an Executive Grant of Clemency, which is a full pardon, to Dwight and Steven Hammond. Our family is grateful to the president and all who worked to make this possible, and to bring this about.

From long before our family's legal challenges, through the trial in 2012, the re-sentencing and return to federal prison in 2016, and the last several years while Dwight and Steven were in federal prison, Dwight and Steven and our family have done all we can do to demonstrate faith in our country and in principles of decency, fairness and justice. We have been a cattle ranching family dedicated to basic principles, and a basic life. With Dwight and Steven returning home we will continue on our path, continue ranching and continue believing in America.

The original judge who sentenced Dwight and Steven, openly stated that the laws under which the prosecution took place, specifically the mandatory minimum sentences that were required – were unjust and shock the conscience. Yet, prosecutors appealed his ruling, and today President Trump accurately described that appeal as "an overzealous appeal." We agree that it was overzealous and share the opinion that there is no place in our courts or anywhere else in the administration of our federal government for overzealousness, and the kind of animus that has been directed at our family by federal officers for years.

Again, we express gratitude for the support we've received from our local community, for all those who wrote letters of support, for those who worked behind the scenes, and for those who have stood by our family through these hard times. While we recognize that our path forward will still be difficult, like it is with virtually all ranching families, we are hopeful that this action by President Trump today, will also help signal the need for a more measured and just approach by federal agents, federal officers and federal prosecutors – in all that they do.

During this whole ordeal there has been a lot of false information in the media. Our family has already paid $400,000 related to the civil damages alleged by the government in this matter, in addition to the combine 7 years Dwight and Steven have spent in prison. We are hopeful that respected media outlets will use professional discretion and judgment before repeating false and misleading stories about the history of this legal ordeal. All of us have a duty to stand up for core American principles. Today, the President of the United States has blessed our family by doing so. As Susie said earlier this morning, "We've been waiting a long time" but today's decision by the President, "is wonderful." We are very anxiously looking forward to seeing Dwight and Steven home.

* * *

For Immediate Release

Contact: Attorney Morgan Philpot,
Phone: 801.891-4499
morgan@jmphilpotlaw.com

Update on Hammond Family
Following Dwight and Steven Hammond's Return Home after Pardon

Tuesday July 17, 2018--Burns, OR.

Since receiving a full Presidential Pardon, Dwight and Steven Hammond have started to have some time to come together with family and evaluate their situation and the future, and to reflect and discuss matters with other family members. As a result of those discussions, the family has asked that an announcement be made that neither the family nor the family business has any plans to take any civil action.

The family asks for privacy as they reunite and focus on the future.

* * *

Note by Morgan Philpot: It has been my pleasure, personally and professionally to work with and assist members of the Hammond Family as part of my legal practice representing many diverse ranching families spread out across the western states. I was originally hired by a member of the family earlier this year, and while I have not worked for Steven or his family specifically – it was a privilege to meet with him and Dwight and other Hammond family members during this past week as a culmination of what so many have worked hard for over the last several years. The President was right to issue the pardon, and I agree with the sentiment expressed by the Wall Street Journal Editorial Board last week, that the pardon was a welcome correction to government injustice.

Chapter 12: Where the Rubber Meets the Road

JAMES MADISON SPEECH OF LIMITED CONTROL GRANTED TO THE NATIONAL GOVERNMENT DURING THE DEBATES IN THE SEVERAL STATE CONVENTIONS OF THE ADOPTION OF THE FEDERAL CONSTITUTION.

"Mr. MADISON. It is supposed, by some gentlemen, that Congress have authority not only to grant bounties in the sense here used, merely as a commutation for drawback, but even to grant them under a power by virtue of which they may do anything which they may think conducive to the general welfare! This, sir, in my mind, raises the important and fundamental question, whether the general terms which have been cited are [428] to be considered as a sort of caption, or general description of the specified powers; and as having no further meaning, and giving no further powers, than what is found in that specification, or as an abstract and indefinite delegation of power extending to all cases whatever — to all such, at least, as will admit the application of money — which is giving as much latitude as any government could well desire.

I, sir, have always conceived — I believe those who proposed the Constitution conceived — it is still more fully known, and more material to observe, that those who ratified the Constitution conceived — that this is not an indefinite government, deriving its powers from the general terms prefixed to the specified powers — but a limited government, tied down to the specified powers, which explain and define the general terms.

It is to be recollected that the terms "common defense and general welfare," as here used, are not novel terms, first introduced into this Constitution. They are terms familiar in their construction, and well known to the people of America. They are repeatedly found in the old Articles of Confederation, where, although they are susceptible of as great a latitude as can be given them by the context here, it was never supposed or pretended that they conveyed any such power as is now assigned to them. On the contrary, it was always considered clear and certain that the old Congress was limited to the enumerated powers, and that the enumeration limited and explained the general terms. I ask the gentlemen themselves, whether it was ever supposed or suspected that the old Congress could give away the money of the states to bounties to encourage agriculture, or for any other purpose they pleased. If such a power had been possessed by that body, it would have been much less impotent, or have borne a very different character from that universally ascribed to it.

The novel idea now annexed to those terms, and never before entertained by the friends or enemies of the government, will have a further consequence, which cannot have been taken into the view of the gentlemen. Their construction would not only give Congress the complete legislative power I have stated, — it would do more; it would supersede all the restrictions understood at present to lie, in their power with respect to a judiciary. It would put it in the power of Congress to establish courts throughout the United States, with cognizance of suits between citizen and citizen, and in all cases whatsoever.

This, sir, seems to be demonstrable; for if the clause in question really authorizes Congress to do whatever they think fit, provided it be for the general welfare, of which they are to judge, and money can be applied to it, Congress must have power to create and support a judiciary establishment, with a jurisdiction extending to all cases favorable, in their opinion, to the general welfare, in the same manner as they have power to pass laws, and apply money providing in any other way for the general welfare. I shall be reminded, perhaps, that, according to the terms of the Constitution, the judicial power is to extend to certain cases only, not to all cases. But this circumstance can have no effect in the argument, it being presupposed by the gentlemen, that the specification of certain objects does not limit the import of the general terms. Taking these terms as an abstract and indefinite grant of power, they comprise all the objects of legislative regulations — as well such as fall under the judiciary article in the Constitution as those falling immediately under the legislative article; and if the partial enumeration of objects in the legislative article *does not, as these gentlemen contend, limit the general power, neither will it be limited by the partial enumeration of objects in the judiciary article.*

There are consequences, sir, still more extensive, which, as they follow clearly from the doctrine combated, must either be admitted, or the doctrine must be given up. If Congress can employ money indefinitely to the general welfare, and are the sole and supreme judges of the general welfare, they may take the care of religion into their own hands; they may appoint teachers in every state, county, and parish, and pay them out of their public treasury; they may take into their own hands the education of children, establishing in like manner schools throughout the Union; they may assume the provision for the poor; they may undertake the regulation of all roads other than post-roads; in short, everything, from the highest object of state legislation down to the most minute object of police, would be thrown under the power of Congress; for every object I have mentioned would admit of the application of money, and might be called, if Congress pleased, provisions for the general welfare.

The language held in various discussions of this house is a proof that the doctrine in question was never entertained by this body. Arguments, wherever the subject would permit, have constantly been drawn from the peculiar nature of this government, as limited to certain enumerated powers, instead of extending, like other governments, to all cases not particularly excepted. In a very late instance — I mean the debate on the representation bill — it must be remembered that an argument much used, particularly by gentlemen from Massachusetts, against the ratio of 1 for 30,000, was, that this government was unlike the state governments, which had an indefinite variety of objects within their power; that it had a small number of objects only to attend to; and therefore, that a smaller number of representatives would be sufficient to administer it.

Arguments have been advanced to show that because, in the regulation of trade, indirect and eventual encouragement is given to manufactures, therefore Congress have power to give money in direct bounties, or to grant it in any other way that would answer the same purpose. But surely, sir, there is a great and obvious difference, which it cannot be necessary to enlarge upon. A duty laid on imported implements of husbandry would, in its operation, be an indirect tax on exported produce; but will anyone say that, by virtue of a mere power to lay duties on imports, Congress might go directly to the produce or implements of agriculture, or to the articles exported? It is true, duties on exports are expressly prohibited; but if there were no article forbidding them, a power directly to tax exports could never be deduced from a power to tax imports, although such a power might indirectly and incidentally affect exports.

In short, sir, without going farther into the subject, which I should not have here touched at all but for the reasons already mentioned, I venture to declare it as my opinion, that, were the power of Congress to be established in the latitude contended for, it would subvert the very foundations, and transmute the very nature of the limited government established by the people of America; and what inferences might be drawn, or what consequences ensue, from such a step, it is incumbent on us all to consider."[433]

Chapter 20: Beautiful Yet Frightening Duty

DIVINE DESTINY OF AMERICA

Contemplating the supernal aid in developing the rule of law, leaves an expanding mind wondering… what is the divine role for the nation that has become an ensign to all other nations? Harmony presides in the notion of America's divine destiny being much bigger than simply gaining independence from Great Britain.

Ezra Taft Benson, a modern-day prophet of the Lord, boldly declared this nation's destiny was to become "the Lord's base of operations in …latter days", an ensign to all other nations, a means to fulfill promises made long ago by God to our fathers of old; Abraham, Isaac, and Jacob."[434]

Seeing the grand tapestry of America's destiny as Ezra Taft Benson did is clearly visible to those who work toward understanding God's covenant with Abraham found in Genesis. As these promises are truly understood, there's an eager transformation from being a mere spectator to an active participant and beneficiary of the blessings that flow from the Abrahamic covenant.

Let's review:

> *Abraham is at the heart of all God's covenant people throughout ancient history. The father of the faithful...*
>
> *...[He] first received the gospel by baptism (which is the covenant of salvation). Then he had conferred upon him the higher priesthood, and he entered into celestial marriage (which is the covenant of exaltation), gaining assurance thereby that he would have eternal increase. Finally, he received a promise that all of these blessings would be offered to all of his mortal posterity. Included in the divine promises to Abraham were the assurances that (1) Christ would come through his lineage, and that (2) Abraham's posterity would receive certain lands as an eternal inheritance. These promises taken together are called the Abrahamic covenant. It was renewed with Isaac and again with Jacob.*[435]

It is from Jacob, Abraham's grandson, that the Twelve Tribes of Israel sprang. It's important to note the different applications of the name Israel. The scriptures use the name Israel to parallel various frames of reference. Israel denotes

> *One who prevails with God or Let God prevail. This name [Israel] was given to Jacob at Penuel (Gen. 32:28) and at Bethel (Gen. 35:10). It also applies to his descendants and to their kingdom (2 Sam. 1:24; 23:3). After the division of the kingdom, the northern tribes, as the larger part, retained the name Israel, while the southern kingdom was called Judah. The land of Canaan is also called Israel today. And in another sense, Israel means the true believer in Christ, as explained by Paul (Rom. 10:1; 11:7; Gal. 6:16; Eph. 2:12). The name Israel is therefore variously used to denote (1) the man Jacob, (2) the literal descendants of Jacob, and (3) the true believers in Christ, regardless of their lineage or geographical location.*[436]

In reviewing Jacob's (also known as Israel's) descendants, we learn one of his twelve sons (Reuben) lost his birthright due to immorality.[437] Furthermore, Jacob's son Joseph had two sons who shared an equal inheritance, thus constituting individual tribes. Each son who had right to inheritance includes Simeon, Levi, Judah, Dan, Naphtali, Gad, Asher, Issachar, Zebulon, Manasseh, Ephraim, and Benjamin. Each son was a tribe. These are the Twelve Tribes of Israel that were eventually scattered and carried captive to Babylon.

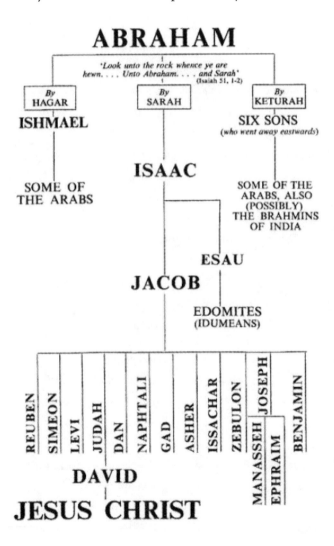

Just as Israel has various meanings, so does the gathering of the lost Twelve Tribes of Israel. This gathering pertains to both a physical and spiritual restoration. The physical restoration will bring people back to the land of their inheritance. The spiritual restoration will provide the opportunity for all to either accept Christ, through a covenant path, or deny Christ by choosing a life of "eat, drink, and be merry for tomorrow we all die."

It is important to note that the focus of the Abrahamic covenant, which was ultimately renewed with Jacob and his twelve sons, is mainly on

> *personal salvation and eternal increase [which is] renewed with each individual who receives the ordinance of celestial marriage. Those of non-Israelite lineage, commonly known as gentiles, are adopted into the house of Israel, and become heirs of the covenant and the seed of Abraham, through the ordinances of the gospel.*
>
> *...To fulfill the covenant God made with Abraham—having particular reference to the fact that the literal seed of his body would be entitled to all of the blessings of the gospel—a number of specific and particular things must take place in the last days:*
>
> *(1) The gospel must be restored.*
> *(2) The priesthood must be conferred again upon man.*
> *(3) The keys of the sealing power must be given again to mortals.*
> *(4) Israel must be gathered.*
> *(5) The Holy Ghost must be poured out upon the gentiles.*[438]

To accomplish such a feat required a land void of the instability that war and carnage create. The only way to even get close to accomplishing this prerequisite, was to have a system set in place to safeguard the people against tyrants who rule in unrighteousness. The development of the American constitutional republic was key to this needed stability. Time has witnessed the implementation of America's governmental system to be the springboard for the genesis of fulfilling the long foretold Abrahamic covenant.

The spirit of freedom that took flame in the Americas not only set the stage for forward movement in seeing the Lord's promises of old come to pass, but it also illuminated all aspects of life. It is fascinating to contemplate the butterfly effects of both freedom and captivity. For now, let's focus on the factual results of freedom.

> The climate of free-market economics allowed science to thrive in an explosion of inventions and technical discoveries which, in merely 200 years, gave the world the gigantic new power resources of harnessed electricity, the internal combustion engine, jet propulsion, exotic space vehicles, and all the wonders of nuclear energy.
>
> Communications were revolutionized, first by the telegraph, then the telephone, followed by radio and television [and now the internet].
>
> The whole Earth was explored from pole to pole—even the depths of the sea.
>
> Then men left the Earth in rocket ships and actually walked on the Moon. They sent up a space plane that could be maneuvered and landed back on Earth.
>
> The average length of life was doubled; the quality of life was tremendously enhanced. Homes, food, textiles, communications, transportation, central heating, central cooling, world travel, millions of books, a high literacy rate, schools for everybody, surgical miracles, medical cures for old age diseases, entertainment at the touch of a switch, and instant news twenty-four hours a day. That was the story.
>
> Of course, all of this did not happen just in America, but it did flow out primarily from the swift current of freedom and prosperity which American Founders turned loose into the spillways of human progress all over the world.
>
> In 200 years, the human race had made a 5000-year leap.[439]

This *5000-year Leap* is absolutely spellbinding. This perspective leaves one in sacred reverence when one realizes how such advancements are indeed manifestations of greater things at play. All it took was a few years of functioning under the American system to foster the beginning of the massive movement toward fulfilling the Abrahamic covenant.

Let's go back to the year 1820 to paint the picture of the beginning of this massive movement. Just a short 33 years after the ratification of the Constitution, a young teenage boy sincerely sought to know which church, of all the rising churches, was the correct one to join.

As with all other advancements, religious freedom, too, was on the rise. As such, the development of many different sects was the result. In the 1830s a French diplomat, political scientist, and historian by the name of Alexis de Tocqueville traveled to the New World to study the culture and climate of the newly formed constitutional republic. He wanted to understand this freedom. After spending quite a bit of time in America, he wrote *Democracy in America*, which was published in 1835. In his published work, Tocqueville wrote about the rise of religious sentiment.

The young boy, seeking to know which church to join, recognized how each sect seemed to possess elements of truth. The conflict and competition between the different religions caused much unrest, which he called "unusual excitement."[440] He witnessed countless members of his county being affected by this unrest. Many joined different sects, which he witnessed to be the cause of much division. There was "priest contending against priest, and convert against convert; so that all their good feelings one for another, if they ever had any, were entirely lost in a strife of words and a contest about opinions."[441] Rather than a sincere conversion to God, it was a war of words.

This young boy deeply wanted to unite with the correct denomination because he desired the promised blessings he read of in the Bible. In his adolescent mind, he understood God to be one of law and order. How else were the *laws of nature* to ensure, as apostle John Taylor would later write, "Earth[s] ...roll [up]on its axis, [while] ...regulate[ing] the planets in their diurnal and annual motions? Their revolutions and spheres are fixed by nature's God, and they are so beautifully arranged...."[442] Having reached such enlightenment, for him to assume God officiated His work through countless, competing, contentious denominations felt erroneous. He sincerely questioned, how it was that a God of perfect order could conduct the work of salvation is such chaos?

Despite this young boy's *old soul*, the great confusion and strife among the different denominations influenced him to feel as if he was too young and unacquainted with the things of the world "to come to any certain conclusion who was right and who was wrong." Little did he know the Lord's pattern through humanity's history has been to use the young and unlearned to confound and lead those presumed wise.

Amid his insecurities, his personal study of James 1:5, which invites all who lack wisdom to ask God, led him to faithful, humble prayer. What he did not expect was to have his sincere prayer answered in the way that it was. He was informed by God the Father and His Son Jesus Christ that none of the current churches had full truth and that he should not join any of them.

How interesting! Let's briefly review why this might be.

This lack of truth was due to the world being in a widespread apostasy since the time of Jesus Christ's crucifixion and death of His Apostles.[443] While countless individuals desired and sought after full truth during the great apostasy (Dark Ages), their search was in vain. Even though there were many who taught about the Savior and served with genuineness, no one possessed the fulness of the truth because during the great apostasy because aggrandizing "people changed some of the doctrines and ordinances of the gospel."[444] Nor was the priesthood any more upon the earth. Priesthood is the proper authority given directly from God to officiate in His ordinances.[445] This was lost with the deaths of Jesus Christ's apostles who walked with Him in the flesh.[446]

Bringing to light the reality of the awful state the people were in during the great apostasy is in no way to suggest that God favors one people over another. Doing so would be blasphemy. God loves all His children equally. Remember, God patiently works within the scope that freedom of choice creates; freedom was a gift from Him. Because the people in ancient time chose contrary to His law, God mercifully removed His gospel truth and priesthood from the earth. This was to be just for a time.

How is this merciful, one might ask? When a people sin against a greater light they are bound to the consequences that pertain to the higher law. The tender heart of mankind's Father understood His obligation to justice and deeply desired to provide the greatest room possible for mercy while still ensuring the demands of justice. The aim of removing the fullness of the gospel truth and the priesthood was not to cause His children to live in darkness forever. A restoration was imminent, but only when the time was right. He wanted His people ready to receive it. Remember, a restoration of the gospel is the first item on the list to fulfill the covenant God made with Abraham.

For anyone to successfully continue forward in understanding, a connection must be made between the gospel's restoration and the most fundamental truth of the Abrahamic covenant. The restoration of the gospel is the means by which "ALL of Heavenly Father's children on both sides of the veil [will] ...hear the message of the restored gospel of Jesus Christ." The restoration of the gospel would be the means by which any "who have neither made crucial covenants with God nor have received their essential ordinances [for whatever reason, will get] ...to [accept or deny the opportunity to] follow Jesus Christ, to accept and receive His gospel with all its blessings, yes all the blessings God promised the lineage of Abraham, Isaac, and Jacob...."[447]

In layman terms, this means all, the living and the dead, would have the chance to accept the gospel by baptism (which is the covenant of salvation) and the opportunity to enter into celestial marriage (which is the covenant of exaltation), thus working out personal salvation and working toward eternal increase, which is the sole focus of the Abrahamic Covenant. If such work is not done while in the flesh, it is the charge of the living to serve in temples to see to it that saving ordinances are accomplished by proxy for each individual who has died. Once the work is done in the flesh for them, that soul then will have the opportunity to either accept or reject. This is why there are 159 temples in operation in 51 different countries, 83 of which are in the United States, to perform such proxy ordinances for the dead.[448]

This opportunity is all-inclusive, especially for those who lived during the great apostasy. Nature's God knew what He was doing. Removing His authority from the earth for a period of time was not disingenuous by any means. On the contrary, that act alone was a tender gesture of perfect, patient, love.

All throughout the human experience the Lord has been intimately involved with freedom's establishment. Why? To enable availability of His gospel truth and priesthood. Why? Because the results give strength to its beneficiaries. This strength helps people to successfully press through this difficult mortal existence. Some might suggest the Lord's hand within the complicated process of organizing stable freedom for *all* people has been anything but streamlined. I humbly submit such a perspective is only the result of a limited viewpoint. We are always down on something we are not up on.

Please don't forget that man's government has, for ages, failed and will continue to fail, as reliance is solely put upon the wisdom of the man alone. Even though humanity is limited to time, God is not subject to it. Fortunately for humankind, God is perfectly patient, long suffering, merciful, and just in His officiation of His work and glory to bring about the "immortality and eternal life' of His children."[449] While humanity has forever wrestled with trusting in the fallen nature of man's wisdom, to God, the span of man's learning curve is but a blink of an eye. As man continues to wrestle, God works wonders to fulfill his promises of old and, as a result, builds His kingdom upon the earth.

The question is, what route has, and will the Lord take to establish His kingdom upon the earth? It is safe to suggest the answer to such a question demands more than just human reason. I believe it requires revelatory communications between mankind and God. For if the literal government of God is to be organized upon the earth in preparation for the return of Jesus Christ, "it must receive its laws, organization, and government from heaven." For God to set up His standard as an ensign for all truth seekers to flow unto, it would require a form of communication with man to make him acquainted with His laws. "As the Father of the human family," He tenderly brings about His work.

> *We cannot conceive of Him thundering from the heavens and terrifying the inhabitants of the earth, nor yet sending angels with flaming swords to coerce obedience. This would be using physical power to control the mind; but as man is a free agent, He uses other means to act upon [mankind's]*

mind, ...judgement, and...will; and by the beauty and loveliness of virtue, purity, holiness, and the fear of God, [God] captivate[s] [mankind's] feelings, control[s] his judgement, and influence[s] him to render that obedience to God which is justly His due; not until these means fail, will others be exercised.

As the world are ignorant of God and His laws, not having had any communication with Him for eighteen hundred years; and as all those great and important events must transpire, and as the Lords says He will "do nothing but what He reveals to His servants the Prophets," it follows, that there must be revelations made from God; and if so, as necessary consequences, there must be prophets to reveal them to. How did God ever reveal His will and purposes to Enoch, Noah, Abraham, Moses, the Prophets, Jesus, and His Disciples, and they to the people? God's messengers make known His will, and the people obeyed, or rejected it. If they were punished by floods, fire, plagues, pestilences, dispersions, death, etc., it was in consequence of their disobedience.

As God has dealt in former times, so will He in the latter, with this difference, that He will accomplish His purposes in the last days; He will set up his kingdom; He will protect the righteous, destroy Satan, and his works, purge the earth from wickedness, and bring in the restitution of all things. The above, while it is the only rational way, is evidently the only just, and scriptural way.

...Now it would not be just for the Lord to punish the inhabitants of the earth without warning. For if the world are ignorant of God, they cannot altogether be blamed for it; if they are made the dupes of false systems, and false principles, they cannot help it; many of them are doing as well as they can, while, as we have before stated, it would be unjust for the world to continue as it is. ...Before the Lord destroyed the inhabitants of the old world, He sent Enoch and Noah to warn them. Before the Lord destroyed Sodom and Gomorrah, He sent Lot into their midst. Before the Children of Israel were carried captive to Babylon, they were warned of it by the Prophets; and before Jerusalem was destroyed, the inhabitants had the testimony of our Lord, and His Disciples. And so will it be in the last days; and as it is the world that is concerned, the world will have to be warned.

...From the above it is evident, that the everlasting gospel will be restored, accompanied with a warning to the world. Now if the everlasting gospel is resorted, there must be the same principles, laws, officers or administrators, and ordinances. If, before, they had apostles, they will again have them; the sacred laws and ordinance will be introduced, and the same method for receiving members into the kingdom. They will also have prophets, pastors, teachers, and evangelists. If they baptised by immersion for the remission of sins and laid on hands for the gift of the Holy Ghost formerly brought things past to the saints' remembrance, led them into all truth, and showed them things to come, it will do the same again, for it is the everlasting Gospel.

If formerly it caused men to dream dreams, and to see visions, it will do the same again; if to one was given the gift of tongues, to another the gift of healing, to another power to work miracles, to another the gift of wisdom, the same will exist in latter days, for it is the everlasting Gospel which is to be restored. If it put men in possession of a knowledge of God, and of his purposes, and brought life and immortality to light in former days, it will do the same again. If it dispelled the clouds of darkness, unveiled the heavens, put men in possession of certainty, and gave them a hope that bloomed with immortality and eternal life, it will do the same again. If it caused men to know the object of their creation, their relationship to God, their position on the earth, and their final exaltation and glory ,it will do the same again, for it is the everlasting Gospel.

In short, it is the will of God to man, the government of God among men, and a portion of that light, glory and intelligence, which exist with God and angels, communicated to mortals, and obtained through obedience to his laws and ordinances. If the Gospel formerly was to be proclaimed to all nations, so it is now, with this difference, associated with it there is to be a cry, "Fear God, and give glory to Him, for the hour of

His judgment is come." From this, then, we may expect a proclamation to be made to all people; messengers to go forth to every nation, and the same principles with once existed to again restored in all their fullness, power, glory, and blessings.

The above is the way pointed out in the scriptures and is the only just and rational way to deal with rational, intelligent beings; for intelligence must be appealed to by intelligence, and it would be unjust to punish the world indiscriminately without first appealing to their reason, judgment, and intelligence.[450]

Returning to that young boy who sought out his God to receive guidance as to which church had full truth in the 19th century, imagine how he must have felt. The answer was to not join any of the churches. His mind must have questioned, what does that mean? What is one to do without a fullness of truth?

After receiving what felt like to him as an undeserving answer to his humble prayer, the Lord began to tenderly raise him up by sending heavenly messengers to teach and train him while in his youth. This was to prepare him for the sacred, yet very difficult work commissioned to him. Whether he liked it or not, he was the Lord's chosen individual to be the prophet of God who would restore the true and living gospel upon the earth once again. The time for the eminent restoration had arrived after much preparation to ensure its safety. It was time to labor one last time in the vineyard of the Lord, preparatory to the return of Jesus Christ. This young boy's name was Joseph Smith.

So, Joseph's journey began with training. He was privileged to be taught on the 22nd day of September each year for four years by the resurrected being Moroni who was the last ancient American prophet of his time. It was this Moroni who finished the compilation of the sacred record of his people who were led by God to the Americas to avoid the inevitable destruction of Jerusalem. Moroni's people inhabited the New World for many years and Moroni was given charge to safeguard the record until the Lord decreed it ready to come forth. Within the record was found key truths that had been omitted from the Bible and lost.

To stay on track on how this all pulls together, let's return to the five things needing to be accomplished in order to see the Lord's fulfillment of promises made long ago.

(1) THE GOSPEL MUST BE RESTORED

After ample training, on September 22, 1827, seven years after Joseph's life changing prayer, he received the gold plates from Moroni at the Hill Cumorah, which is the place Moroni hid the record.[451] The work of translating the record into English commenced. On March 26, 1830, the first printed copies of the Book of Mormon became available in Palmyra, New York. Within the pages of this scripture contained the fullness of lost the gospel.[452]

(2) THE PRIESTHOOD MUST BE CONFERRED AGAIN UPON MAN

On May 15, 1829, while translating, "having read about baptism for the remission of sins…, Joseph Smith and his scribe Oliver Cowdery went to a secluded area to inquire of the Lord concerning the matter. There, on the banks of the Susquehanna River near Harmony, Pennsylvania, they received the answer to their prayer."[453] Nine short years after Joseph's first humble prayer in asking what church to join, the priesthood was restored to the earth in answer to another heartfelt prayer. John the Baptist, a resurrected being, conferred upon Joseph Smith and Oliver Cowdery the Aaronic Priesthood. This Priesthood enabled the covenant of salvation to commence.

Next, the ancient apostles Peter, James, and John conferred the Melchizedek Priesthood upon Joseph Smith and Oliver Cowdery.[454]

On April 6, 1830. The Church was organized in Fayette Township, New York, beginning with six members.

This was only 43 years after the ratification of the American constitutional republican system of government. Fascinatingly so, this was only a mere three years after the American beloved founders Thomas Jefferson (83) and John Adams (88) passed. Providence had a hand in seeing these two freedom and liberty giants give up the ghost on the same day, July 4, 1826, the nation's annual day set aside to celebrate the establishment of freedom and liberty.

(3) THE KEYS OF THE SEALING POWER MUST BE GIVEN AGAIN TO MORTALS

March 27, 1836. The Kirtland Temple, the first temple built [after the restoration of the Gospel], was dedicated. The Prophet Joseph Smith offered the dedicatory prayer, which had been given to him by revelation.[455]

On April 3, 1836. The Savior appeared to Joseph Smith and Oliver Cowdery in the Kirtland Temple. Moses, Elias, and Elijah also appeared and gave priesthood keys to Joseph and Oliver. Elijah brought the keys of the sealing power, which [made] it possible for families to be sealed together forever, commencing the covenant of exaltation.[456]

The fulfillment of the first three steps in seeing the Abrahamic covenant come to pass took place in these short 16 years. How momentous! Note that the timestamp of these accomplishments is only 33 years after the ratification of the Constitution—no coincidence.

For review, to fulfill the covenant God made with Abraham—having particular reference to the fact that the literal seed of his body would be entitled to all of the blessings of the gospel—a number of specific and particular things must take place in the last days:

(1) The gospel must be restored.

(2) The priesthood must be conferred again upon man.

(3) The keys of the sealing power must be given again to mortals.

Done! Praise goes to the man Joseph Smith, who became the first president and prophet of the restored Church of Jesus Christ of Latter-day Saints. He spearheaded the movement and now one can track throughout the last 190 plus years, since the restoration of the Church, apostolic leaders diligently working toward the fulfillment of the last two elements:

(4) Israel must be gathered.

(5) The Holy Ghost must be poured out upon the Gentiles.

Spencer W. Kimball, who was the twelfth President of the Church and prophet of God outlined an easy way to understand the three-fold mission of the Church:

1. Proclaim the gospel
2. Perfect the Saints
3. Redeem the dead.

Russell M. Nelson, who is the current president and prophet of the Church, in 2018 concisely communicated the sole aim of the Church being progression toward fulfilling the Abrahamic covenant (gathering Israel). Therefore, all decisions of apostolic leaders continue to be, and will forever be, devoted to this cause alone. They labor the best they can to lead a worldwide church in a fallen world to accomplish this great work of salvation. This is a heavy burden not envied.

While the above is the sole aim of the Church, take great caution from the popular notion that civic duty is not necessary. The reality is quite contrary. Let it never be forgotten that maintaining freedom and liberty ultimately rests upon the individual shoulders of those who are the beneficiaries of such blessings. "The individual Church members must step up and get involved. It must come from the people, not General Authorities."[457] Why, one might ask? This manuscript addresses that question in its entirety, and be it known, anyone who does this *maintenance righteously,* in wisdom's balance, will be "eternally vindicated and rewarded [for their] stand for freedom."[458]

Below is the data found in the 2017 statistical report delivered in the 2018 April annual general conference, which is a report issued for members of the Church to be apprised of the progress in its goals.

CHURCH UNITS
Stakes.. 3,341
Missions.. 421
Districts... 553
Wards and Branches.. 30,506

CHURCH MEMBERSHIP
Total membership.................................... 16,118,169
New children of record during 2017......... 106,771
Converts baptized during 2017................. 233,729

MISSIONARIES
Full-time Missionaries 67,049
Church-service Missionaries........................ 36,172

TEMPLES
Temples dedicated during 2017............................. 4
(Paris France, Tucson Arizona, Meridian Idaho, Cedar City Utah)
Temples rededicated during 2017....................... 1
(Idaho Falls Idaho)
Temples in operation... 159[459]

If the fundamental truths about the Abrahamic covenant are understood, one can clearly see great progress toward fulfillment of the last two elements of the Abrahamic covenant in just reviewing this report. While the world continues in commission, providing the necessary opposition in all things, God presses forward in keeping promises made long ago. Make no mistake, He is establishing His kingdom upon the earth while humankind continues in a war of words and blood. Be that as it may, Jesus said himself, "render to Caesar the things that are Caesar's, and to God the things that are God's...."[460]

The destiny of The United States of America truly is to be "the Lord's base of operations in ...latter days", an ensign to all other nations, a means to fulfill promises made long ago by God to our fathers of old; Abraham, Isaac, and Jacob."[461] Commencing with Adam, the record tells of every prophet's revelatory experience in seeing the present day. They all prophesied of Israel's gathering and how the world would be prepared for the second coming of the Savior. Nations have, through time, been scattered as a result of wickedness and this is the dispensation of gathering foretold of long ago. The present day is the eleventh hour in the Lord's olive vineyard as metaphorically documented in Jacob 5 of The Book of Mormon.

It is hoped that one might now see a little more clearly how America's divine destiny is much more than sole divorcement from tyrants. Such authenticity is a type of things to come. The American phenomenon is preparatory for the return of the true author of freedom and liberty. Its divine destiny is to prepare a people willing to participate in the maintenance process of governing as well as a willingness to be peacefully governed by the government of God, where perfect justice and mercy preside. The grand tapestry of America encompasses the establishment of the kingdom of God upon the earth with Jesus Christ as its literal king.

What an exciting time it is to be alive, when the quality of life is at its all-time best, when the fulfillment of things foretold of since the beginning of time are well underway, and when the Holy Ghost is being poured out upon all of earth's inhabitants!

In reading, did more questions arise? Might there be kindled a small desire to be an active beneficiary of all blessings that are available and a participant in the most important work foretold by all ancient and modern prophets? Schedule an appointment with missionaries to begin your journey by visiting: *ChurchofJesusChrist.org*

NOTE: As of early 2019, as result of the Church changing the names of many of the Church's global communications channels, in an effort to be true to the charge of being called The Church of Jesus Christ of Latter-day Saints, LDS.org will become ChurchofJesusChrist.org and Mormon.org will be changed to ComeUntoChrist.org.

APPENDIX C

EXTRAS

FINICUM FAMILY MISSION STATEMENT

We, the Finicum Family,
seeking to better understand,
maintain and defend
our God-given rights
to further our eternal happiness,
will virtuously let our voices be heard,
educating on the principles of the Constitution
and let our testimonies be seen for
personal property rights, liberty, freedom
and, one that has become even more near
and dear to us as of late,
the importance of LIFE.

A SHORT HISTORY OF THE BUNDY STANDOFF AND WHAT MOVED AMMON BUNDY TO GO TO THE AID OF THE OREGON HAMMOND RANCHING FAMILY

After having sat in Oregon prisons for the duration of his federal trial, after having been acquitted by a jury of his peers, and while sitting in Nevada prison, Ammon narrates the history of the abuses his family suffered at the hands of agents from federal agencies.[462] At this point, he had sat in prison for almost two years, suffering cruel punishment, often forced to sit in solitary confinement for months.[463] Gavin Seim, a friend of liberty, shared his time and talent to produce the recording of Ammon's voice to a video. This had to be done in three segments as Ammon's phone calls were time restricted. Each segment was separately released on YouTube and shared on social media before the Nevada mistrial with prejudice verdict. The three segments were eventually put into one video.

> *My name is Ammon Bundy. I am speaking to you today from a maximum-security jail. I am the son of [a] Nevada cattle rancher. My father, brothers, and myself have been incarcerated for many months, leaving our wives and twenty-six children altogether without fathers to care for them. I ask that you listen to our story and judge us. Yes, judge us. Ask yourself if we were justified in standing for our ranch and the rights of our neighbors. Or should we have just let federal agencies take our heritage? Ask yourself what you would have done. Ask yourself what is right. Let me explain our story.*
>
> *My brothers and I grew up on a family cattle ranch in southern Nevada. It was established by our great-great-grandfathers in 1877. We were raised in humble circumstances in the same ranch home as our father, Cliven Bundy, built by my grandfather Dave in 1940. For five generations our family has run cattle along the Bunkerville mountain. Our ancestors were the first pioneers to settle in the southern Nevada desert. They carved their living out of leveling and farming land next to the Virgin River and ran cattle on the hills. Their homesteads were established before Las Vegas had even one person living in it. Nevada had*

only been a state for thirteen years. Discovering multiple springs on the foothills of the mountains, our forefathers began to build water troughs and holding tanks to supply water for cattle. This made it so the cattle did not have to travel too far for water. In the Arab desert where our ranch is, it takes approximately 100 acres to feed one cow. In his lifetime, my father has improved upon this watering system by installing pipes throughout the lower hills from eleven different water sources over a thirty-mile span. This has allowed the cattle to benefit from feed in areas where otherwise they could not live because they would have to walk too far for water.

This has also greatly benefited the desert wildlife and made hunting and camping plentiful. As a true environmentalist, my father, by expanding the water system and caring for the land and the road, has tremendously promoted wildlife, increased game, improved camping, and generally made the area more enjoyable to be on. Even the desert tortoise would thank Cliven Bundy for the water close by if they could speak. All of this was done at my father's expense and effort, costing the taxpayers nothing. With his banged-up Dodge pickup, my father would spend many days a month, blowing out the water lines with air and repairing the leaks, making sure each water tank was full. My family has brought life to the southern Nevada desert for over one hundred years. Imagine what would happen to all the wildlife if this watering system was not maintained or if it was destroyed.

Before I move on, it is important that you have a little more background about the legality of our water and grazing rights. In 1890, the state of Nevada created a registry so that ranchers and others could deed their water and grazing rights. In Nevada, as with other western states, the livestock watering rights include title to graze. Each deed in print designates how many cattle the owner of the deed is typically grazing around the water. This is the way grazing rights are recorded and protected by the state of Nevada. Just to be clear, these livestock grazing and water rights are vested property, just like a mineral right or deeded right to your home. *These grazing rights are real property. They can be sold, traded, borrowed against, or adversely taken. They are the lifeblood of our ranch and a valued heritage to our family. Many people have desired to purchase them over the years, but my father has chosen to remain raising cattle in the desert. Without these stockwater grazing rights, our ranch has almost no value. My father owns eleven of these stockwater grazing rights deeded with the state of Nevada.*

In the early 1990s, the Bureau of Land Management, also known as the BLM, an agency of the executive branch, tried to trespass my father for grazing cattle on our deeded range where my family has run cattle for 138 years. The BLM adopted and extreme environmental 'no-cattle policy' designed to remove all ranching from the land. On the wall of the southern Nevada BLM district office, they displayed their motto. It reads, "no moo by 92, cattle free by 93."[464]

Seeing their intent to destroy his ranch, my father stood on the fact that his ranch was inside the boundaries of the state of Nevada and that the Federal agencies were violating the constituted laws between the state and the federal government and that he owned the deeded right to graze and water his cattle established over a century ago. When agents from the BLM told my father, the federal government didn't recognize his grazing rights and that my father must remove his cattle, he told them they had no authority to take his family's heritage away. When they said they were going to take it away anyway, he said, "No." And then he said, "Hell no."

Several times the BLM tried to drag my father in to federal court so they could strip him of his rights like they have done with thousands of others. Being land inside the state of Nevada, not ceded to the federal government, my father held the constitutional position that federal agencies have no legal constituted authority to administrate the land inside the state. Therefore, they had no jurisdiction to trespass or prosecute him. Watching other ranchers, miners, and loggers try to defend themselves in federal court when the federal government was the plaintiff, my father often said, "Going into federal court to defend yourself against federal agencies is like as if a man broke into your home and beat your wife and children, to get justice you take him to court and when they say all arise to the honorable judge, in walks a man in a black rob and he is the very man who assaulted your wife and children."

Of over 100 thousand cases in the western states where the federal government is the plaintiff in federal court, federal judges have sided with federal agencies every single time. Taking century-old vested property rights from good hard-working families. In our area, my dad is the last rancher out of 53. In the state of Nevada alone, federal agencies have taken 5072 water rights from the people and deeded them to themselves. It is astonishing to think about this when the United States Constitution was specifically designed to prohibit this very thing from happening. We the people have ignorantly allowed federal agencies of the executive branch to be modern day conquerors, gobbling up our land and resources. They are inserting themselves into every facet of our lives, our homes, schools, churches, jobs, manufacturer industries, housing industries, agricultural industries, mineral industries, financial industry. Everywhere there is wealth, they seek to control and take. They will not stop expanding and growing on their own. They will not limit themselves because they do not produce a product in order for them to survive, gain, and grow. They must take from the people who produce a product.

The judicial branch of government, the courts and judges, have not been an effective check and balance to these agencies for over sixty years. They have given them a free pass to prey upon the wealth of the American people. The United States Congress has tried to stop them twice in the last decade by defunding them. We saw through this that the executive agencies are too powerful for even the United States Congress to limit.

So how did people come to know about the Bundy family, my family? Well, in April 2014 the BLM joined forces with four other federal agencies to enforce their unlawful trespass and destroy our ranch. They set up a massive military-like compound on the range with 200 hired guns, mercenaries. They surrounded our ranch and put it under siege. They began to brutally round up our cattle with helicopters, running them to death, shooting them from the air, and leaving the newborn calves out on the range to thirst to death or be eaten by coyotes. The dead cattle were dumped in a mass grave, dug by the federal backhoes. They also began to destroy the water infrastructure that had been established over 100 years ago. The family was threatened by BLM personnel that said, if we resisted in any way that this would be another Waco or Ruby Ridge.

Knowing beforehand the abuses that they were about to cause would bring public outcry, the BLM built two first-amendment areas in non-conspicuous places and threatened the public with arrest and federal charges if anyone protest[ed] outside these areas. Our family, friends, and other local people began to protest first. They insisted to not have their first amendment rights corralled and refused to protest in these remote designated areas. With hired snipers on the hill, federal agents began to gang beat protestors for filming their abusing actions. For several days they body slammed us to the asphalt, sicced dogs on us, tazed us, and threatened to open fire on us for protesting on what they said was their property. Even standing next to state highway 170 with the guns to our heads and our children's heads, the federal agent said the road belonged to the state but the earth under it belonged to them.

Much of this abuse was caught on video and was posted on the internet. Within hours, millions had viewed the gross actions of these federal agencies. People from all over the United States began flowing to the ranch. That Saturday, thousands had assembled and demand[ed] the Clark County Sheriff Department and the State Governor to do their jobs in protecting the people from [an] out-of-control federal agency.[465] The Clark County Sheriff's Department finally stepped in and ended the abuse. All federal agents left the area within an hour and the surviving cattle were brought back to the ranch to be doctored or turned out on the range and we went back to the ranching.

This infuriated the bureaucrats. People such as Harry Reid who had personally made millions off of land deals with the BLM, publicly came out against our family and the people that stood up to them, calling us domestic terrorist[s], threatening that this was not over.[466] Many of us wore name tags that read, "Hi, my name is so-and-so, and I am a domestic terrorist." Great-grandmothers, little children and everyone in between wore them proudly.

Since then federal agencies [have] mounted continual media campaigns to demonize my family and those that stood against their horrific actions. In defense, we have had to respond by publishing the truth. My mother, sisters, and many of our friends and family have done the best they could to stop them from controlling the narrative. We knew if they could change the public sentiment they would once again justify forceful action against us. In an effort to make sure that this did not happen to any more families in Nevada, in early 2015, my family, along with many state representatives, entered a bill into the Nevada legislature. This bill would end the federal land grabs in the state and force the federal government to follow the Constitution to not to control land inside the state. Bill AB 408. It was the most publicly-supported bill in Nevada history. Despite its popularity, bureaucrats united together from within and changed the text of the bill right before it was voted on. The new text gave them more power rather than take it away. It was a full ray of politics at its finest. On the last day of the house vote, we had to kill our own bill, hoping that the Nevada legislatures would stand up to federal agencies and protect families like ours. We left Carson City, Nevada with our heads hanging low and went back to ranching, working, and raising children.

Before I go on, I need to say that even though our family is suffering great pain and sorrow right now, we do not hate or harbor anger for anyone. We pray daily and diligently for those who have and continue to harm us. We love the Lord Jesus Christ and desire for all of us, even those who have spitefully put us in these jails, to find peace and happiness through His forgiveness and example. Through these great tribulations, we have strived to follow the Lord and do only as He has asked. Now let me go on.

Toward the end of 2015 many became aware of another ranching family in Oregon, the Hammonds, where the father Dwight, 74, and the son Steven, 43, had been put in prison for resisting federal agencies of the executive branch in taking their lands. The abuse to this family for over two decades [is] terrible. Federal agencies of the executive branch teamed together and have taken their water rights, destroyed much of their ranch, restricted use of private property and access to it. Through the courts they have taken hundreds of thousand[s] of dollars in fines. Forced them to sign that they would only sell their ranch to the BLM and put them in prison a second time for doing maintenance on their ranch without a permit from the BLM. All of this was done inside the state of Oregon on private property or land that federal agencies do not have constituted authority to administrate. These same tactics are being used to take established property rights all over the U.S. The EPA, an agency of the Executive Branch, is using the same play book in the eastern states.

Before federal agencies diminished ranching and destroyed logging in Harney County, where the Hammonds live, the county had the highest family incomes in the state of Oregon. Now families in Harney County struggle with the lowest incomes in the state. Over the last thirty years, Harney County has consistently declined in incomes, population, and jobs because of the federal government overtake of the land and resources. The best hope of employment now in Harney County is working for a federal agency of the executive branch, BLM, Forest Service, or Fish and Wildlife. Government employment tallies at 58% of Harney County income. This does not include those on government assistance. Together, approximately 70% of Harney County residents depend on the government for their living. The remaining minority, the producers, are choking from forceful regulation and live in fear of retaliation if they speak out. Those that do speak out against the federal agencies, like the Hammonds, are targeted, demonize[d]. Their lands are taken. They're prosecuted and thrown in prison.

What has happened to us, the Hammonds, and the people of Harney County is a type and shadow of what is happening to our entire country. We must stop federal agencies of the executive branch from taking over and controlling the producing class. Federal agents have shown they are willing to destroy entire state and county economies and put the American people in prison to protect, increase, and justify their gain and control. It is rapidly coming down to federal agencies gaining control over the American working class. These federal agencies of the executive branch have been building up heavy military forces to make sure their projects of ambitions are not limited.

Look at what they put us in jail for—"conspiracy to impede a federal officer's duties." Or in other words, resisting them from doing what they want to do. Federal agencies have conspired for years in impeding the jobs and taking the income of the American working class, diminishing states, counties and destroying more incomes and livelihoods than any other people of the history of this county. When someone finally stands up and says no more, when someone boldly points out that their so-called duties are unlawful and are destroying our livelihoods, states, counties, our future and our children's future, when this message becomes loud enough that people take notice, federal mercenary hired by agencies of the executive branch move in, shoot, and arrest the messengers and drive fear into anyone who might stand up.

Federal agencies of the executive branch are willing to kill and destroy families to protect their ambitions to get gain. Just ask the Finicum family, or the twenty-six Bundy children with their fathers locked up, if I speak the truth. No moral principle, tradition, heritage, livelihood, way of life, or life itself appears to be more important than their ambitions to get gain. Produce nothing, take everything. Modern-day robbers. In my forty years, I have seen my hardworking neighbors lose their homes incomes, heritage, and freedoms at the hands of these wool-covered predators. Often I have asked myself, what is to be done? What are we to do? How can we allow this to continue? Do people care about what is happening to our country?

Seeing directly what the federal agencies did to the Hammonds and to the citizens of Harney County, experiencing firsthand at the Bundy ranch how federal agencies are willing to kill everyday American men and women to keep them self in power, if the Lord had not directed so many people to show up at the Bundy ranch in 2014, I am certain that federal agents would have taken our lives. Something had to be done. How could we pass these gross and growing deterioration of our rights and liberties over to our children? What would be left by the time they were raising their children?

Feeling a providential urge, a love for my neighbors, and a great concern for my country, I used the public connections made during the Bundy ranch standoff to inform everyone I could about the abuses to the Hammond family and how adverse federal agencies took over and destroyed the economy in Harney County. Many, including myself, began to petition the county and state representatives to do their duty and protect the liberties and pursuit of happiness of the people in the county. All of this fell on deaf ears. The elected representatives did not respond to one of our emails. We know they received thousands. We learned later that the FBI, an agency of the executive branch, contacted the sheriff, state, and county representatives and directed them not to respond to the people's petitions. This lack of response created a[n] extreme environment of frustration with the people. No matter what the people did, even after filing an official notice of redress of grievance, the representatives would not respond.

It is my belief that if the FBI would have stayed out of it, elected representative would have responded and taken a lead. This would have ended the mass frustration, and the people would have gotten behind their representatives with major support, satisfying any need for the people to act on their own. The entire protest at the wildlife refuge could have been avoided if the FBI would have stayed out of the way of our republican *form of government. But then again, the FBI could not justify their jobs or have a reason to play with their war toys if the American system of government was allowed to work properly. This reminds me of a John F. Kennedy quote, "Those who make peaceful revolutions impossible, make violent revolutions inevitable."*

The Hammond case was setting a very dangerous precedent in federal court. The abuse has been too great to turn a blind eye. Elected representatives were ignoring the people. What were we were to do? Feeling inspired to do so, on January 2nd, 2016, less the an hour before the rally in support of the Hammonds, I purposed to a group of people, including a sheriff deputy, that we need to do more to bring attention to the abuses and to educate the American people of their rights.[467] I shared how I felt and expressed that we should use adverse possession law to reverse the actions of these federal agencies and give the land that has been stolen back to the people of the county.[468] This was legal and beneficial to the people and would bring a lot of immediate exposure to these abuses.

With [a] majority in agreeance, we took residence of a federal-controlled wildlife refuge thirty miles outside of town. To create this refuge over, one hundred families lost their ranches, homes, and lands to the U.S. Fish and Wildlife Service, another agency of the executive branch.

As adverse possession law requires, we changed the name of the refuge to the Harney County Resource Center, changed the signs, including the vehicles and equipment, contacted the utilities companies, flew the American flag high, opened a post office address, and created a land registry to adjudicate the parcels back to the people of Harney County. Oh, and meanwhile we attracted international media attention who had no idea what adverse possession was. At times it was quite comical watching the controlled mainstream media who had free access to roam the facilities, talking to us openly and then report how we were somehow dangerous armed militants. We shook our head over this many times.

In just a couple of weeks, we attracted over 1000 visitors. Men, women, children, even elementary students came to the center to do homework reports on the events. The local people began supplying all our food, supporting us financially, and took care of us well. They also shared their horror stories of the U.S. Fish and Wildlife, BLM, and Forest Service's action over the past several decades. Out of our many visitors, hundreds attended our seminars on property rights, including state representatives from five different western states.

These people were taking the message back to their hometown and organizing community meetings for us to attend. Meanwhile, the FBI, need I remind you, an agency of the executive branch, took over a high school, county buildings in downtown Burns and the airport, terrorizing the local people, trying to scare them into believing that their force was necessary to protect them against us. As time went on, the local people started to see through this. The FBI knew they had to act quickly. This is what federal agencies of the executive branch have been doing to the American people. Emails from government officials read, "the virus is spreading," indicating that our message was too effective and had to stop.

January 26th [2016], while on our way to a community meeting in Grant County, Oregon, the FBI and Oregon State Police ambushed us and opened fire without cause, shooting my brother Ryan and killing our friend and fellow Arizona rancher, LaVoy Finicum. They shot him multiple times in the back with his hands in the air. The FBI tried to cover up their participation by denying that they shot and hiding the bullet casings. If we would have not filmed the attack, they would have gotten away with it. Never did we hold a gun or show any type of threat to them. We were carrying laptops, projectors, and a PA system, planning on having another effective meeting with the people of Grant County, including the sheriff. We were invited to meetings like this every day that week. Our schedule was filling up.

With millions of dollars [and] thousands of federal agents controlling the main media, federal agencies were still not able to suppress the truth. So, they resolved to use force, much like a big bully who is not intelligent enough to convince people to follow him. He just beats them up if they *don't. Our message is one of freedom and choice. Their message is one of coercion and force.*

With my brother Ryan and I arrested and others, the FBI went on a massive witch hunt, arresting people from all over the United States. Many had nothing to do with Oregon but were in support [during the] 2014 [standoff] in Nevada. I suppose they thought this was their chance to completely destroy any opposition to their ambitious agenda. My father, a 70-year-old man was met with thirty or so operators in the airport. He was on his way to visit my brother and [me]. My brother Dave, they tacitly converged on him when he was unloading lumber for the house he is building. There were over forty agents with assault rifles and full tactical gear in the little town of Delta, Utah, shooting flash things at him. Dave is one of the most reserved, kindest men I know. My brother Mel was in Arizona when they converged on him. Now with the men of the Bundy family locked away in prison cells, charged with pretended offences, the Bundy women are left to tend to our children and our livelihoods, including the ranch. Meanwhile, federal agencies of the executive branch are making plans once again to take our homes, the ranch, remove the cattle, sell them for their profit, destroy the water infrastructure and take all our assets of value. This would force my mother, our wives and children out of our homes with nothing to our names. Meanwhile, we the providers and protectors are locked away facing vindictive charges that if convicted could put us in prison for the rest of our lives.

We never once hurt anybody, threatened anybody or used force in any way. We simply stood for our rights and the rights of our neighbors. Adding salt to our wounds, the extreme environmental group that call themselves the Center for Biological Diversity that has worked hand in hand for several years with the BLM, Forest Service, and other federal agencies, had the audacity to go to Mother at the ranch and offer to buy our century-old family grazing rights for next to nothing. They indicated that they would offer us some money before they took them from us. My mother kindly asked them to leave. They have followed up by phone and continued to harass her.

At the beginning of this I asked you to judge us, to form an informed conclusion in your mind if we were justified to stand for our rights. Time will only allow me to express a hundredth part of what has happened to us. However, before making that judgment, consider a couple more points.

Our Founding Fathers principally understood and documented clearly that the central government, the federal government, has very limited power, especially inside the state and particularly in controlling the land and resources inside the state. The Founders made detailed statements about their intent when they drafted the Constitution. These statements are known as the federalist and anti-federalist papers. Federalist #45 reads, "The powers reserved to the several States will extend to all the objects, which, in the ordinary course of affairs, concern the lives, liberties and properties of the people; and the internal order, improvement, and prosperity of the State."

Federal agencies in direct opposition to the Founders' intent are claiming over 51% of the lands in the western states, approximately 600 million acres and 72% of the subsurface mineral rights. It is estimated that the West has more mineral concentration in the world. It is no wonder why these federal agencies of the executive branch are building up standing armies and are willing to kill their own people for it. By ignoring the constitutional limitations on the federal government, people are being abused, the land and resources in the states are being held and sold for federal profit, and the people are left begging for the crumbs, just as the Founders predicted would happen if the states lost their giant patriotism and stopped enforcing the limitations on the central government.

Unfortunately, a state cannot properly protect the people without the taxes from the land and resources. The people cannot put food on their table, clothe themselves, or build their homes without the lands and resources. And federal agencies cannot sustain themselves or continue to build their standing army, or manipulate the states, counties, and people through welfare, contracts, and grants without the profits from the land and the resources. All wealth and power derives from the land and resources. Everything we eat, live in, wear, use, need or find physical comfort from comes from the earth. Control the land and the resources, you control the people. To protect the people from the evil design of men who would use government to gain ultimate power, our Founders limited the amount of land and resources our government may control. These limitations are found in the powers granted to the federal government through the Constitution, the supreme law of the land, see Article 1 Section 8 Clause 17.

Our family ranch was put under siege by an army of federal agents, 200 hired mercenaries. Our lives were openly threatened at gunpoint for many days in a row, our cattle were run to death by helicopters, shot from the ground and the air, then buried in mass graves right in front of us. Our century-old water infrastructure was being destroyed by federal backhoes, we were body slammed to the asphalt, tazed, gang beaten, detained, and interrogated. They had dogs sicced on us. Our children multiple times had the red dots from hired snipers on their little bodies. The Hammond family and thousands of others across the Western states have had their lands stolen, water rights taken, and experienced a full list of similar abuses by these federal agencies of the executive branch.

Agents of the executive branch claim to have legal unlimited authority to abuse the people and control the land and resources. We the people are in danger. The Constitution prohibits their action. Everything that is American is against it. The United States is not a communist form of government, where the government owns and controls everything. This is against our founding principles and our Founders made it against our laws. The only way they have gotten away with it is because of the Department of Justice, an agency of the executive branch—yes, the Department of Justice is another agency of the executive branch, not the judicial branch—the largest legal team ever known to man. With over 7000 U.S. attorneys, with unlimited budgets, assistance, support, and resources, all paid for by the American people. They have deceitful and forcefully, through the courts, shoved down the throats of the American people that agencies of the executive branch have no limit and that the Constitution does not apply to them. They have destroyed federalism and infiltrated our checks and balances, all in an effort to centralize power, to funnel it into one body so that they can control it for their own gain.

The only safe for power, especially the land and the resources, is to distribute it into millions of people's hands all across this great country, from sea to shining sea, allowing each person to live in liberty while enjoying the benefits of the increase of the earth through the law of the harvest. Land and resources equal power. It is what all ancient and modern conquerors desire. The land and resources must not fall into the hands of a small group of people. It must not be centralized or nationalized. Our food, water, homes, clothing, transportation, communication, everything that sustains us, and find physical comfort from hangs at risk if the heads of these federal agencies obtain their ultimate objective. Control the food, water, air, lumber, iron and other resources, control the use of the earth and you have obtained an ultimate power over the people.

Never was this just about some cattle running in the desert or just about some poor rancher trying to hold onto his way of life. This is about God and country, about standing so the bad doesn't overcome the good. It is about each individual. It is about you, your children and your grandchildren. It is about food on your table about having a home to put table in. This it is about agency, the ability to choose. This is about life, liberty, and the pursuit of happiness for many generations to come.

This is about freedom... or maybe, just maybe, the horrible pain from being kept from our families for this long has driven us insane.

You be the judge. I know the Lord has protected us, kept us from falling into despair. I know He loves us, and, in time, I know, I am certain that He will allow us to go home and have that so desired reunion with our little families and all the others we love so very much.

Thank you for listening.

Ammon Bundy

THE FUNERAL REMARKS OF DAD'S BISHOP

"The Finicums have lived around this part of the country for a lot of years, several generations. I am their neighbor over the hill in Moccasin and I have always wondered about that name Finicum. It seemed like it was kind of a peculiar name. I only knew one family that had the name Finicum so one day I asked one of the Finicum boys if the name Finicum came from Finland and he said, "No, it comes from Cane Beds."

No, I didn't really ask that. I made that story up so I could say what I would like to say next. You younger generations of Finicums have a lot to live up to. You have a legacy to live and examples such as LaVoy's life to live up to.

As LaVoy's bishop, I would like to tell you LaVoy was a committed, faithful, temple-worthy member of the Church of Jesus Christ of Latter-day Saints.

I know our time is short. I would like to say a couple of things. A few months ago, LaVoy and Jeanette were in the bishop's office with me and we were talking about a church calling. As usual, we talked about a lot of other things. I remember one thing that I have never forgotten from that day in the office was LaVoy saying the most important thing to him in this life was his temple covenants and temple blessings.

I know that that is true. I think of the beauty and simplicity of that as we sing a primary hymn called "Families Can Be Together Forever." I just want to give you my testimony that I know that is true, that families can be together forever.

I am going to skip over some of my notes because of time. Yesterday morning, I was lying in bed reading my scriptures, the Book of Mormon in the book of Enos Chapter 1:26-27. I thought, "Boy, this is beautiful." Enos said,

> And I saw that I must soon go down to my grave... And I soon go to the place of my rest, which is with my Redeemer; for I know that in him I shall rest. And I rejoice in the day my mortal shall

put on immortality and shall stand before him; then shall I see his face with pleasure, and he will say unto me, ye blessed, there is a place prepared for you in the mansions of my Father, Amen.

That is my testimony.

I would like the Finicum family to know that I love them and I appreciate them. They are a great family. If there is a way to tell a great man, just look at his family. I leave that with you in the name of Jesus Christ, Amen."[469]

HOW DAD BECAME KNOWN AS TARP MAN

On Wednesday, January 6th, 2016, four days after the occupation started, around 3:30 a.m., dad was peppered with leading questions from a National MSNBC reporter, Tony Dokoupil. Dad sat in a chair under a blue tarp in the center of the entrance to the refuge as he was questioned. Large spotlights were stationed there for the *Associated Press*. Dad's choice was to sit in the light. Transparency was always the goal.

A highly credible source had informed the occupiers that five federal warrants had been issued for their arrest. Dad said to the reporter, "If that is true and is the case, I do not want the FBI/federal agents having to go running around in the dark, kicking in doors looking for me. I want them to know exactly where I am at."[470]

Why the blue tarp?

It being January, there was sleeting rain. In an effort to keep himself dry he covered himself with the tarp. I'll admit, the footage of him under the blue tarp was quite funny. It wasn't twenty-four hours before he became the focus of trending jeers on social media. This is how he came to be known as #tarpman. He definitely made a spectacle of himself trying to keep dry and I would have done the same in his position.

It seems most watching the footage could only focus on the blue tarp. As result, their ears were shut off to the message Dad was delivering. Tony asked his leading question that implied Dad had a death wish: "So, you are out here prepared to die over what principle exactly?" Dad calmly responded by saying,

It's about our country. It's about federalism. It's about the government closest to the people governs best. What has happened is that the powers in the government have been brought back up into a centralized government. And so, the counties and states, the things dealt with at a county and state levels are now so regulated by the federal levels that our freedoms and our ability to have contact with our representatives on a one-and-one, face-to-face basis is gone. It is gone. I have sat down with my county sheriff face-to-face. I have sat down with my county commissioner face-to-face. John McCain is not going to sit down with me face-to-face and if he does, he'll promise lots of things, but he won't be able to change anything. That doesn't happen. Let the states manage and govern the things that pertain to the state. Let the county manage and govern the things pertaining to the counties and let the federal government go back to managing pertaining to protecting our borders and defending our nation. That's what they need to do. Keep commerce regular and a few narrowly defined things that the Constitution lays down. Let's just go back to that. I believe in government, okay.

Social media exploded with various memes of him and his blue tarp. Some were in support and some not. My favorite meme was one that used Leutze's renowned canvas of George Washington crossing the Delaware. Whoever created this meme inserted the shape of Dad under his blue tarp right behind the standing George Washington in between the two seated men in the boat. The shape of the blue tarp fit perfectly in the meme. I wish I could include the meme in my book for you to see. In looking at the following photo, you can imagine.

Washington Crossing the Delaware (1849–1850)
Original painting by Leutze

When I arrived at the refuge two days later, Dad was not self-effacing or self-deprecating about his new brand of #tarpman. Rather, he possessed a peculiar strength wherein he was peaceably agreeable in that "today's superhero indeed had a *blue* cape."[471]

GLOSSARY

Abrahamic Covenant. Abraham received the gospel and was ordained a high priest.[472] He later entered into celestial marriage, which is the covenant of exaltation.[473] In connection with the covenants he made, he received great promises from the Lord concerning his family. Among these promises were the following:

> - His posterity would be numerous.[474]
> - His seed, or descendants, would receive the gospel and bear the priesthood.[475]
> - Through the ministry of his seed, "all the families of the earth [would] be blessed, even with the blessings of the Gospel, which are the blessings of salvation, even of life eternal."[476]

Together, all the covenants and promises that Abraham received from the Lord are called the Abrahamic covenant. It is an everlasting covenant that extends to all of Abraham's descendants.[477] To be counted as Abraham's seed, an individual must obey the laws and ordinances of the gospel. Then that person can receive all the blessings of the Abrahamic covenant, even if he or she is not a literal descendant of Abraham.[478]

Members of The Church of Jesus Christ of Latter-day Saints are children of the covenant.[479] They have received the everlasting gospel and inherited the same promises given to Abraham, Isaac, and Jacob. They have the right to the blessings of the priesthood and to eternal life, according to their faithfulness in receiving the ordinances of salvation and keeping the associated covenants. Nations of the earth will be blessed by their efforts and by the labors of their posterity.

Adverse Possession Law. "A method of acquisition of title to real property by possession for a statutory period under certain conditions.[480] It has been described as the statutory method of acquiring title to land by limitation.[481] Because of the statute of limitations on the bringing of actions for the recovery of land, title can be acquired to real property by adverse possession. In order to establish title in this manner, there must be proof of non-permissive use which is actual, open, notorious, exclusive and adverse for the statutorily prescribed period.[482] State statutes differ with respect to the required length of possession from an upper limit of 20 years to a lower one of 5 years, with even more extreme time periods covering certain special cases. There may be different periods of time even within a single state, depending on whether or not the adverse possessor has color of title and/or whether or not taxes have been paid. In some cases, a longer possession is required against public entities than against individuals. Adverse possession depends on intent of occupant to claim and hold real property in opposition to all the world,[483] and also embodies the idea that owner of or persons interested in property have knowledge of the assertion of ownership by the occupant.[484] Adverse possession consists of actual possession with intent to hold solely for possessor to exclusion of others and is denoted by exercise of acts of dominion over land including making of ordinary use and taking of ordinary profits of which land is susceptible in its present state[485]."[486]

Agency. "Your Heavenly Father has given you agency, the ability to choose and to act for yourself. Agency is essential in the plan of salvation. Without it, you would not be able to learn or progress or follow the Savior. With it, you are 'free to choose liberty and eternal life, through the great Mediator of all men, or to choose captivity and death, according to the captivity and power of the devil.'[487]

"You had the power to choose even before you were born. In the premortal Council in Heaven, Heavenly Father presented His plan, which included the principle of agency. Lucifer rebelled and 'sought to destroy the agency of man.'[488]

As a result, Lucifer and all those who followed him were denied the privilege of receiving a mortal body. Your presence on the earth confirms that you exercised your agency to follow Heavenly Father's plan.

"In mortality, you continue to have agency. Your use of this gift determines your happiness or misery in this life and in the life to come. You are free to choose and act, but you are not free to choose the consequences of your actions. The consequences may not be immediate, but they will always follow. Choices of good and righteousness lead to happiness, peace, and eternal life, while choices of sin and evil eventually lead to heartache and misery.

"You are responsible for the decisions you make. You should not blame your circumstances, your family, or your friends if you choose to disobey God's commandments. You are a child of God with great strength. You have the ability to choose righteousness and happiness, regardless of your circumstances.

"You are also responsible for developing the abilities and talents Heavenly Father has given you. You are accountable to Him for what you do with your abilities and how you use your time. Do not idle away your time. Be willing to work hard. Choose to do many good things of your own free will."[489]

Bureaucracy. A system of government in which most of the important decisions are made by state officials rather than by elected representatives. Within this system, such unelected agents write regulatory legislation as well as enforce said laws.

Committee of Correspondence and Safety. Before, during, and after the American divorcement from the crown of Great Britain, there began a formation of the committees of correspondence and committees of safety for the purpose of enabling the American people to become the sole arbiters of their own political destiny.

> "The primary movement was to bring people to understand their interests and act in concert, and the first means used to attain this end was the establishment of committees of correspondence in different parts of the country. These committees were chosen in towns, counties, parishes,

> *districts, or smaller neighborhoods. ...So necessary was the system in itself, and so well adapted to promote the general welfare, that it was succeeded to everywhere, and in a short time committees were so universally appointed throughout the colonies that the friends of liberty had speedy and direct channels opened with each other in every part of the continent. This increased their mutual intelligence, gave them confidence and encouragement, harmonized their sentiments, and sowed the seeds of union."*[490]

In the era of American Independence such committees were the tools used by the people as the last line of defense for the protection of the people's life, liberty, and pursuit of happiness (property) so to avoid at all costs, war. Such committees were always about enforcing law to keep those hold government control switches in check.

Members of such committees were not wannabe anarchists. The committees were "conciliatory indeed! This was the spirit that permeated an organization unrivaled in its time and place. John Adams judged truly when he said that its conception embodied the whole Revolution."[491] The American founders called the King's actions "unconstitutional," thus unlawful and the people had to advocate for themselves or be slaves.

There is just as much need for committees of correspondence and safety in today's modern world as there was in American primitive time. The real-life stories found within the pages of this book is concise enough answer to any questioning why this is the case.

One goal of the Oregon occupation was to establish and nurture a local committee of safety as the last line of defense for the protection of Harney County, Burns, Oregon citizens' right to life, liberty, and pursuit of happiness (property).

Community of Keep the Republic. A dear friend and mentor of mine offered this definition of what a 'community of keep the republic' is in today's political culture:

> *A collection of individuals who mutually pledge to each other to maintain balanced order by first, maintaining their own paradigms of maintenance principles because for an object [in this case, the governmental*

system] to animate, it requires an external power source [human beings] (i.e. government is a system, political power is only inherent in human persons, government control is either separated or combined, etc.). [In other words, realize government does not have the power, government does not have too much power, and that it is human beings that have power. Realize the governmental system is not a living thing but an 'it' that is controlled by human beings who possess power.] "Remember, the governmental system and those controlling it are not a golden calf unless the people worship it and treat it as if it is superior and animate."[492]

Second, maintaining the meaning of foundational and weaponized words, such as person, governance, government, governing, governed, hero, villain, victim, dual federalist, cooperative federalist, layer cake federalist, marble cake federalist, terrorism, terrorist, extremist, white supremacist, right-wing, alt-right, far-right, etc.

Third, maintaining relationships between the governed and their layered governments.

Fourth, maintaining the boundaries of layered governments.

Fifth, preventatively maintaining leaky control [breaching Constitutional bounds] between the governing of layered governments.

Sixth, empowering, enlightening, and encouraging other governed [people] to maintain political boundaries and prevent leaky control.

Seventh, building and sustaining a perpetual maintenance team in every community across a nation (Herr, 2019).

As my friend and I continued our discussion, he suggested the phrase 'balanced order' summed up the possibility of personal and communal captivity as result of inappropriately applied maintenance or no maintenance at all. We marveled together as we discussed the reality of God creating humanity. We agreed it is He who breathed life into the human soul. Mark then went on to express further that it is God who 'animated human with His breath' and then asked the rhetorical question, "What animates the human relationship?" He followed his question with the answer, "Words"! He went on to say, "Government is the application of the meaning of words in a human relationship. For an object to animate, it requires an external power source. God used words to create and to instruct, man uses words to define and Satan uses words to confuse."[493]

Cooperating Federalist. The exact opposite of Dual federalist.

Dual Federalist. "A legal geographical boundary where control is exercised by separate multiple sources."[494]

> *"No, my friend, the way to have good and safe government, is not to trust it all to one; but to divide it among the many, distributing to every one exactly the functions he is competent to. let the National government be entrusted with the defense of the nation, and it's foreign & federal relations; the State governments with the civil rights, laws, police & administration of what concerns the state generally; the Counties with the local concerns of the counties; and each Ward direct the interests within itself. it is by dividing and subdividing these republics from the great National one down thro' all it's subordinations, until it ends in the administration of every man's farm and affairs by himself; by placing under every one what his own eye may superintend, that all will be done for the best. what has destroyed liberty and the rights of man in every government which has ever existed under the sun? the generalising & concentrating all cares and powers into one body, no matter whether of the Autocrats of Russia or France, or of the Aristocrats of a Venetian Senate."[495]*

The purpose of the multiple sources is so each level of government can check and balance each other, so when one level steps outside its responsibility or controls that the social contract gives, it can be put back in its place. The different jurisdictions are not to be friends with one another. There must be a level of tension as the multiple sources interact to conduct business.

Federalism. As scary as the word federalism sounds, the Constitution's language invented its practice. The backbone of federalism is a shared *control* between both the governed and the governors. Federalism's doctrine springs from the idea where there is no such thing as subordination because everyone carries within them equal *power* that originates from "'the laws of nature and of nature's God."

The role of federalism is for the individuals working within each jurisdiction (level) of government to provide the necessary checks and balance when one level steps outside its responsibilities or controls that the social contract (state or federal constitution) gives them. It was not meant for the different level of governments to be tight-knit friends.

The United States Constitution is a binding contract that brings the states together into a federal republic. The sole purpose is to protect God-given rights against the human tendency to violate said rights for personal gain. The purpose of this binding contract with its separations of control was to prevent a centralized power. Checking and balancing those working within the governmental system, using the Constitution as a guide, is federalism.

FIVE MAIN CATEGORIES

1. **Monarchy**: rule by one. A monarchy most assuredly provides arbitrary authority whose dubious governance has been the means of destruction to countless people's life, liberty, and the pursuit of happiness (property). "The way to safe government is not to trust it to one but to divide it among the many."[496]
2. **Anarchy:** rule by none.
3. **Oligarchy:** rule by few. An oligarchy was described by Thomas Jefferson as a dangerous doctrine that leads to despotism: "Our rights are not defined by five men in black robes [i.e. the Supreme Court]."[497]
4. **Democracy:** rule by majority. Benjamin Franklin is well known to have described a democracy as two wolves and a sheep sitting down to decide what's for dinner.
5. **Republic:** control by elected representative who are to follow and defend the rule book, which is the law created within the limits defined by the Constitution. The Constitution creates political boundaries that require continual maintenance by both the governed and governors to prevent it from becoming a tyranny.

Freedom. "A state of exemption from the power or control of another."[498]

Governed. Any person, including all types of persons as defined by law, who are governed in any way by a governmental system that is controlled by the governors (see below).

Governors. Any appointed, elected, or employed persons controlling governmental switches.

Israel. *"One who prevails with God* or *Let God prevail.* This name [Israel] was given to Jacob at Penuel[499] and at Bethel.[500] It also applies to his descendants and to their kingdom.[501] After the division of the kingdom, the northern tribes, as the larger part, retained the name Israel, while the southern kingdom was called Judah. The land of Canaan is also called Israel today. And in another sense, Israel means the true believer in Christ, as explained by Paul.[502] The name Israel is therefore variously used to denote (1) the man Jacob, (2) the literal descendants of Jacob, and (3) the true believers in Christ, regardless of their lineage or geographical location."[503]

Label Lynching. "Using labels, by one person, including all types of persons as defined by law, without due process or remedy, appearing to intend to coerce or intimidate, destroy the reputation of, disrupt the private or political business or enterprise of another person, including all types of persons as defined by law."[504]

Sticks and stones can break my bones, but *words CAN KILL YOU!*

Liberty. "Unobstructed action according to our will: but rightful liberty is unobstructed action according to our will, within the limits drawn around us by the equal rights of others."[505]

Natural-Born Person. "The term applying to the person who is born in the country in which they are a citizen. By definition a natural-born person is different than an artificial person, judicial person, employed person, or third person."[506]

Remember, "government is the application of the meaning of words in a human relationship."[507] Do you know what kind of person you are according to law? Do you know what rights are granted to artificial persons, judicial persons, employed persons, or third persons and how that impacts your rights? Are you willing to be ever learning so to enable yourself to powerfully "maintain the meaning of foundational and weaponized words" for the sake of preserving your rights? There is no satire in the phrase, sticks and stones can break my bones, but *words can kill you!* Do you think my father was killed by mere happenstance? No. He was labeled with weaponized words found in law book lexicons and the agents were trained with words to bring about a desired result.

Natural Law or the Laws of Nature. "A rule of conduct arising out of the natural relations of human beings established by the Creator, and existing prior to any positive precept. Thus, it is the law of nature, that one man should not injure another, and murder and fraud would be crimes, independent of any prohibition from a supreme power."[508]

"True law is right reason in agreement with nature; it is of universal application, unchanging and everlasting; it summons to duty by its commands, and averts from wrongdoing by its prohibitions.... It is a sin to try to alter this law, not is it allowable to repeal any part of it, and it is impossible to abolish entirely. We cannot be freed from its obligations by Senate or people, and we need not look outside ourselves for an expounder or interpreter of it. And there will not be different laws at Rome and at Athens, or different laws now and in the future, but one eternal and unchangeable law will be valid for all nations and all times.... Whoever is disobedient is fleeing from himself and denying his human nature, and by reason of this very fact he will suffer the worst penalties, even if he escapes what is commonly called punishment."[509]

Opposition in All Things. "The purpose of mortal life for the children of God is to provide the experiences needed 'to progress toward perfection and ultimately realize their divine destiny as heirs of eternal life.' As President Thomas S. Monson taught us so powerfully this morning, we progress by making choices, by which we are tested to show that we will keep God's commandments.[510] To be tested, we must have the agency to choose between alternatives. To provide alternatives on which to exercise our agency, we must have opposition.

"The rest of the plan is also essential. When we make wrong choices—as we inevitably will—we are soiled by sin and must be cleansed to proceed toward our eternal destiny. The Father's plan provides the way to do this, the way to satisfy the eternal demands of justice: A Savior pays the price to redeem us from our sins. That Savior is the Lord Jesus Christ, the Only Begotten Son of God the Eternal Father, whose atoning sacrifice—whose suffering—pays the price for our sins if we will repent of them.

"One of the best explanations of the planned role of opposition is in the Book of Mormon, in Lehi's teachings to his son Jacob. 'It must needs be, that there is an opposition in all things. If not so, ... righteousness could not be brought to pass, neither wickedness, neither holiness nor misery, neither good nor bad.'

"As a result, Lehi continued, 'the Lord God gave unto man that he should act for himself. Wherefore, man could not act for himself save it should be that he was enticed by the one or the other.'[511] Similarly, in modern revelation the Lord declares, 'It must needs be that the devil should tempt the children of men, or they could not be agents unto themselves.'[512]"[513]

Ordinances. "In the Church, an ordinance is a sacred, formal act performed by the authority of the priesthood. Some ordinances are essential to our exaltation. These ordinances are called saving ordinances. They include baptism, confirmation, ordination to the Melchizedek Priesthood (for men), the temple endowment, and the marriage sealing. With each of these ordinances, we enter into solemn covenants with the Lord.

"Other ordinances, such as naming and blessing children, consecrating oil, and administering to the sick and afflicted, are also performed by priesthood authority. While they are not essential to our salvation, they are important for our comfort, guidance, and encouragement.

"Ordinances and covenants help us remember who we are. They remind us of our duty to God. The Lord has provided them to help us come unto Him and receive eternal life. When we honor them, He strengthens us.

"You may receive many opportunities to participate in priesthood ordinances. Whenever you have such an opportunity, do all you can to prepare yourself, whether you are performing the ordinance or receiving it. You can prepare by praying, fasting, counseling with priesthood leaders, and studying the scriptures and the words of latter-day prophets. If you are a priesthood holder, you should always be spiritually prepared to perform an ordinance. Live a clean, worthy life, and strive to receive the constant companionship of the Holy Ghost."[514]

Priesthood. The priesthood is the eternal power and authority of God. Through the priesthood God created and governs the heavens and the earth. Through this power He redeems and exalts His children, bringing to pass "the immortality and eternal life of man."[515]

Property. Property is the result of an individual mixing their labor (life/time and liberty/choice) with unclaimed natural resource from the earth. Locke said, "Every man has a property in his own person. This nobody has a right to but himself."[516] However, property is not limited to one mixing their labor with natural resources. It is also the natural results of one's use of their life and liberty separate from earth's resources. For a few examples of this type of property think about relationships, health, joy, pain, knowledge, wisdom, and ignorance.

"Thou shalt not steal." "This admonition against stealing presupposes the existence of private property." "Thou shalt not covet thy neighbor's house, thou shalt not covet thy neighbor's wife, nor his manservant, nor his maidservant, nor his ox, nor his ass, nor anything that is thy neighbour's."[517] This also presupposes the existence of private property.[518]

Alexander Hamilton said in Federalist #79, "In the general course of human nature, a power over a man's subsistence amounts to a power over his will."

Alexander Hamilton said in Federalist #73, "In the main it will be found that a power over the man's support is a power over his will."

John Adams said, "All men are born free and independent, and have certain natural, essential, and unalienable rights, among which may be reckoned the right of enjoying and defending their lives and liberties, that of acquiring, possessing, and protecting property; in fine, that of seeking and obtaining their safety and happiness."[519]

Pursuit of Happiness. The bold statement "pursuit of happiness" presupposes that not all are guaranteed happiness. Such an idea is an interesting concept, often convoluted by the 21st-century culture bred to *expect fairness*. In reality, to achieve the outcome of happiness, personal liberty must be used in obedience to natural law as it pertains to the matter of happiness, so as to avoid atrophy as it pertains to happiness. The byproduct of such pursuit becomes one's personal property, and that property either contributes to or withdraws from personal happiness. Thus, as long as humanity has a heartbeat (life) and choice (liberty) they are in *"pursuit of happiness"* (property).

"Life plus liberty equals the pursuit of happiness", which is one's property."[520]

Regionalism: Center for Self Governance describes regional government in this way:

> *"Regional government is an effort to address the challenges the interstate compact clause in the US Constitution poses to intergovernmental cooperation where a perceived common problem may exist. [Despite the mindset of those wishing to use this system of government], the division of constitutional powers between jurisdictions is inherent to the framework of the United States [to avoid the nation morphing into an empire]. [In the mind of those converted to regionalisms doctrine, there is] conflict between jurisdictions, [which] limits cooperation between those jurisdictions. Regional Government is seen, by a growing number of public personnel through all levels of government, as the solution to this perceived problem.*
>
> *Region Government is where public officials from multiple units (jurisdictions) of government (schools, cities, counties, states, and federal government agencies, etc.) enter into contracts or otherwise to share control, functions, organization, and financing to address a problem (e.g. utilities) or a set of common problems (e.g. housing, transportation, environment, water etc.) On agreement, the representatives of the member units will form a board that is recognized by the state or state encompassing the regional government.*

The newly formed regional government can be a non-profit corporation or a stand-alone jurisdiction. In some cases (and expanding), regional government is authorized by the state government to legislate, tax, and assess. In most regional governments, representatives are selected by the member unit of government. Representatives can be either an elected, proxy, or employee of the participating member unit.

All 50 states have incorporated regional government into either the state constitution or state law. Most counties and municipalities, across the United States, have become or participate in municipal planning commissions, metropolitan planning organizations, regional planning agencies, council of governments, etc."[521]

RECOMMENDED READING

Adam, John. *A Defense of the Constitutions of Government of the United States of America*

Allen, Gary. *None Dare Call it Conspiracy*

American Political Writing During the Founding. Edited by Charles S. Hyneman and Donald S. Lutz

Andrews, Joseph. *A Guide for Learning and Teaching The Declaration of Independence and The U.S. Constitution*

Barruel, Augustin. *Memoirs Illustrating the History of Jacobinism* (1798)

Barton, David. Any title.

Bastiat, Frederic. *The Law*

Benson, Ezra Taft. *The Constitution: A Heavenly Banner* and *Stand for Freedom: Teaching on Liberty*

Bentley, Christopher S. *A Glorious Standard for all Mankind* and *The Hidden Things of Darkness*

Blackstone, Sir William. *Commentaries on the Laws of England*

The Book of Mormon

Bradley, Scott N. *To Preserve The Nation*

Cicero. De re publica (*On the Commonwealth*)

Colonial Origins of the American Constitution. Edited by Donald S. Lutz

Engels Friedrich and Karl Marx. *The Communist Manifesto*

Gibbon, Sir Edward. *The Decline and Fall of the Roman Empire*

Griffin, G. Edward. *The Creature from Jekyll Island*

Hamilton, Alexander and James Madison. *The Federalist Papers*

Hazlitt, Henry. *Economics in One Lesson*

Henry, Patrick, et al. *The Anti-Federalist Papers*
Herr, Mark and Bill Norton. *Speaking the Language of Liberty*
The Holy Bible
Horowitz, Jerome. *The Elders of Israel and the Constitution*
House, Edward Mandell. *Philip Dru: Administrator* (1912)
The Humanist Manifestos I, II, and III
Jefferson, Thomas. *Notes on the State of Virginia* and *The Thomas Jefferson Papers*
Locke, John. *First and Second Treatises on Civil Government* and other works
McKay, David O. "Two Contending Forces"
Monnett, John D. *Awakening to Our Awful Situation*
Montesquieu. *The Spirit of Laws*
Newquist, Jerreld L. *Prophets, Principles and National Survival*
Paine, Thomas. *Common Sense*
Perloff, James. *The Shadows of Power*
Plato. The Republic
Political Sermons of the American Founding Era. Edited by Ellis Sandoz
Pratt, R. Stephen. *Why the Constitution*
Robinson, John. *Proofs of a Conspiracy* (1798)
Romney, Marion G. "Is Socialism the United Order?"
Skousen, W. Cleon. *The Making of America, The Five Thousand Year Leap, The Naked Communist, The Majesty of*
God's Law, and *The Cleansing of America*
Smith, Adam. *The Wealth of Nations*
Taylor, John. *The Government of God*
de Tocqueville, Alexis. *Democracy in America*
Tucker, St. George. *View of the Constitution of the United States*
The United States Constitution and the Declaration of Independence
Wallison, Peter J. *Hidden in Plain Sight: What Really Caused the World's Worst Financial Crisis and Why It Could*
Happen Again
George Washington's Farewell Address
Webster, Noah. *An American Dictionary of the English Language* (1828)
Your State Constitution

ENDNOTES

1. A series of trials held in the city of Nuremberg, Germany after World War II that were intended to bring to justice the principle leadership of Nazis Germany who were deemed responsible for the war crimes of the Nazis war machine, and the Holocaust.
2. Adolf Eichmann was a Nazi functionary who helped organize and carry out the Holocaust in Europe during World War II. He was captured in Argentina by Israeli agents in 1960, tried in Jerusalem in 1961, and executed in 1962.
3. Remember these rights were not created by government, for these rights pre-existed all forms of mortal government and were Divine in their origins.
4. *Habeas corpus* is the assurance of judicial review of arrest and incarceration.
5. *Bills of attainder* declare a person to be a criminal without a trial and conviction.
6. *Ex post facto law* is creating a law that made something illegal that had been legal when an individual engaged in the activity and then charging the person with a crime after the new law was enacted.
7. Hosea 4:6
8. Isaiah 5:13
9. Ephesians 6:12
10. Revelations 6:9-11
11. Thomas Paine, *The Crisis No. I*, 1776.
12. The essential or characteristic customs and conventions of a community.
13. The Constitution cannot mean anything other than what it says. It was written in plain English. Nobody needs thousands of meandering, perverse interpretations of hundreds of court cases. It was written for the common person to be able to easily understand. Thomas Jefferson said, "Laws are made for men of ordinary understanding and should, therefore, be construed by the ordinary rules of common sense. Their meaning is not to be sought for in metaphysical subtleties which may make anything mean everything or nothing at pleasure." ("Letter to William Johnson," June 12, 1823)
14. Some foundational writings include the Federalist Papers, Washington's monumental "Farewell Address," Tucker's expansive View of the Constitution of the United States, and other fundamental policy statements, such as the Monroe Doctrine.

15. If you are unfamiliar with the story, there is a brief history on the Bundy Standoff found in the appendix.
16. Our family went through several lawyers before officially filing a wrongful death complaint. The two-year process was anything but easy. It is interesting to look back and recognize the many unqualified individuals who inserted themselves into the situation with motives of their own rather than serving the best interest of our family. Finding the right legal team required interviewing over 30 different law firms, starting working relationships with four different legal teams, and negotiating before signing on the dotted line with the legal team that would spearhead the wrongful death suit.
17. Read official family statement after the murder of Dad in appendix.
18. *Only by Blood and Suffering: Regaining Lost Freedom*, which can be found on our family website: onecowboystandforfreedom.com
19. Please see appendix for the lyrics of the song.
20. Chris Lawrence, "'No Land Alternative' Prompts bin Laden Sea Burial," *CNN*, May 2, 2011.
21. LaVoy Finicum, *Only by Blood and Suffering: Regaining Lost Freedom*, 2015, pg. 199.
22. We prepared and practiced this: "I do not have all the answers to the questions, thank you and goodbye."
23. Read the chapter titled, *A Force to be Reckoned With*, for more details on our family dynamic.
24. I remember as a child lying on the living room floor listening to Dad read to us kids. Dad really enjoyed reading, and, naturally, we kids followed suit.

    After Dad's murder, my mind would often drift to memories like this, of him and us. Even before he was taken from us, I could never think of books without also thinking of Dad. Except now, it's different.

    Children's classics, such as *The Hobbit, The Lord of the Rings, Harry Potter,* and many others, give a unique opportunity for the reader to develop a keen understanding into the complexities of social life. This happened for me as my perspective broadened into being able to see into the minds of characters as they experienced hardship and fulfillment. Whereas, in real life, only assumptions can be made into the *why* behind the state of others.

    While wrestling with the emotions of grief, anger, sadness, loneliness, frustration, and duty while being overwhelmed, lost, and exhausted after the loss of my Father, it was natural for me to identify, on an entire new level, with the characters from the books that we had come to know and love together. It felt natural to include many quotations from these works in telling the story of Dad's murder.
25. Read Thara and Tierra-Belle script for press conference after funeral in appendix.
26. Please see appendix for the lyrics of the song.
27. Victoria Sharp, the young woman who was one of the passengers in Dad's truck the day he was murdered, was also there with her family. Their family sang a few songs and Victoria gave her chilling eyewitness account of his murder.
28. LaVoy Finicum, *Only by Blood and Suffering: Regaining Lost Freedom*, 2015, pg. 210.
29. LaVoy Finicum, "LaVoy Publicly Announcing the Cancellation of His BLM Contract," Personal

interview by Bryan Hyde, *HD Radio Show*, June 25, 2015.
30 J.K. Rowling, *Harry Potter and the Sorcerer's Stone*, 1998.
31 See the glossary for a definition of *federalism*.
32 See the appendix to read the occupiers' redress of grievance.
33 Maxine Bernstein, "15 Confidential Sources Fed FBI Info from Malheur National Wildlife Refuge," *The Oregonian*, October 14, 2016.
34 Shawna Cox, Personal interview conducted by L. Champion, *Liberty's Champion*, February 2, 2016.
35 Elliot Njus, "Oregon Standoff: Harney County Group Felt Betrayed by Occupation, But Working to Take Up Cause," *The Oregonian*, January 17, 2016.
36 See glossary for definition of *The Committee of Safety*.
37 The 2016 Harney County, Oregon Committee of Safety was comprised of local citizens who courageously broke through very justifiable fear. The tactics of lawlessness and intimidation on the part of government officials had been at play in this community for a long time. Local people watched life, liberty, and the pursuit of happiness stripped from their friends. The fear of reprisal was raw and real and, as a result, the newly formed committee members' stand at first was very precarious. The local ranchers Dwight and Steven Hammond reporting back to prison for a second time was the ongoing reminder of what might be the committee members' fate. The leadership of this committee included a man by the name of Chris Briels, who was the local fire chief for many years. Only a few days into the occupation of the Malheur National Wildlife Refuge, Chris publicly announced his resignation as fire chief to the *Associated Press* stationed at ground zero. He expressed he could no longer in good conscience sustain certain local governors due to clear, unlawful infringements upon the life, liberty, and pursuit of happiness of local residents. (Chris Briels, "Harney County Fire Chief Resigns FBI Caught Audio Enhanced," Malheur National Wildlife Refuge Press Conference, January 14, 2016.)
38 Brent Weisberg, "Militia at Malheur: 'Virus was spreading,'" *Koin 6*, January 29, 2016.
39 "Burns Oregon-Ranchers Sign to End Their Contract With the BLM," Shuf1111, January 25, 2016.
Maxine Bernstein, "Oregon Standoff: Ranchers, Including Ex-con, Renounce Grazing Permits," *The Oregonian*, February 22, 2016.
40 "Shawna Cox Cell Phone Video from Inside LaVoy Finicum's Truck," *The Oregonian*, March 14, 2016.
41 Shawna Cox, Personal interview conducted by L. Champion, *Liberty's Champion*, February 2, 2016.
42 ibid.
43 Their suspicion was substantiated eighteen months later during the trial for the FBI agent W. Joseph Astarita in charge that day. A grand jury indicted him for five counts of obstruction of justice in regard to the murder scene. During trial the witness on the stand revealed "FBI agent Justin Travis Elkins said he had his eyes trained on [Ryan] Payne at the initial police

stop, and the state police officer's firing of a rubber round "was totally unexpected." Dugan turned to the state police officer and yelled, "W[hat] T[he] F[u#*] was that?!" Elkins confirmed. He said Payne was complying with commands, and the officer's shot escalated the vehicle stop." (Maxine Bernstein, "Indicted FBI Agent's Flippant Remark When asked if he fired his gun recounted at trial," *The Oregonian*, July 31, 2018.)

44 Harney County Judge Steve Grasty held a meeting with several elected officials during the occupation with the aim to "get the terrorists out of his county." Grasty started the meeting with a threat to all the elected officials, making it very clear he would smear their political names if they did not conform to what he wanted them to do in regard to dealing with the occupation. Nevada Assemblywoman Michele Fiore was in attendance of this meeting via phone. Matt Shea, a member of the Washington House of Representatives was physically present, along with other elected officials. Local state and federal officers were present for questioning as well. After Grasty set the tone of the meeting with his brief on the occupiers, label lynching them as armed dangerous terrorists who need swift action followed by his threat to the elected officials, the elected officials asked what laws exactly the occupiers had broken. No one could give a straight answer. Matt said in interview about Grasty's conduct, "Are you presuming somebody is guilty until proven innocent instead of the other way around, which our American system. Due process demands that question be upfront and at the first, not waiting until after the fact." (*Dead Man Talking Trailer: Part Two of the Governing vs. Governed Documentary Series*, 2018.)

45 See glossary for the definition of *adverse possession*.

46 Marcus R. Mumford and J. Morgan Philpot, "Trial Memorandum and Opposition to the Government's Motion in Limine RE: Adverse Possession," August 17, 2016.

47 "Mr. Bundy has ...made repeated and consistent efforts to apprise the Court of his statutory and common law rights to attempt adverse possession under the Color of Title Act, 43 U.S.C. § 1068, as justifying his and his fellow defendants' presence on the Refuge.
Mr. Bundy's defense: regardless of whether Mr. Bundy's attempted adverse possession of the Refuge would have been successful – it was unquestionably legal to try.
If Mr. Bundy and his colleagues were intentionally engaged in a statutorily protected attempt at adverse possession as part of their lawful protest – regardless of the merits of their attempt, and regardless of the actual outcome – they were not engaged in an illegal conspiracy to do something else. And because their presence at the Refuge was in furtherance of their statutory rights of adverse possession, the government cannot argue that Mr. Bundy and the other defendants cannot avail themselves of their rights under the First and Second Amendments.
...Mr. Bundy's and others' "knowledge that the land is owned by the United States" was one of the primary purposes of their protest. The protesters asserted their adverse possession claim in hopes that it would force the government to bring their civil ejectment action, where Defendants and their group, the Citizens For Constitutional Freedom, could raise, inter alia, an argument under Article 1, Section 8, Clause 17 of the U.S. Constitution to challenge the federal government's illegal ownership

Mr. Bundy and the Citizens for Constitutional Freedom, by admission of the government, did in fact occupy and exclusively possess the property at the refuge, both the land and other property, and protected that occupation, and exercised control over that property. This fundamentally changed the nature of the property from what it was – to what its new possessors say it is. See The Uneasy Case for Adverse Possession, 89 Geo. L.J. 2419, 2424 (2001) (recognizing that adverse possessors must "act as a true owner would act" and this includes all typical elements of "control" and full "exercise of dominion"); see also Blumrosen, 1995 WL 918312, at *6 ("[B]efore the court's quieting of title, the adverse possessor can maintain an action for trespass against all who allegedly enter onto the adversely possessed property without his consent"). Thus, at the time of the occupation, the property at issue was not the Malhuer National Wildlife Refuge, it was the "Harney County Resource Center" as its occupiers had so determined, and the rules and control of the property was firmly Case 3:16-cr-00051-BR Document 1052 Filed 08/17/16 Page 24 of 28 Opposition to Government's Motion In Limine to Exclude Defense of Adverse Possession – 25 in the hands of the adverse possessors, and should have remained so, until the government lawfully succeeded at retaking possession – assuming it could.

Ammon Bundy should not be impeded from presenting his complete defense – that he did not engage in a conspiracy to impede federal officers, but rather that he engaged in a legitimate political protest, using the lawful principles and rights pertaining to setting up and attempting an adverse possession claim – and it was the government's overreaction, political motivations, and disdain for his personal political views that have distorted the nature of the protest and occupation, and tragically altered the course of what took place in January 2016. While at the "Harney County Resource Center," the occupiers exercised the well-recognized characteristics and requirements of adverse possession, and the government now admits that for its own strategic reasons, neither Mr. Bundy nor any other occupiers were ever expressly told to leave, and there is no evidence that the federal government ever sought to a) establish its lawful ownership; or b) challenge the adverse possession. Instead, the government skirted the issue entirely, used overwhelming force, arrested Mr. Bundy and his co-defendants, and charged them with conspiracy and federal firearms violations." (Marcus R. Mumford and J. Morgan Philpot, "Trial Memorandum and Opposition to the Government's Motion in Limine RE: Adverse Possession," August 17, 2016.)

48 Maxine Bernstein, "Indicted FBI Agent's Flippant Remark When Asked If He Fired His Gun Recounted at Trial," *The Oregonian*, July 31, 2018.
49 They asserted their 4th amendment right. "Th[eir] right... to be secure in their persons, houses, papers, and effects, against unreasonable searches and seizures" was being violated (U.S. Constitution, 4th Amendment).
50 "Shawna Cox Cell Phone Video from Inside LaVoy Finicum's Truck," *The Oregonian*, March 14, 2016.
51 Despite the very dangerous situation, the passengers in the truck did not employ foul language. What strong character. Sadly, the same can not be said about the agents in play. There is a very

telling memo from the lead investigator, Larry Wooten, who had been the lead case agent and investigator for the U.S. Bureau of Land Management after the tense NV Bundy Standoff. He discloses federal officers handling missions with far-reaching misconduct, recklessness, and unrestrained antipathy. You can find a copy of the memo in the appendix, section 3.

52 For the agents in dad's story to have employed the "Deadman's Roadblock" on that bend in the road requires justification in a court of law. Such a roadblock is designed to create a collision where there is no way to pass through. Such a tactic may only be used in exigent circumstances. Based on the adjudicatory process, the site of the roadblock was prepared beforehand on a blind curve, which shows no "exigency." These premeditated efforts on January 26th, 2016, on U.S. Route 395, are thus defined as an ambush. ("Vehicular Pursuits C," *Washington State Patrol Regulation Manual*, 2010.)

In a U.S. Supreme Court case, the late Justice Scalia saw that strict policy be in play when considering the use of a Deadman's Roadblock. Such policies on the topic mirror each other across state, federal, and bureaucratic lines as result of Justice Scalia's pen. To neglect adherence to such policy would be a seizure under the 4th amendment (Justice Antonin Scalia, *Brower v. Inyo County* (vol. 87-248), March 21, 1989).

53 In the planning of the ambush, the predetermined location of the deadman's roadblock was deliberately moved from Grant County to Harney County for the sole reason that Grant County is a United Nations (UN) free zone. The report from the investigation into the shooting, conducted by the Oregon Deschutes County Sheriff's office, provides continued evidence that the ambush was indeed premeditated. In the report, the questioned officer said that Grant County made it very clear "they were not friendly to law enforcement conducting any enforcement actions, and mainly the Federal Bureau of Investigation and federal agencies" by simply reiterating the counties status of a UN free zone. When the investigator asked, "Was that a factor in moving the location from Grant County to where you made the incident?" The officer answered, "Absolutely." What the legal ramification are for conducting Federal Bureau agency enforcement actions within a UN free zone, I do not know. I assume we will discover this in our trial. Be that as it may, it was enough to cause the ambushers to move their deadman's roadblock. ("Tri-County Major Incident Team Released Reports (Redacted), Officer Involved Shooting January 26, 2016 — Robert 'LaVoy' Finicum," Deschutes County Sheriff's Office, March 9, 2016).

54 Maxine Bernstein, "Acquits FBI Agent Accused of Lying in Finicum Shooting Case," *The Oregonian*, August 10, 2018.

55 "Shawna Cox Cell Phone Video from Inside LaVoy Finicum's Truck," *The Oregonian*, March 14, 2016.

"Ryan Bundy cell video from first traffic stop," *The Oregonian*, January 26, 2016.

56 The police photo showing the gun on Dad's person at the scene of his murder is all the evidence needed to prove that the gun was planted. A reenactment was done of a person drawing a similar gun from a side jean jacket pocket. The person performing the reenactment was sure to position the gun in the pocket just as the police photo indicated. This showed the effect of

drawing a gun in the position of the police photo. The viewers of the reenactment get to see that when the gun is drawn it is upside down in the person's hand. The person performing the reenactment also reenacted the natural position a person would have taken in planting a gun on a person who was lying on the ground. This natural motion that a person would have taken to plant the gun is what caused the gun to be planted incorrectly. To plant it correctly, the agent must recognize the gun had to be flipped to ensure its proper position in the jacket for it to be ready for draw. But flipping the gun as one is planting it is not natural and very easily overlooked. (Curt Kruse and Elias Alias, "The Assassination of LaVoy Finicum 3: The Planted Gun," *YouTube*, March 27, 2017.)

57 See appendix for the family's statement in response to March 8th, 2016, Bend, Oregon's news conference regarding the investigation of Dad's death.

58 It was discovered during testimony in the trial of FBI agent W. Joseph Astarita that there were two airplanes recording the scene. Part of the video footage viewed during court showed infrared footage of the agents walking back and forth in the small triangle area of where the agents were standing when the shots were fired. The video also showed the agents bending down several times as if they were picking something up. That day in court, it was also discovered that the scene had been left insecure for *nine* hours. No marking, no tape, vehicles were moved, and casings were moved and now are conveniently lost. Expert witness after expert witness testified on the stand during this trial how such conduct is in violation of standard protocol. Victoria Dickerson, who is a forensic scientist with the Oregon State Police, testified on the stand that she observed a well-worn path from Dad's body and his truck. It was also discovered during the trial that the agents in charge insisted on the standard agent interviews after a scene to be done in a group setting rather than individually. It was implied on the stand that this was done as a form of intimidation to the agents to keep any who might have a conscience quiet. (Jeanette Finicum, Press Conference live stream on Liberty Rising Facebook page, August 3, 2018.) We believe the gun they claimed Dad had on his person was planted. Many questions still stand. What were the agents hiding? Why were they not following protocol?

59 Jeanette Finicum, Press Conference live stream on Liberty Rising Facebook page, August 3, 2018.

60 For further understanding, study Brower v. County of Inyo, 489 U.S. 593 (1989), (penned by the late Justice Scalia). It was in this case that the U.S. Supreme Court ruled that the use of such a roadblock in a similar situation as Dad's, was a seizure under the 4th amendment. and that such a roadblock in and of itself was the lethal use of force. Thus, such lethal use of force must be justified.

61 Shawna Cox told me in an interview after Dad was killed, she and the others in the truck were forced to sit outside in the freezing air for five hours. FBI agent W. Joseph Astarita aggressively hit Ryan Bundy's hat off his head. (The video footage shows the agents doing the same to Dad's hat after they had shot and killed him, but Dad's hat was kicked off his head.) Her observation of the agents was one of panic. To her, it appeared that the agents were trying

to resolve on what their story would be for reporting. Shawna and the others were eventually taken to Portland, Oregon where they all stayed the night behind bars. Shawna was provided with a criminal complaint of which included everyone's name but Dad's. (Shawna Cox, Personal interview conducted by Thara Tenney, February 2016.)

[62] "Since the 1890s, cooperative federalists have been working toward collapsing political boundaries that safeguard life, liberty, and the pursuit of happiness. They have successfully changed the meaning of words (liberty and freedom) for those people who support the Constitution. LaVoy Finicum was label lynched as a domestic terrorist, a right-wing extremist on the verge of committing a Title 18, Section 2331 Act of Domestic Terrorism. As result, Oregon's local, state, and federal law enforcement, i.e. the FBI were engaged. LaVoy was profiled and considered the top threat in the Oregon occupation. The outcome was the agents' trapping him and the others on that highway in Oregon. [It seemed] they felt justified because in their view, as local, state, and federal law enforcement, they were stopping a potential domestic terrorist act from being committed by a potential domestic extremist who was either considered anti-government and/or a sovereign citizen who was rejecting federal authority. This language, defining these buzzwords, is found in the Department of Homeland Security lexicon on domestic extremism, which is a result of the 2001 Patriot Act. This is when the definition for domestic terrorism was redefined and added to title 18 of the federal code. This is how a person like LaVoy Finicum is shot in the back three times despite both hands being up in the universal sign of surrender.

If we continue to play complacent political checkers, the cooperative federalist will continue to play strategic political chess and collapse political boundaries. This will only result in needing more people like LaVoy to boldly stand to defend freedom and liberty and lose their lives in order to preserve America's Constitution." (M. Herr, "Beyond the Matrix," personal interview conducted by G. Edward Griffin, Red Pill University Expo, May 7, 2018.)

[63] Maxine Bernstein, "Jury Finds All Oregon Standoff Defendants Not Guilty of Federal Conspiracy, Gun Charges," *The Oregonian*, October 28, 2016.

[64] Mark Albright, "Missionary Moment: The Helmuth Hubener Story–Three LDS Teenagers who Defied Hitler." *Meridian Magazine: Latter-Day Saints Shaping Their World*. October 15, 2012.

[65] Adolf Hitler, *Mein Kampf*, 1925.

[66] Six days before Dad's life was taken, Kate Brown, the governor of Oregon, delivered two letters. One of the letters was to President Obama and the other to U.S. Attorney General Loretta Lynch and FBI director James Comey. In her correspondence Governor Brown label lynched the occupiers calling them "armed radicals" and requested "swift resolution." (Les Zaitz, "Kate Brown Presses Top Federal Officials for 'Swift' Action against Occupiers," *The Oregonian*, January 21, 2016.) You can find the letters in the appendix. Please see glossary for an explanation on *label lynching*.

[67] Paradoxically, despite the modern conviction rate favoring the side of the United States, it being 97 percent, the prosecuting team from both the Nevada and Oregon Bundy trials

openly expressed the Bundys and their friends were the *most dangerous defendants* they had ever tried. Ammon questioned how they, a church-going, cow-tipping, yes-ma'am and yes-sur kind of folk, could be the *most dangerous defendants* in the history of these seasoned U.S. prosecuting attorneys. They, in their tenure as prosecuting attorneys, must have crossed paths with some pretty scary people.

Was the root of their fear that the defendants had no criminal record? Did the fear stem from the reality that nothing they did warranted over five months in solitary confinement, over two years in prison, and the taking of their friends' life? While mentioning these possibilities, Ammon said the only plausible explanation for the United States prosecuting attorneys' *telling* statement was that they, just as described above, didn't control the mind. The outcome of these cases was not going to be easily manipulated with circumvented fiat. The innocent defendants understood their rights and possessed the strong ability to conceptualize, analyze, and evaluate information. They had proven that guile and intimidation wouldn't thwart their stand. The prosecution's fear was legitimate, and they did lose both cases. (Ammon Bundy, "What Really Happened," Speech at *Prophets, the Constitution, and Utah's Gadianton Robbers* in South Jordan, Utah, September 29, 2018.)

The U.S. prosecution's team inadvertently disclosing the root of their fear brings light onto why Dad was murdered on January 26, 2016. The motto of *the powers that be* working within the 21st century is just as those of old: be judge, jury, and executioner in order to eradicate those whose mind can't be controlled.

[68] History always repeats itself, if not learned from. Perhaps this is why the admonition has forever been to study scripture. Many historically recognizable people understood this. Patrick Henry, a leading figure in the American Revolutionary period, said, "I have but one lamp by which my feet are guided and that is the lamp of experience. I know of no way of judgment of the future but by the past" (Patrick Henry, *Give Me Liberty or Give Me Death!*, March 23, 1775). Solomon, the third king of Israel who is a direct-line ancestor of Jesus Christ, commented, "the thing that hath been, it is that which shall be; and that which is done is that which shall be done: there is no new thing under the sun" (Ecclesiastes 1:9). Alexander Hamilton, a New York delegate to the 1787 constitutional convention said in Federalist #20, "experience is the oracle of truth and where its responses are unequivocal they ought to be held sacred and conclusive" (James Madison and Alexander Hamilton, "The Insufficiency of the Present Confederation to Preserve the Union," *New York Packet, Federalist #20*, December 11, 1787). An unidentified writer said, "doing the same thing over and over again, but expecting different results" is indeed insanity.

We must study. The good of humanity urging the study of history is for the hoped probability of producing a positive butterfly effect from choices that reflect enlightenment gained through study. The types and shadows in scripture become pearls of great worth if likened in wisdom for current happenings to bring about better futures. The American founders understood this and took great care to be informed while never anticipating becoming key characters in a great work.

69 Adolf Hitler, *Mein Kampf*, 1925.

70 Dad briefly expressed this during a press conference on January 4th, 2016. He said, "Maybe I can bring this down to more of an emotional level, or a human level. Each one of you, each one of you here today are important. Individually! Individually! Each one of you are important. Not collectively. We are talking about you as an individual, as a human being." (*PBS NewsHour*. Video filmed in Burns, Oregon, January 4, 2016.)

71 Moroni 7:15.

72 Thomas Monson, "Choices," April 2016 LDS General Conference.

73 "Likewise shall we walk the path of pain; we cannot go to heaven in a featherbed. The Savior of the world entered after great pain and suffering. We, as servants, can expect no more than the Master. Before Easter, there must be a cross" (Thomas S. Monson, "The Paths Jesus Walked," April 1974 LDS General Conference).

74 Avraham Gileadi, *The Book of Isaiah: A New Translation with Interpretive Keys from the Book of Mormon*, 1988.

75 LaVoy Finicum, personal interview, January 2016.

76 On January 3rd, 2016, CNN analyst Juliette Kayyem published an article titled "Face it, Oregon building takeover is terrorism." (Juliette Kayyem, "Face It, Oregon Building Takeover is Terrorism," *CNN*, January 3, 2016.)

77 A reporter named Tim Walker who works for a news agency in the United Kingdom named Independent published an article wherein he referred to the occupiers as gun-toting farmers, armed wing-nuts, and "right-winged radicals." (Tim Walker, "Oregon Occupation: Inside the Malheur National Wildlife Refuge Where Armed Farmers are Protesting against Land Laws," *Independent*, January 6, 2016.)

78 On January 8th, 2016 video journalist Dena Takruri uploaded a video to their news politics YouTube channel wherein she peppered Dad with leading questions asking what would happen if they were brown, black or Muslim and chosen to occupy a federal building. (Dena Takruri, "Oregon Standoff: What If the Armed Men Were Black or Muslim?," *Direct from With Dena Takruri - AJ+*, January 8, 2016.)

On February 10, 2016, a *Washington Post* journalist boorishly commented, "The patriot movement would never let a good martyr go to waste. ...Born out of the whitewashed remnants of the radical racist-right movements of the 1960s and '70s...provided the structural framework for most of today's claims by so-called 'constitutionalists' and 'Patriots' — this movement has a long history of attracting violent actors who are willing both to kill and be killed in the name of their extreme worldview." (David Neiwert, "The Right-Wing Oregon Occupiers Have a Martyr Now, And That Should Worry Everyone," *The Washington Post*, February 10, 2016.)

79 Oregon Senator Ron Wyden likened the occupation unto a spreading virus. (Brent Weisberg, "Militia at Malheur: 'Virus was Spreading,'" *Koin 6*, January 29, 2016.)

80 On January 3rd, 2016, the *Washington Post* published an article wherein the first sentence read, "A group of armed anti-government activists…." (Carissa Wolf, Peter Holley, and Wesley

Lowery, "Armed Men, Led by Bundy brothers, Take Over Federal Building in Rural Oregon," *Washington Post*, January 3, 2016.)

81 On January 4th, 2016, Katie Herzog, a writer for *Grist* dedicated her column to suggest the ranchers thrive off "welfare" (Katie Herzog, "Here's What You Need to Know about the Crazy Ranchers' Standoff in Oregon," *Grist*, January 4, 2016).

82 The article title says a million words: "FBI footage shows Oregon militia member LaVoy Finicum reaching for waistband."
This small list of articles is just a hand full of thousands upon thousands of articles with headlines that were fabricated. (Evan Anstey, "FBI Footage Shows Oregon Militia Member LaVoy Finicum Reaching for Waistband," *WIVB.com*, January 29, 2016.)

83 Despite all the passionate negative responses and political maneuvering, the principle of *opposition in all things* in this context did not fail us. There were many who reached out in tender love, expressing their deepest respect. Occasion after occasion, people quietly offered to us their time, talent, and monetary assistance. It seemed it was always by divine design, because each time we were ministered to, it just so happened that it was in a time of most dire need. We witness that God is in the details.

84 Matthew 24:12

85 "Nearly a dozen Burns-area schools [were] closed. A voice message to parents on the Harney County School District 3 phone line said, 'staff and student safety is our greatest concern.'" (Anna King, "Schools in A Wide Swath Around Burns Close Down for Security," *Northwest News Network*, January 4, 2016.)

86 Control the mind, conquer a nation.

87 While Plato's reference to philosopher kings can be solely interpreted as a compliment, as such a class typically was found among the elite who on the surface esteemed knowledge, intelligence, wisdom, and simplicity of life as fundamentals in their effort to govern; I am suggesting philosopher kings can either bring about much good or bad depending on what lord they serve. Keep that in mind as I continue to use Plato's philosopher king term in this chapter.

88 "Occupation Leader Robert 'LaVoy' Finicum Speaks to Supporters, Protestors and the Media," *The Oregonian, YouTube*, January 18, 2016.

89 Dena Takruri, "Oregon Standoff: What If the Armed Men Were Black or Muslim?," *Direct from With Dena Takruri - AJ+*, January 8, 2016.

90 "Robert 'LaVoy' Finicum shooting in slow-motion," *The Oregonian, YouTube*, January 26, 2016.

91 Maxine Bernstein, "FBI Told State Police Not to Wear Body Cameras for 2016 Stop of Refuge Occupation Leaders," *The Oregonian*, February 3, 2018.

92 Department of Justice U.S. Attorney's Office District of Oregon, June 28, 2017.

93 Maxine Bernstein, "Judge Throws Out 2 of 5 Charges Against Indicted FBI Agent One Week Before Trail," *The Oregonian*, July 16, 2018.

94 Maxine Bernstein, "LaVoy Finicum Shooting: Prosecutors Seeking Missing Shell Casings, Metal Fragment from Ryan Bundy's Shoulder," *The Oregonian*, August 3, 2018.
As of October of 2018, the U.S. Department of Justice's Office of Inspector General is

investigating Astarita and several other FBI agents who responded to the 2016 occupation of the Malheur National Wildlife Refuge for a "lack of candor." Despite a jury not being able to convict him due to too much reasonable doubt, justice seekers are working to hold him accountable administratively (Conrad Wilson, "DOJ Investigates FBI Agents Who Responded to Malheur Occupation, *OBP*, October 25, 2018).

95 Maxine Bernstein, "Juror in FBI Agent Acquittal: 'It's Possible Someone Is Lying,'" *The Oregonian*, August 11, 2018.

96 Special Agent Larry Wooten, "Disclosure and Complaint Narrative in Regard to Bureau of Land Management Law Enforcement Supervisory Misconduct and Associated Cover-ups as well as Potential Unethical Actions, Malfeasance and Misfeasance by United States Attorney's Office Prosecutors from the District of Nevada, (Las Vegas) in Reference to the Cliven Bundy Investigation," *U.S. Department of Interior, Bureau of Land Management*, Boise, Idaho, 2018. Brian Maffly, "Interior Boss Blasts Fired Utah BLM Law Enforcement Agent," *The Salt Lake Tribune*, September 25, 2017.

97 Ibid.

98 See appendix for a short history of the Bundy Standoff and what moved Ammon Bundy to go to the aid of the Oregon Hammond ranching family.

99 To learn about this alteration, study the federal court proceedings from the 2017 U.S. v. Bundy, in which the judge declared a mistrial with prejudice. You can also begin your study by turning to the appendix to read the whistleblower memo by BLM chief investigator Larry Wooten that came forth in this trial just before the judge declared a mistrial.

100 Bryan Hyde, "NV Bundy Mistrial Report," 2018.
Richard Pérez-Peña and Julie Turkewitz, "Mistrial Declared in Bundy Armed Standoff Case," *The New York Times*. December 20, 2017.
Bryan Hyde, "Perspectives: Bundy Ranch, 4 Years Later," *St. George News*. April 16, 2018.
It was in this trial that we discovered Dan Love's falsification of the threat assessment, which was handed off to the Oregon FBI agent Greg Bretzing. This was two years after dad was shot and killed as result of label lynching, which the altered threat assessment contributed to. Bretzing is the new director of global security and special projects for the Lake Oswego-based Greenbrier Companies. Greenbrier transports uranium for the federal government. Could Greenbrier recruitment of former top FBI agents, the transport of uranium, and the ongoing Clinton Foundation uranium conspiracy be connected? Only time will tell. (Maxine Bernstein, "Oregon's Top FBI Agent Greg Bretzing to Retire in January," *The Oregonian*, November 30, 2016; "Greenbrier Enhances Senior Management Team with Addition of Experienced National Security Executive," February 7, 2017; National Archives and Records Administration, Part III, 49 CFR Parts 171, 172, and 173, Pipeline and Hazardous Materials Safety Administration of the US Department of Transportation, 2014; John Solomon, "FBI's 37 Secret Pages of Memos about Russia, Clintons and Uranium One," *The Hill*, October 1, 2018.)

101 Unfortunately, the innocent American citizens who were the victims of these agent's

misconduct were not afforded the same grace by the media. While in the thick of the abuse, they were relentlessly humiliated on a national level. It is this very type of human behavior that reflects Gileadi's sentiments of Isaiah's governing themes mentioned above. The wicked "exalt themselves now, persecuting the humble, but in the end God humiliates them." Isaiah has foretold the fate of all those who unrighteously persecute the humble. Such fate is one not desired.

[102] David Fry, "Occupant of the 2016 Oregon Malheur Wildlife Refuge Occupation and Acquitted Defendant," personal interview, 2016.

[103] See appendix the read the Larry Wooten Memo.

[104] Special Agent Larry Wooten, "Disclosure and Complaint Narrative in Regard to Bureau of Land Management Law Enforcement Supervisory Misconduct and Associated Cover-ups as well as Potential Unethical Actions, Malfeasance and Misfeasance by United States Attorney's Office Prosecutors from the District of Nevada, (Las Vegas) in Reference to the Cliven Bundy Investigation," *U.S. Department of Interior, Bureau of Land Management*, Boise, Idaho, 2018.

[105] Maxine Bernstein, "Bureau of Land Management Supervisor Contradicts Whistleblower's Concerns in Bundy Case," *The Oregonian*, December 17, 2017.

[106] Thara Tenney, "Daddy-Daughter Council," Personal interview, December 2015.

[107] Patrick Henry, *Give Me Liberty or Give Me Death!* speech, Richmond, Virginia, March 23, 1775.

[108] Luke Easter and Dee Cheeks, "A Strong Woman Versus a Woman of Strength."

[109] Sara Bibel, "6 Lesser-Known Facts About Audrey Hepburn," May 3, 2015.

[110] Our family was invited back January of 2018 and January of 2019 by local residents who took it upon themselves to host the second and third annual Oregon event reenactment, each year on the anniversary of Dad's murder, as a way to honor him and our family. We feel so honored and are grateful for these Oregonians courage to work toward building a community that maintains their political boundaries. It is our hope that each county within the United States has such a community maintaining their political boundaries.

[111] Maxine Bernstein, "Jury Finds All Oregon Standoff Defendants Not Guilty of Federal Conspiracy, Gun Charges," *The Oregonian*, October 27, 2016.

[112] This was the cowboy who was in the truck with Dad the day he was killed. One of the disputed shots discussed in the previously-before mentioned FBI agent W. Joseph Astarita trial hit Ryan in the shoulder that day. The metal fragment is still in his arm. What is interesting is how, during Ryan's detainment before his acquittal in Oregon, which was almost a year ago, one morning the guardsgarudes came into his cell abnormally early. I want to say it was before five a.m.. Of course, Ryan wasn't going to comply not knowing where they were taking him and what for. He knew his rights and was going to see to they were not infringed upon anymore then they already were. The guards would not inform him of the purpose. It ended up with the guards forcing him out of the cell and pushing and kicking him down the stairs. There was a fight. Ryan ended up finding out that they were taking him to an "emergency surgery" to have the metal fragment removed from his shoulder without asking for his consent. Of course, Ryan did not allow them to cut into his flesh and steal the evidence (Ryan Bundy,

Recorded phone call from prison, Oregon Federal Prison, 2016.)

113 The acquitted defendants who were involved in the 2014 Nevada Bundy standoff were being ruthlessly detained in the state of Nevada with what felt like no end in sight. The 2014 incident and the 2016 incident were fueled by the same issues, just different state and different date. Despite their innocence, wives and children continued to suffer the effects of jailed husbands and fathers. Tyranny was playing its course, and many were raw from the impact.

114 J.R.R. Tolkien, *The Lord of the Rings: The Return of the King*, 1955.

115 J.K. Rowling, *Harry Potter and the Deathly Hallows*, 2007.

116 Read the details of FBI and BLM Colorado event encounter in appendix.

117 Read the letter I wrote in appendix.

118 "Sovereign citizens are anti-government extremists who believe that even though they physically reside in this country, they are separate or 'sovereign' from the United States. As a result, they believe they don't have to answer to any government authority, including courts, taxing entities, motor vehicle departments, or law enforcement" ("Domestic Terrorism: The Sovereign Citizen Movement," Federal Bureau of Investigation, April 13, 2010).

119 The day was Thursday, October 27, 2016. Impeccable timing. We got the news literally in the middle of the event that evening.

120 Doctrine and Covenants 122:7

121 It's interesting to note that in today's world, this place they called their *promised land* is now known as the Americas.

122 1 Nephi 11:1

123 Even if I had, I would not publicly share without direction because I believe doing so would show great disrespect for the gift of a deeply sacred experience.

124 See glossary for the definition of *opposition in all things*.

125 D. Michael Stewart, "What Do We Know about the Purported Statement of Joseph Smith that the Constitution Would Hang by a Thread and that the Elders Would Save It?", lds.org, June 1976.

126 Mark Herr and B. Norton, *Speaking the Language of Liberty*, 2019.

127 Boyd K. Packer, "Little Children," LDS General Conference, November 1986.

128 Ezra Taft Benson, who served as the 15th United States Secretary of Agriculture for eight years and as an apostle for the Church of Jesus Christ of Latter-day Saints for 51 years, nine of which he was the 13th president of the Church, highly recommended a book called *None Dare Call It Conspiracy*, wherein it boldly states, "...the first job of any conspiracy, whether it be in politics, crime or within a business office, is to convince everyone else that no conspiracy exists." It goes on to interestingly say, "The most effective weapons used against the "conspiratorial theory of history" are ridicule and satire. Those who believe that major world events result from planning are laughed at. Of course, no one in this modern day and age really believes in the "conspiracy theory of history" - except those who have taken the time to study the subject.

[Be that as it may] FDR once said, "In politics, nothing happens by accident. If it happens you can bet it was planned that way." He was in a good position to know. If we were dealing with mere incompetence, our leaders should occasionally make a mistake in our favor. We shall attempt to prove that we are not really dealing with coincidence or stupidity, but with planning and brilliance.

[129] The opposite of this extrinsic influence of broadcasting conspiracy is understanding that it is "true doctrine [that] changes attitudes and behavior" and thus destiny. Such study "will improve behavior quicker than a study of behavior will improve behavior" (Boyd K. Packer, "Little Children," LDS General Conference, 1986). This simple truth gives credence to why all who love freedom and liberty must become an investigative student, on the lookout for the specific political truths that preserve said rights. Once found and deeply understood, the next task is an application of the principles. This unmatched technique to influence change is intrinsic.

[130] See glossary for definitions of *governed* and *governors*.

[131] See glossary for definition of *label lynching*.

[132] I don't remember exactly all I or he said that night, but I do remember saying, after I informed him I was a constituent of his, that I understood he was chairman of the United States House Committee on Oversight and Government Reform. I told him who my father and I were and, with uncontrollable tears welling in my eyes, I inquired as to what it was he was going to do to facilitate an investigation and much needed reform. He looked at me with a slight smirk (and no sign of human concern whatsoever) and said, "I can't believe we are even having this conversation." He proceeded to convey his hands were tied and that he could do *nothing*. On his part, there was no word or even effort to pretend he had any concern whatsoever for my father's loss of life, liberty, and pursuit of happiness. Not only was I shocked by his poor manners but disgusted with his hypocrisy. He failed epically when it came time to put his actions where his mouth was. He failed epically to be a human being and servant to the people whom he serves. He failed epically when it came time to uphold his oath to defend the Constitution. It seemed more energy went into his pretentious meet-and-greet speech than to the real-life human being sitting in front of him who was suffering as result of an out-of-control government.

[133] Frederic Bastiat, *The Law*, 1850, p. 24. See glossary for definitions of *governed* and *governors*.

[134] Ibid, p. 44.

[135] Mark Herr, Personal interview conducted by Thara Tenney, 2017.

[136] Mark Herr and B. Norton, *Speaking the Language of Liberty*, 2019.

[137] Numbers 21

[138] LaVoy Finicum, "Defend the Constitution: An Appeal to 50 Million Americans," *YouTube*, September 18, 2014, 5:50-5:57.

[139] Examples: limiting, contentious, manipulative, discouraging, pretentious, selfish, contemptuous, fearful, destructive, clingy, bewildered, etc.

[140] John 16:33

[141] Luke 12:32

[142] Mark 6:50

[143] Doctrine and Covenants 6:34

144 Doctrine and Covenants 45:33-35

145 Many fail to understand the improvements a steward brings to an untamed land. Those who exercise their liberty to live within today's modern world of virtual existence don't understand the relationship created between property owners, the land, and the property owners' fellow neighbors. The relationship of ownership is one of accountability, respect, and a recognition of humanity's dependence on earth's natural resources for survival. In Alma 44:5 of the Book of Mormon we learn ownership binds its people to the land. It is a relationship of giving. It is a partnership of work so humanity might be provided with life's necessities. There is no truer environmentalist than a God-fearing ranching cowboy.

146 See glossary for definition of *cooperative federalist*.

147 See glossary for definition of *label lynching*.

148 James Madison, et al., *The United States Constitution*, 1787.

149 It was Locke who described the origination of personal property to be the result of an individual mixing their labor (life/time plus liberty/choice) with unclaimed natural resource from the earth. Locke said, "Every man has a property in his own person. This nobody has a right to but himself" (Locke, *Second Treatise of Civil Government*, 1689). This principle is always on the forefront as Congress continues to write property right law.

150 "Fat and sassy cattle" is not necessarily a cattle term. It is simply a phrase Dad used when there were full water holes and plenty of tall green grass.

151 "Malheur National Wildlife Refuge, Oregon," *U.S. Fish and Wildlife Service*, January 5, 2016.

152 Each state defines water property rights of individuals in written law. In general, to have more than one water property right means the individual has ownership of water from three separate locations as defined by law. A rancher often has ownership of multiple water rights to ensure the operation of his business in cattle movement/grazing is successful.

153 Steven Hammond, "Hammond Family Facts and Events," Interview conducted by Ammon Bundy, *Bundy Ranch blog*, December 31, 2015, par. 3.

154 "Malheur National Wildlife Refuge, Oregon," *U.S. Fish and Wildlife Service*, January 5, 2016.

155 Steven Hammond, "Hammond Family Facts and Events," Interview conducted by Ammon Bundy, *Bundy Ranch blog*, December 31, 2015, par. 5.

156 Ibid., par. 6

157 Language within the 1986 study reveals clear apathy federal bureaucracy agents had toward the concept of private property ownership and the current owners of the land. Rather than allow the state and county to tend to the things of the state and county by correspondence with the property owners, seventeen federal agencies were listed at the top of these reports recipients as if they were the sole arbiters and owners. The language in the study suggests annoyance leveled at property owners who provide speed bumps in the process of federal land management. It suggested property owners had no say, whatsoever, as to what was going to happen to their private property. (*Malheur Lake Flood Damage Reduction Feasibility Study and Environment Impact Statement: Harney County, Oregon*, Walla Walla District Corps of Engineers, September 1986).

158 No wonder tensions were high between the citizens of Harney County and bureau agents:

"Refuge officials [even] acknowledge[d] that some people in the community resent[ed] the federal agency" (Rachel Odell, "Ranchers and Officials Feud Over Water Rights," *Bend Bulletin*, May 16, 2004).

[159] Fast forwarding a few years, this very binder was shared with Ammon Bundy during their correspondence before the Oregon occupation. Ammon Bundy was one of the acquaintances mentioned at the beginning of the chapter that also was studying the Hammond case. Ammon was the driving force behind the occupation. When he was arrested the day Dad was murdered, all of Ammon's things were taken into custody and, since then, he has not had returned to him any of his items, including that three-ring binder (Ammon Bundy, Telephone interview, 2018).

[160] Steven Hammond, "Hammond Family Facts and Events," Interview conducted by Ammon Bundy, *Bundy Ranch blog*, December 31, 2015, par. 32.

[161] If struggling to understand what the language "wildlife is considered as an accepted beneficial use" means, it is helpful to learn the nature of water, forage, and right-of-way laws. Not having access for continual beneficial use puts the property owner at risk of losing their ownership. "In Oregon, water rights may be lost through common law abandonment, if a water user ceases beneficial use with intent to abandon. Without intent to abandon, however, a water right (or part thereof) can be lost through non-use" ("Oregon Water Law," *Red Lodge Clearinghouse*, October 15, 2010). The federal agents were not ignorant of this fact, which is why their pattern of tactics over the years was to prevent the family's continual beneficial use. As long as the cowboy was running his cattle on his recorded section of land, for the cattle to drink the water, eat the grass, and travel on their cow trails from point A to point B, then the cowboy was getting continual beneficial use of his property rights. At any point that the cowboy decided to stop running cattle, causing the natural resources to no longer be continually used, law stated to that, in time, the cowboy would forfeit his right to his recorded water, forage, and right-of-way property rights.

[162] See the glossary for definition of *natural-born person*.

[163] The pool of blood in the shape of the Finicum cattle brand at the foot of this Malheur Refuge red-crowned crane creates a disturbing imagery of Dad's murder scene. Our story is one that witnesses law to be granting wildlife more rights than a human. See the appendix for the story behind Dad's cattle brand, which is the L V symbol in the art.

[164] Kathie Durbin, "Ranchers Arrested at Wildlife Refuge," *High Country News*, October 3, 1994.

[165] Dwight and Steven were "taken into custody by nine federal agents, five of whom were armed. The Hammonds were charged with two counts, each a felony: 'disturbing and interfering with' federal officials or federal contractors. They spent one night in the Deschutes County Jail in Bend, Oregon, and a second night behind bars in Portland." Dwight then was forced to appear before a federal magistrate, at which point he was released without bail. A hearing on the charges was postponed and the federal judge never set another date (Ibid).

[166] Steven Hammond, "Hammond Family Facts and Events," Interview conducted by Ammon Bundy, *Bundy Ranch blog*, December 31, 2015, par. 10.

[167] "Open or Closed Range," Oregon Department of Agriculture, *Oregon.gov*.

168 In addition to acting as if they were above the law in regard to Oregon open range law, they also conducted their business as if they were above the Steens Mountain Cooperative Management and Protection Act of 2000, which states in section 113, E2 that "the Secretary shall be responsible for installing and maintaining any fencing required for resource protection within the designated no livestock grazing area" ("H.R. 4828, 106th Cong., 20 (2000) (enacted). Steens Mountain Cooperative Management and Protection Act of 2000," Section 113. Land Use Authorities, E, 2).

Gregory Paul Walden, who is the U.S. Representative for Oregon's 2nd congressional district and helped to author the act said in an interview, "The intent was pretty clear that the government had the responsibility to do the fencing (related to the no livestock grazing area), not the ranchers" (Andrew Clevenger, "Fence Fight on Steens Mountain," *The Bulletin*, April 25, 2014, par. 14). And yet the Hammond family was removed from the land and their ranch was cut in half. Walden went on to say, "[I am] frustrated with BLM's efforts to circumvent Congress' intent" (ibid, par. 18).

169 Steven Hammond, "Hammond Family Facts and Events," Interview conducted by Ammon Bundy, *Bundy Ranch blog*, December 31, 2015, par. 10.

170 "Antiterrorism and Effective Death Penalty Act," 1996, Section 18 U.S.C. 844 (f) (1)

171 Fire #1. In 2001, Steven Hammond performed a routine prescribed burn on their ranch, which was properly reported. It is most important to note how prescribed burns are a common method that Native Americans and ranchers have used for centuries to improve upon the health and productivity of forage. Furthermore, United States Code (USC) 18-1855 exempts property owners from prosecution for reasonably setting fire to their land as doing so is exercise of proprietary rights. This U.S. code will later be reiterated as this discussion deepens with the hope to have this concept really resonate in your mind. We need to understand that fire setting is not solely an unlawful pyromaniac act.

Unfortunately, the fire in 2001 got onto public land and burned 127 acres of grass. The Hammonds put the fire out. There was zero concern about the burn breaching the boundary from federal agents at that time.

Fire #2. In 2006, five years after the first incident, an unprecedented lightning storm caused multiple little fires that quickly joined together. The entire countryside was inflamed ("Annual Fire Report Pacific Northwest Area," 2006). With the intent to protect forage property and their homestead, Steven Hammond started a backfire on their private property. This act alone was the catalyst that choked the fire's quick movement that had already destroyed thousands of acres. Steven's mother, Susie Hammond said, "There was fire all around them that was going to burn our house and all of our trees and everything. The opportunity to set a backfire was there and it was very successful. It saved a bunch of land from burning. ...The BLM asserts that one acre of federal land was burned by the backfire but determining which fire burned which land is 'a joke' because fire burned from every direction" (Carrie Stadheim, "Two Members of Oregon's Hammond Family to Serve Time in Prison After Burning 140 Acres of BLM Land," November 14, 2015, par. 23-24).

What did the local federal agents do in response to this second fire? They promptly visited the Harney County Sheriff's office and filed a police report accusing Dwight and Steven Hammond of arson for starting the backfire. A few days later a Range Conservationist, i.e. Range Con. or Rangeland Management Specialist from the Burns, Oregon District BLM office invited Steven to meet over coffee in town. Steven accepted. Just as coffee time was coming to a close, he was arrested by the Harney County Sheriff, Dave Glerup and BLM Ranger Orr. Steven was ordered to return home and bring his father Dwight back to the station. Both Dwight and Steven were again charged with several offenses against Oregon State law. The Harney County District Attorney reviewed the accusation, evidence, and charges, and determined that the accusations against Dwight and Steven Hammond did not warrant prosecution and dropped all the charges (Steven Hammond, "Hammond Family Facts and Events," Interview conducted by Ammon Bundy, *Bundy Ranch blog*, December 31, 2015).

172 Dwight and Steven's faces burned through the screens of all sizes with the headline "Domestic Terrorist" and "Arsonists." Susie Hammond (wife and mother) said, "I would walk down the street or go in a store, people I had known for years would take extreme measures to avoid me" (Steven Hammond, "Hammond Family Facts and Events," Interview conducted by Ammon Bundy, *Bundy Ranch blog*, December 31, 2015). Now, after the occupation, the Hammonds take extreme measures to avoid anything associated with Dad or the Bundy family (Carrie Stadheim, "Two Members of Oregon's Hammond Family to Serve Time in Prison After Burning 140 Acres of BLM Land," 2015).

173 "United States of America v. Steven Dwight Hammond and Dwight Lincoln Hammond Jr.," 2012, p. 17, l. 25.

174 James Madison, et al., *The United States Constitution*, 1787, Article 3, Section 2, Clause 1. "United States of America v. Steven Dwight Hammond and Dwight Lincoln Hammond Jr.," 2012, p. 26, ll. 3-9, 18-19

175 Chocolate cake was served in the courtroom promptly after the Justice's last verdict of his career. Dwight and Steven were also provided cake. Why didn't the agents wait to serve the cake until after the defendants had left the room? If I were the defendant, it would be very difficult to pretend to enjoy the cake as my new reality of unjust imprisonment was soberly sinking in. If it were me, watching a room full of people who successfully violated my life, liberty, and pursuit of happiness, glut themselves with smiles and cake would have made me sick. What a morbid twilight zone. The Hammonds did not have to be convicted and yet everyone ate their cake.

176 The United States Code (USC) 18-1855 Timber Set Afire, which reads,
Whoever, willfully and without authority, sets on fire any timber, underbrush, or grass or other inflammable material upon the public domain or upon any lands owned or leased by or under the partial, concurrent, or exclusive jurisdiction of the United States, or under contract for purchase or for the acquisition of which condemnation proceedings have been instituted, or upon any Indian reservation or lands belonging to or occupied by any tribe or group of Indians under authority of the United States, or upon any Indian allotment while the title to the same shall be held in trust by the Government, or while the same shall remain inalienable by the allottee without the consent of the United States, shall be fined under this

title or imprisoned not more than five years, or both.

This section shall not apply in the case of a fire set by an allottee in the reasonable exercise of his proprietary rights in the allotment. ("18 U.S. Code § 1855 - Timber set afire")

177 Alexander Hamilton said in Federalist #79, "In the general course of human nature, a power over a man's subsistence amounts to a power over his will."

178 Ruth Danielsen, "Denial of Application for Grazing Permit Renewal 3602564 - Hammond Ranches Inc.," Letter to Bureau of Land Management, Burns District Office Rhonda Karges – Andrew/Steens Field Manager, Frenchglen, Oregon, August 11, 2014.

179 "United States of America v. Steven Dwight Hammond and Dwight Lincoln Hammond Jr.," 2014

180 James Madison, et al., *The United States Constitution*, 1787, 5th and 8th Amendments.

181 All too often alcohol and drugs are used to cope with the depression associated with not being successful at putting food on the table. The effects of addiction are very toxic, and the sting is felt for generations. This negative energy is amplified as dignity is extinguished when such communities regulated out of business are compelled to live off of government subsidy, starve, or be forced to abandon their choice of pursuit of happiness-their heritage.

182 Mohave County, Arizona

183 Steven Hammond, "Hammond Family Facts and Events," Interview conducted by Ammon Bundy, *Bundy Ranch blog*, December 31, 2015.

184 The numbers of Harney County, Oregon:
> Number of Oregonians drawing unemployment benefits...: 166,526
> Benefits paid to Harney County in 2008: $3 million
> Average check amount in Harney County: $294.64
> Benefits paid statewide in 2008: $947.1 million
> Average check amount statewide: $308.45
> Highest average check amount: Washington County, $329.53
> Lowest average check amount: Malheur County, $232.60

(Amy Hsuan, "Harney County Losing Jobs, Hopes", September 29, 2009; *State of Oregon Employment Department*).

185 The crazy results of the ebb and flow of presidential policy in each new administration, birthed by the fifteen executive departments, restricting or reopening the use of natural resources across the nation, is one reason why the things of the state and county were to be managed by the state and county (Amy Hsuan, "Harney County Losing Jobs, Hopes," *The Oregonian*. September 29, 2009, par. 23).

186 LaVoy Finicum, *The Objective*, interview, Burns, Oregon, January 2016.

187 Please understand, rural poverty in the West is known to be greater than urban poverty in the West (Alemayehu Bishaw and Kirby G. Posey, "A Comparison of Rural and Urban America: Household Income and Poverty," *United States Census Bureau*, December 2016).

188 Mark Herr, et al. *Macro Understanding of Centralized Governance 3.4* [Level 2 Student

Workbook]. Center for Self Governance, Murfreesboro, Tennessee, 2015.
189 You will read of regionalism in a later chapter.
190 See glossary for the definition of *adverse possession*.
191 LaVoy Finicum and Ammon Bundy, interview, Burns, Oregon, January 2016.
192 See appendix for "A short history of the Bundy Standoff and what moved Ammon Bundy to go to the aid of the Oregon Hammond ranching family."
193 LaVoy Finicum, interview by P. Openshaw.
194 Mark Herr, *LaVoy: Dead Man Talking*, Video interview of LaVoy showcased in Documentary number 3, 2018.
195 Dena Takruri, "LaVoy Finicum Talks Oregon Standoff," AJ+, *YouTube*, January 7, 2016.
196 Mark Herr, "Beyond the Matrix," Interview by G. Edward Griffin, Red Pill University Expo, May 7, 2018.
197 LaVoy Finicum, "The Objective," Interview, Burns, Oregon, January 2016.
198 See appendix to read my social media post explaining my experience at ground zero.
199 There is something peaceful about the song of a bird. Whenever I hear the sound, it always takes me back to a moment in time when Dad shared with me why he enjoyed his morning runs so much. He loved the song of the *mourning* dove.
200 See glossary for definition of *adverse possession*.
201 To set the stage, it is helpful to know that, for most of Dad's life, he cherished the bald eagle. Its symbolism spoke to his soul. Whenever speaking of the bird, there was always a deep reverence in his tone that left us kids feeling its majesty.
202 Ezra Taft Benson, "Christ and the Constitution," LDS General Conference, Salt Lake City, Utah, April 1967, par. 7.
203 The day prior she had inadvertently made a large bean soup for a church activity that was actually scheduled for a different date. Rather than toss it out, she brought it to the refuge.
204 Russ Ramsey, "Tell Me A Story, Louis L'Amour," *The Rabbit Room*, January 7, 2009, par. 5.
205 See appendix to read the statement from the Hammond family on President Trump's pardon as well as their updated statement upon their return home.
206 "Hammonds Out of Prison After Presidential Pardon," *News Channel 21 KTVZ.com*, July 10, 2018.
207 Exactly three years and two days after Dad's murder, on January 28th, 2019, Public Lands Council (PLC) President Bob Skinner and National Cattlemen's Beef Association (NCBA) President Kevin Kester gave the following statement in response to the reissuance of Bureau of Land Management (BLM) grazing permits to Hammond Ranches:
In light of a full and unconditional presidential pardon, the reissuance of the Hammond Ranches' grazing permits is the final step in righting the egregious injustices the Hammonds faced. This is the culmination of years of effort on behalf of this industry to restore a family's livelihood. We speak on behalf of the livestock producers nationwide in saying thank you to Acting Interior Secretary David Bernhardt and his team who worked to correct the hardships this family faced. (Bob Skinner and Kevin Kester, "Ranching Industry Praises Department of Interior After Agency Reissues Hammond Ranches' Grazing Permit," *NorthernAg.net*,

January 28, 2019).

[208] Dad said, lamenting about the Hammond case, "If they [the federal government] have the power to do good, as they have the power to do bad, they shouldn't have the power. Look what they have done to the Hammonds." On February 6th, 1792 James Madison argued the same principle of limited control granted to the federal government during the debates in the several state conventions of the adoption of the federal Constitution. Please see the appendix to read a portion of his speech.

[209] Thomas S. Monson, "In Quest of the Abundant Life," *Ensign*, March 1988.

[210] James Madison, et al., *The United States Constitution*, 1787.

[211] See glossary under *five main categories* for further explanation of each.

[212] A republic is indeed control elected representative who are to follow and defend the rulebook, which is the law created within the limits defined by the Constitution. The Constitution creates political boundaries that require continual maintenance by both the governed and governors to prevent it from becoming a tyranny. See Federalist # 51.

[213] John Adams, *A Defence of the Constitutions of Government of the United States* (Vol. 1), 1787, preface III, par. 2 and preface IV, par. 1.

[214] John Locke, *Second Treatise of Civil Government*, 1689, ch. 16.

[215] Thomas Jefferson, et al., *The Declaration of Independence*, 1776.

[216] Ibid, p. 1, par. 2.

[217] Land and resources equal power, which is why all ancient and modern opportunist desire it. The American way is to divide the land and resources amongst its people from one side of the nation to the other in the form of personal property, thus avoiding centralized control.

[218] John Adams, *A Defence of the Constitutions of Government of the United States* (Vol. 1), 1787, preface III, par. 1.

[219] Ibid, preface VI, par. 2

[220] Ibid, preface IX, par. 1

[221] Review "Chapter 3: Lords of the Message" to rediscover some of the tactics used to achieve this "one great mission."

[222] Look to your state constitutions to understand the controls of the state executive and legislative branches. (LaVoy Finicum, "LaVoy vs. BLM part 1 - 8/14/15," *YouTube*, August 14, 2015, 19:20-29:56).

[223] "The Administration," *WhiteHouse.gov*, 2018.

[224] Ibid.

[225] "The Cabinet," *WhiteHouse.gov*, 2018.

[226] To view the list of 411 agencies, bureaus, services, commissions, departments, and administrations that dot the nation, visit https://www.usa.gov/sub-agencies

[227] Fundamental to a republic is law that applies equally to all people while protecting the rights of both the majority and minority.

[228] This is a huge red flag because CFR is the executive branch 'writing' law.

[229] In Federalist #47, James Madison stated, "The accumulation of all powers, legislative, executive, and judiciary, in the same hands, whether of one, a few, or many, and whether hereditary,

self-appointed, or elective, may justly be pronounced the very definition of tyranny." See the appendix to read some of his words.

[230] John Adams, *A Defence of the Constitutions of Government of the United States* (Vol. 1), 1787, preface IX, par. 1.

[231] You read of this in the Hammond case.

[232] Thomas Jefferson, "Letter to Edward Carrington," *Jefferson Papers*, January 16, 1787, p. 1, par. 4.

[233] My family's story as well as the those of the Bundy and Hammond families are good modern-day examples of the fruits of administrative law birthed from the different departments of the executive branch. Our stories illustrate why it is so dangerous for the executive department to make the law, adjudicate the law, and enforce the law. The only available due process is to go through the department wearing all three hats. Such a formula clearly explains the modern conviction rate favoring the side of the United States, it being 97 percent.

Unfortunately, there are other ways in which the executive is assuming the legislative controls. One is through executive order. Executive orders take effect and are forced upon the people. Another modern-day breach of the legislative political boundary set up in the United States Constitution is through judicial activism. They make a declaration on what protocol will be and it is enforced upon the people. Both executive orders and judicial declarations are treated as if the mandates had passed through the constitutional legislative process-congress. The attitude is that such a breach is okay. As this continues the powder keg will continue to heat until enough people's unalienable rights begin to be trampled upon, then the bloody political pendulum swings to mob rule and anarchy. The founders could see this and, as result, set up the parameters to work toward avoiding this dangerous, violent swing.

[234] This dangerous consolidation of control is happening not only within the federal government but also *in each* state government.

[235] See appendix for "A short history of the Bundy Standoff and what moved Ammon Bundy to go to the aid of the Oregon Hammond ranching family."

[236] My pointing out and focusing on the consolidation of control between the legislative and executive branches is merely to suggest that there are other methods used wherein the Constitution of the United States isn't followed. There are many ways the Constitution is violated. I have chosen to focus on this topic because of its application to our story.

[237] The BLM is one of those 411 agencies briefly mentioned before. These agencies write and enforce—at gunpoint—their own regulatory law. Remember the BLM has no legislative control granted by the United States Constitution.

[238] The cattle were placed, for the summer, on a feedlot where there was access to water. Her father-in-law kindly organized this place at the Finicum homestead just a few miles from her home. This was such a relief to Mom during this most difficult time after losing her husband. Furthermore, at no charge, friends provided and hauled enough feed for the cattle to get through the summer. You readers who are not in the ranching business, understand that this is a significant financial donation. I thank God that there are good people in this world who truly follow the biblical admonition to tend to widows.

This miracle was the beginning of many as Mom continued to choose to press on, advocating for her rights. People would just show up out of the blue. Well-to-do strangers would contact her, ready to give. These types of miracles were a continued witness that her God was well aware of her fight and was providing a way through the storm.

By the kindness of others, she and her cattle made it through the summer. Toward the end, she strangely found herself taking a deeper liking to the cattle as she daily tended to their sustainment. She now better understood Dad's emotional connection to his herd.

[239] While fighting with them in a way continued to legitimize their supposed authority, Mom was not in a position to stand as Dad had in asserting his rights. Just as I honor Dad's sacred freedom of conscience, I too honor my mother in hers.

[240] With the help of Dr. Angus McIntosh, who has a Bachelor's in Animal Science from BYU, a Master's in Range Science from CSU, and a Doctorate in Range Science and Agricultural Economics from NMSU, is the executive director of Range Allotment Owners Assn., director of Natural Resource Law and Policy Research for the Land and Water U.S. Foundation, academic member of the American Society of Farm Managers and Rural Appraisers, an adjunct professor of agricultural and natural resource economics, was an expert witness in the U.S. Court of Federal Claims and Federal District Courts of AZ, CO, NV, and OR, and has given testimony before the State Legislatures of AZ, NM, MT, and NV on water rights, range management, and federal regulatory impacts on property rights, Mom edited and signed the contracts knowing her late husband was rolling over in his grave. Her expressed sentiment was that she was not LaVoy and had to do things her way. Her way was that she was willing to try to work with the BLM, but that the contract was no longer going to one-sided, hence the edits. She wrote the outrageous check to cover the fees and fines, which was to be hand delivered by her mother-in-law the day she was to begin driving the cattle to her winter range.

[241] In 2015, Dad publicly announced on the Bryan Hyde radio show his cancelation of the contractual relationship he had with the Bureau of Land Management (BLM) (LaVoy Finicum, "June 25, 2015; LaVoy Publicly Announcing the Cancellation of his BLM Contract," *YouTube*. March 23, 2016; Mori Kessler, "Arizona Rancher Follows in Bundy's Footsteps," *St. George News*, November 1, 2015).

[242] To further your study of the patterns of tyrants, read *The Suffering of the Saints* by Jack Monnett, which is an account of a community of people who suffered greatly.

[243] Years prior, during a campout, Dad while lying awake with Mom in their bedroll under the stars, gave Mom a specific star. Her star shone brightly that lonely sleepless night as she contemplated what she was going to do. Its glow gave her courage and comfort.

[244] This political philosophy will be discussed in the following chapter. It is there where I review the dangers of regionalism's practice in more detail.

[245] Ironically, after dad had canceled his contractual agreement with the BLM, his water tank, the life blood of his cattle operation, was stolen from and then sabotaged by BLM agents (LaVoy Finicum, "BLM Stealing Water," *YouTube*, August 7, 2015; LaVoy Finicum, "Water Tank Sabotage," *YouTube*, September 10, 2015). Remember, his water property right is just like owning your car. Their taking his water without notice or permission is like if someone

took your car from your garage without notice or permission. These reprisals started before dad went to Oregon. See the timeline of events. Ammon Bundy was right when he said, when they can't control your through their deceptive contractual agreements, they truly resort to the tactics of "a big bully who is not intelligent enough to convince people to follow" (Ammon Bundy and Gavin Seim, "Bundy. The True Story—Official," *YouTube*, December 18, 2017).

246 Please understand what the BLM's original purpose was. It was to advise the President by providing a survey of the land. After all, the purpose of the heads of the fifteen executive departments was to do just that, to advise the president. The intent never was for the 411 agencies working under the fifteen executive departments to become overlords who both legislate and enforce law. Our American Constitution gives no control whatsoever to the executive branch to *author and enforce* law. What does that mean? It means the BLM has no authority to be writing the law they enforce. I might also add that nowhere in the U.S. Constitution does it give authority for the executive branch to own and control mass lands. According to Article 1, Section 8, Clause 17 of the Constitution, the federal government's land use is narrowly outlined. Departments of the executive branch stepping outside their narrowly defined controls is the simplest explanation I can give for the why behind the Bundy standoff, Hammond incarceration, and the Oregon occupation.

247 Base property means: Land that has the capability to produce crops or forage that can be used to support authorized livestock for a specified period of the year, or (2) water that is suitable for consumption by livestock and is available and accessible, to the authorized livestock when the public lands are used for livestock grazing.
Code of Federal Regulations. (CFR). *Transfer of Grazing Preference* [4110.2-3], Title 43.

248 Has not the American people already fought painful, bloody, wars to free themselves of whimsical overlords?

249 In the past Mom was always confronted by male agents.

250 See Timeline of Events in the appendix.

251 There are many other families who have suffered for many years at the hands of federal agencies that I do not want to neglect. Once you start looking, you will be overwhelmed by the number of families who have suffer from these abuses.

252 Even though we all have the right to seek change, it seems in today's culture there is less adherence to "prudence, ...dictat[ing] that Governments long established should not be changed for light and transient causes..." (Thomas Jefferson, et al., *The Declaration of Independence*, 1776, par. 2). This explains the *why* behind the current system's functions resembling more a democratic oligarchy rather than a republic and *why* maintenance to the system is so important to ensure the integrity of life, liberty, and our pursuit of happiness.
Again, if we were currently functioning within the same republican system that was established over 200 years ago, how was it that, in 2014, American agents were pointing guns at a crowd of American civilians who were standing to defend their private property? This event came to be known as the Bundy Standoff. Suggesting the Bundy Standoff to not be a people becoming '*undone*,' I don't know what is. Not to mention the suffrage of the Hammond family and the murder of my father. See the appendix for "A short history of the Bundy Standoff

and what moved Ammon Bundy to go to the aid of the Oregon Hammond ranching family."
253 See glossary under *five main categories* for further explanation of each.
254 A republic is indeed control by elected representative who are to follow and defend the rulebook, which is the law created within the limits defined by the Constitution. The Constitution creates political boundaries that require continual maintenance by both the governed and governors to prevent it from becoming a tyranny. Read Federalist # 51
255 Mark Herr, et al., "Macro Understanding of Centralized Governance 3.4," Center for Self Governance, Murfreesboro, Tennesee, 2015, p. 61, par. 1-4.
256 Let's jump back to earlier when you read of this same president to also be the one who established 51 wildlife refuges during his tenure as president, including the Malheur National Wildlife Refuge in Burns, Harney County, Oregon ("About the Refuge," U.S. Fish & Wildlife Service, January 5, 2016). Please connect the dots by recognizing this president spearheaded the beginning of developing codified regions within the United States over 80 years ago. These regions are governed, not by the voice of the people, but by meritocracy.

You also have read how it was President Franklin D. Roosevelt who also established the Executive Office of the President (EOP) in 1939, just four years after the *Regional Factors in National Planning and Development* report was delivered to him. The question now lies: are the fundamental shifts to the American system of government during President Franklin D. Roosevelt's tenure a coincidence? No, no government action is spontaneous. It is thought out, planned, and strategically executed. On the surface, well thought out governance sounds comforting unless it is the work of the contending force to freedom and liberty.
257 Karl Marx, *The Communist Manifesto*, 1848.
258 Amy Bishaw and Kirby G Posey, "A Comparison of Rural and Urban America: Household Income and Poverty." *United States Census,* December 8, 2016.
259 John Adams, *A Defence of the Constitutions of Government of the United States* (Vol. 1), 1787
260 Scott Bradley, *To Preserve the Nation: In the Tradition of the Founding Fathers,* 2009.
261 Harold L. Ickes, et al., "Regional Factors in National Planning," December 1935, p. 2, par. 8.
262 Remember the earth is a gift to all humanity with the charge for all to pursue their choice (liberty) of creativity to produce useful and beautiful things. This charge indeed creates *private property* for the laborer that no other has a right to without '*just compensation.*' When all people go about using their life and liberty to pursue their chosen form of happiness, by nature, *private property* becomes convoluted, demanding a need for governance. But when aggrandizing dispositions refuse to be tempered, refuse obedience to natural law, refuse respect for others' life, liberty, and private property, refuse mastery of self, it becomes realized that not just any given governance will do. A specifically engineered system becomes necessary to protect humanity against itself.

Remember nature's God left "the world unfinished for man to work his skill upon" (Monson, "In Quest of the Abundant Life", 1988). This also applies to the search, discovery, development, and experimentation of systems of governance. There was no '*user manual*' per say, with all the intricate details of successful governance. The people's charge was to toil, search, and then develop. As with any system's beta, each system of governance called for troubleshooting, maintenance of the good, and out with the bad.

263 Ammon Bundy, phone interview, 2018
264 Harold L. Ickes, et al., "Regional Factors in National Planning," December 1935, p. 207.
265 "... Property, per se, has no rights; but the individual—the man [or woman]—has three great rights, equally sacred from arbitrary interference: the right to his life, the right to his liberty, the right to his property.... The three rights are so bound together as to be essentially one right. To give him his life but deny him his liberty, is to take from him all that makes his life worth living. To give him his liberty but take from him the property which is the fruit and badge of his liberty, is to still leave him a *slave*" (George Sutherland, "Principle or Expedient?" 1921, p. 18).
266 Harold L. Ickes, et al., "Regional Factors in National Planning," December 1935, p. viii, par. 8.
267 Ibid., par. 7
268 John Adams, *A Defence of the Constitutions of Government of the United States*, preface III, par. 1, 1787.
269 Harold L. Ickes, et al., "Regional Factors in National Planning," December 1935, p. viii. par. 3.
270 Ibid., par. 6
271 Helaman 6:39, 7:4-5
272 Mark Herr, et al., "Macro Understanding of Centralized Governance 3.4," Center for Self Governance, Murfreesboro, Tennesee, 2015, p. 61, par. 1-4.
273 I hope you recognize the red flag here. CFR is the executive branch *'writing'* law.
274 James Madison, et al., *The United States Constitution*, 1787. Article 4, Section 4.
275 "Republican form of government," *Conservapedia*, 2017.
276 LaVoy Finicum, "LaVoy vs. BLM part 1 8/14/15," *YouTube*, August 14, 2015.
277 James Madison, et al., "The Constitution of the United States," 1787, Tenth Amendment.
278 For a comprehensive training on applied civics please visit: centerforselfgovernance.com. The mission of Center for Self-Governance is to "stabilize civil society and increase political influence, improve networking skills, and expand personal growth and development."
279 George Washington, "Washington's Inaugural Address," April 30, 1789, p. 1, par 4.
280 George Washington, *Washington's Inaugural Address*, April 30, 1789.
281 LaVoy Finicum, "Part 2, June 25, 2015, LaVoy Publicly Announcing the Cancellation of his BLM Contract," *YouTube*, 46:00-48:36.
This is a radio segment LaVoy did with Bryan Hyde in Cedar City, Utah. It was published to LaVoy's YouTube channel three months after he was killed.
282 M. A. Soupios and Panos Mourdoukoutas, *The Ten Golden Rules of Leadership*, 2015.
283 'Know thyself' is an Ancient Greek aphorism known to originate from Thales (Thales, "αλῆς "). This Delphic maxim is also known to be inscribed in the pronaos of the Temple of Apollo at Delphi according to the Greek writer Pausanias. Thales' phrase was later added upon by the philosopher Socrates who said, "The unexamined life is not worth living" (Pausanias). If interested, you many consider reading the works of M.A. Soupios and Panos Mourdoukoutas.

They have organized a powerful short read with classical wisdom for modern leaders titled *The Ten Golden Rules of Leadership.*
284 Ezra Taft Benson, *Stand up for Freedom: Teachings on Liberty*, 2012.
285 To offer a little more detail on how serious I am about Dad never wearing shorts, he would wear Wranglers and boots to the beach, of all places.
286 Please refer to the Good Reads list to springboard into a deeper study. But study is not enough. Robert Welch was an American businessman, political activist, author, sponsor of anti-Communist causes, and co-founder of the John Birch Society conservative group in 1958, where his positive influence was strongly felt until his death in 1985. It was he who was widely known for the slogan, "Education without action leads to frustration and action without education leads to fanaticism." We must get out in the community, build relationships, and mutually pledge with others to maintain the integrity of the local government system.
287 Read President George Washington's 1789 Inaugural address.
288 Ponder how your time is spent. How might there be adjustments made to allow the necessary time needed to understand principles of governance that truly yields freedom and liberty? How might there be adjustments made to allow the necessary time needed to provide the obligatory checks and balance to the systems operators?
289 J.R.R. Tolkien, *The Lord of the Rings: The Fellowship of the Ring*, 1954.
290 Henry B. Eyring, "Mountains to Climb," LDS General Conference, Salt Lake City, Utah, April 2012.
291 See glossary for the definition of *human government.*
292 See *Five Main Categories* in glossary to review these.
293 LaVoy Finicum, *Only by Blood and Suffering: Regaining Lost Freedom* (1st ed.), 2015.
294 George Washington, *Washington's Inaugural Address*, April 30, 1789.
295 Dr. James McHenry, *Papers of Dr. James McHenry on the Federal Convention of 1787*, May 14, 1787.
296 Thomas Jefferson, "Letter to Joseph C. Cabell," February 2, 1816, par. 5.
297 Mosiah 29:16-17, 32, 34
298 Alma 46
299 Alma 48:17
300 Doctrine and Covenants 101:77
301 LaVoy Finicum, "BLM Update," *YouTube*, September 7, 2015.
302 See the glossary for a definition of *community of keep the republic.*
303 For a comprehensive training on applied civics please visit centerforselfgovernance.com. The mission of Center for Self-governance is to "stabilize civil society and increase political influence, improve networking skills, and expand personal growth and development." (Mark Herr, Interview by Thara Tenney, 2017).
304 Helaman 7:4-7
305 2 Kings 6:16
306 Dr. James McHenry, *Papers of Dr. James McHenry on the Federal Convention of 1787*, September

17, 1787.
[307] John Adams, Letter to Abigail Adams, July 3, 1776, par. 5.
[308] Acts 10:38
[309] Gordon B. Hinckley, et al., *The Living Christ: The Testimony of the Apostles*, January 1, 2000, par. 2-3.
[310] Bill Norton, "Understanding Your Most Fundamental Rights, Part 1," *The Language of Liberty* Series, 2017, p.1, par. 1.
[311] Ibid., p. 2, par. 1
[312] The happiness or unhappiness of a person is a form of property that is intangible, of which others have no control of or authority over, no matter how hard they try, to take it away.
[313] 2 Nephi: 2:27
[314] Bill Norton, "Understanding Your Most Fundamental Rights, Part 3," *The Language of Liberty* Series, p.1, par. 1.
[315] George Sutherland, "Principle or Expedient?" New York State Bar annual address, 1921, p. 18.
[316] Frederic Bastiat, *The Law*, 1850.
[317] Karl Marx's theory in *The Communist Manifesto* clearly states an abolition of property as one of the top goals to accomplish communism. The Americanist doctrine is one that promotes and protects the sacred right to personal property ownership. Please re-read the chapters titled "Murder Mayhem," "History of the Hammond Ranching Family," "Dad Crossing the Rubicon," and "Regional Government," as well as "A short history of the Bundy Standoff and what moved Ammon Bundy to go to the aid of the Oregon Hammond ranching family" and whistleblower Larry Wooten Memo sections within the appendix to be reminded of modern-day results of practicing principles of communism.
[318] Frederic Bastiat, *The Law*, 1850.
[319] John Taylor, *The Government of God*, 1830, p. 3 par. 5.
[320] Mark Herr, et al., "Macro Understanding of Centralized Governance 3.4," 2015, p. 13, par. 2.
[321] "This is the heartbeat of our existence. Without, we have no thought, words, or action… the end of which is chaos and oppression" (Mark Herr, Interview conducted by Thara Tenney, 2017).
[322] Mark Herr, et al., *Foundation in Self Governance 3.2*, Center for Self Governance, Murfreesboro, Tennessee, 2015. p. 16.
[323] Frederic Bastiat, *The Law*, 1850, p. 24, par. 5.
[324] Ibid., p. 44, par. 2
[325] Today's abortion laws are one of many very good examples of this (Ibid., p. 31, par. 2).
[326] Mark Herr, Interview conducted by Thara Tenney, 2017.
[327] Frederic Bastiat, *The Law*, 1850, p. 44, par. 2.
[328] Revelations 12:9
[329] Ezra Taft Benson, *Stand up for Freedom: Teachings on Liberty*, 2012, p. 34.
[330] Ephesians 6:12
[331] Mark Herr, et al., "Macro Understanding of Centralized Governance 3.4," 2015, p.13, par. 2.

332 It is foolish to assume one can give that which they do not have. Also read Matthew 26.
333 Matthew 7:3-5
334 Ezra Taft Benson, *Stand up for Freedom: Teachings on Liberty*, 2012, p. 34.
335 Alexander Fraser Tytler, "The Decline and Fall of the Athenian Republic," Lecture, 1801.
336 Dad being moved to action was the direct result of the violent swing of this political pendulum. He personally witnessed the suffering of his fellow ranching neighbors at the hands of bureaucratic rogue agents unwilling to be confined by the rule of law. While the conflict associated with drawing a firm line in the sand to defend personal property was so out of character for him, he understood that doing so often is the last line of defense when all other methods fail at preserving life, liberty, and the pursuit of happiness. Dad never was one to be at the face of trouble. But in April of 2014, he took courage to rise and stand with fellow Americans with the resolve much like unto original committees of safety to be as gentle as possible but as firm as necessary in the defense of their property rights that had been under attack using tactics of pretended legislation and intimidation. Please see the glossary for an explanation on committees of safety.
337 See the "Divine Destiny of America" section in the appendix.
338 Ezra Taft Benson, "Prepare, Then Fear Not," LDS General Conference, April 1967.
339 Frederic Bastiat, *The Law*, 1850, p. 6, par. 5.
340 LaVoy Finicum, "LaVoy Publicly Announcing the Cancellation of his BLM Contract," Radio interview by Bryan Hyde, *HD Radio Show*, June 25, 2015.
341 Remember in a previous chapter John Adams boldly foresaw the outcome should the separation of controls ever combine under one head. He said, "We shall learn to prize the checks and balances of a free government, ...if we recollect the miseries of [history] which rose from their ignorance of them. The only *balance* [emphasis added] attempted against the ancient kings was a body of nobles; and the consequences were perpetual altercations of rebellion and tyranny, and butcheries of thousands upon every revolution from one to another. When the kings were abolished, the aristocracies tyrannized; and then no *balance* [emphasis added] was attempted but between aristocracy and democracy. This, in nature of things, could be no *balance* [emphasis added] at all, and therefore the pendulum was forever on the swing" (John Adams, *A Defence of the Constitutions of Government of the United States*, 1787, preface iii, par. 1). He continues, "Without...an effectual *balance* [emphasis added] between them [the divided governmental controls], ...it must be destined to frequent unavoidable revolutions; if they are delayed a few years, they must come, in time" (ibid., preface vi, par. 2). He continues on, "If there is one certain truth to be collected from the history of all ages, it is this: That the people's rights and liberties, ...can never be preserved without ...separating the *executive* power from the *legislative* [emphasis added]. If the executive power, or any considerable part of it, is left in the hands either of an aristocratical or a democratical assembly, it will corrupt the legislature as necessarily as rust corrupts iron, or as arsenic poisons the human body; and when the legislature is corrupted the people are undone" (ibid., preface ix, par. 1).
342 If America's founders had not been true to their divinely gifted passion to establish a *superior*

system of governance to those that had already been employed and failed, make no mistake, nature's God would have prepared others willing to do the work because this land called America has a divine purpose. It was to become "the Lord's base of operations in ...latter days," an ensign to all other nations, a means to fulfill promises made long ago by God to our fathers of old; Abraham, Isaac, and Jacob (Ezra Taft Benson, "Prepare, Then Fear Not," April 1967, p. 1). Refer to *Divine Destiny* in the appendix to learn more on the topic of America fulfilling promises made long ago.

Doctrine and Covenants 101:79-80.

[343] David Barton, "Evidence of America's Christian Heritage," *YouTube*, November 29, 2016.

[344] Ezra Taft Benson, *Stand up for Freedom: Teachings on Liberty*, 2012.

[345] Many suffering victims of injustice throughout time must have, at one point or another, asked why nature's God allows toxic governance to persist with its abhorrent consequences of blood and bondage. I know many have wondered if lasting peace, freedom, and prosperity is the fate for only a superior class. Disaffected as one may be, it is tender to discern God to be no respecter of persons and piercing to grasp how humanity brings upon itself its own condemnation.

Such are *beautiful yet frightening* fathoms.

Yes, men are that they might have joy and God's work and glory is to see this come to pass, but such a feat can only be accomplished when man chooses obedience to correct eternal laws. It is up to *each individual* to gain enlightenment. Then the charge is to press forward in obedience to the degree of enlightenment gained while always relying on the grace of God for further truth and light. Alas, not all seek enlightenment, nor do all press forward in obedience, as discussed in chapters previous.

Holy scripture rings from the dust, tales of God's dealings with those who have gone before. Examining these vaults of history reveals God's unwavering pattern to tenderly direct all to the path that leads to true living waters. It is a personal choice to drink or not to drink. Scriptural accounts unfold humanity's pattern of disobedience. We read in the Bible how this disobedience always will bring upon ourselves, our families, our communities, and eventually our nations heavy condemnation and sure destruction. It has been decreed in another testament of Christ, "Inasmuch as ye shall keep my commandments ye shall prosper in the land; and inasmuch as ye will not keep my commandments ye shall be cut off from my presence" (2 Nephi 4:4).

Despite the destructive path of disobedience, we also read of God's pattern to always have his hand outstretched. His being is full of mercy. We see, within the same pages of scripture that tell of the people's disobedience, other stories of powerful deliverance as result of repentance and obedience. Such elegies clearly express life's "beauties that pierce like swords" (Lewis, "The Gods Return to Earth", 1954).

While nature's God is all-powerful, infringing upon the agency (choice) of His children is something that cannot be done. Doing so would violate eternal law, by which even God is bound. Humbling it is to contemplate the unyielding patience as He waits for His children to choose to follow His wisdom and guidance. Contemplating the painful consequences associated with humanity's relentless pride cycle is overwhelming. Yet, God perfectly wades through the suffering associated with watching His children consistently destroy possibilities for true happiness and lasting prosperity. His deep desire for His children is that they might learn to apply correct principles so as to experience as much happiness as possible during earth life, but this cannot be done by force. It must be chosen.

346 Thomas Paine, *Common Sense*, 1776.

347 Dr. James McHenry, *Papers of Dr. James McHenry on the Federal Convention of 1787.* September 17, 1787.

348 Could have Franklin grasped the covenant associated with the new nation in that if the people disobeyed "the laws of nature and of nature's God," then their prosperity would cease?

349 See *Committee of Correspondence and Safety* in glossary for definition.

350 Dr. Richard R. Beeman, "Perspective on The Constitution: A Republic, If You Can Keep It," par. 2.

351 Brnjamin Franklin, Address presented at Constitutional Convention, Philadelphia, Pennsylvania, 1787.

352 Doctrine and Covenants 121:39

353 Some refer to this 'naked greed' as the natural man. Such tendencies are not exclusive to just one class of people. This is found in us all, both governed and governors, and must be tempered. To the natural man, it is ever so appealing to live befitting from the toil of others. Such a concept is even better if doing so can be under the guise of culturally accepted, codified, systematic redistribution. This provides comfortable justification for both the participating governors and governed.

354 Frederic Bastiat, *The Law*, 1850, p. 5, par. 3.

355 Thomas Jefferson, et al., *The Declaration of Independence,* July 4, 1776, par. 2.

356 Thomas Jefferson, "Letter to William Charles Jarvis," September 28, 1820.

357 Boyd K. Packer, "Teach Them Correct Principles," Speech presented at Member Finance Fireside, February 18, 1990.

358 Some of the most obvious tactics include and but not limited to torture by hanging, crucifixion, beheading, burning alive, financial ruin, character defamation, tar and feathering, labor/sex slavery, or the taking of personal property without just compensation.

359 LaVoy Finicum, *Only by Blood and Suffering: Regaining Lost Freedom* (1st ed.), 2015.

360 Doctrine and Covenants 98:9

361 Alexander Fraser Tytler, "The Decline and Fall of the Athenian Republic," Lecture, 1801.

362 Ezra Taft Benson, *Stand up for Freedom: Teachings on Liberty,* 2012, p. 34.

363 Russ Ramsey, "Tell Me A Story, Louis L'Amour," *The Rabbit Room,* January 7, 2009, p. 1.

364 William Ernest Henley, "Invictus," *Poetry Foundation*, April 2018.

365 Alma 42:4; 34:32

366 Moses 4:1, 3

367 Moses 4:2

368 See glossary for a definition of *agency*.
Ezra Taft Benson, *Teachings of Presidents of the Church*, ch. 3, par. 7.
369 2 Nephi 2:27
370 Dr. Seuss, *Oh, the Places You'll Go!* 1990.
371 Isaiah 9:6
372 Gordom B. Hinckley, et al., *The Living Christ: The Testimony of the Apostles* January 1. 2000, par. 1.
373 Revelations 12:9
374 A third of the host of heaven were deceived by Lucifer's crafty campaign (Revelations 12:7-9; Doctrine and Covenants 29:36-37; LDS KJV, Bible Dictionary, "Atonement").
375 Revelations 12:7-9; Ephesians 6:12
376 These two forces have been known by different titles throughout history. There is Satan on one hand and Christ, the only begotten, on the other. In Joshua's time in the Old Testament, there were the gods of the Amorites on the one hand and the Lord of Israel on the other. In New Testament time, Paul spoke of the "works of the flesh" on the one hand and the "fruits of the spirit" on the other (Galatians 5). An angel testified to Nephi in the Book of Mormon how there are only two churches, the church of the devil on the one hand and the church of the Lamb of God on the other (1 Nephi 14). Today we often talk of selfishness on one hand and a life of service on the other, domination of the state on one hand and personal liberty on the other, or communism on one hand and free agency on the other (David O. McKay, "Two Contending Forces," Speech delivered at Brigham Young University, May 18, 1960).
377 Doctrine and Covenants 10:27
378 Those who were denied the opportunity for a mortal body suffer in captivity as there is no more progression for them. The opportunity for a body meant the opportunity for progression. It meant the opportunity to prepare for things to come. It meant a chance to practice our freedom of choice to earn our reward, whether great or small. One can only wonder what the eternal fate will be for those who choose to be on the wrong side during morality when "to have been on the wrong side of the freedom issue during the war in heaven meant eternal damnation" (Ezra Taft Benson, "Not Commanded in All Things," 1965, par. 11).
379 LaVoy Finicum, "Defend the Constitution: An Appeal to 50 Million Americans," *YouTube*, September 18, 2014.
380 Daniel 3:17-18
381 The name Helmuth Hubener might be one familiar to some. This young boy, just like Dad, was a member of the Church of Jesus Christ of Latter-Day Saints who had unprecedented courage. Hubener's stand was in countering propaganda of the Nazi regime, while Dad's was in standing for the American rule of law against domestic adversaries. Different eras, countries, and forms of government, but courage to stand for the harder right just the same. Hubener's story, just like Dad's, is one that shocks the conscience. At the age of 17, Hubener became the youngest opponent of the Third Reich to be sentenced to death. He was arrested, brutally interrogated, and later tortured in Gestapo prisons, and finally beheaded by guillotine

for merely authoring, printing, and anonymously disseminating news he heard on forbidden radio broadcasts. He was charged and executed on the pretense of conspiracy to commit treason against the Nazi regime just as the Oregon occupation defendants were charged with conspiracy against the U.S. government. Many thank God for our current American jury system because Hubener's story is a type of what the fate would have been for the remaining occupation defendants if our jury system was not set in place. Instead the defendants were found not guilty by a jury of their peers (Maxine Bernstein, "Jury Finds All Oregon Standoff Defendants Not Guilty of Federal Conspiracy, Gun Charges," October 27, 2016).

Hours before Hubener's scheduled execution, he shared his last thoughts on paper. He said, "I am very grateful to my Heavenly Father that my miserable life will come to an end tonight — I could not bear it any longer anyway. My Father in Heaven knows that I have done nothing wrong. I am just sorry that I had to break the Word of Wisdom at my last hour. I know that God lives, and He will be the Just Judge in this matter. I look forward to seeing you in a better world!—Your friend and brother in the Gospel, Helmuth" (Mark Albright, "Missionary Moment: The Helmuth Hubener Story–Three LDS Teenagers who Defied Hitler," October 15, 2012).

[382] Dr. Seuss, *Oh, the Places You'll Go!* 1990.
[383] Ezra Taft Benson, *Stand up for Freedom: Teachings on Liberty*, 2012. p. 34.
[384] Joshua 24:15; 2 Nephi 31:19.
[385] Isaiah 32:3
[386] Philpot, Attorney for Plaintiff, J. Morgan. The United States District Court For The District Of Oregon. January 25, 2018. Civil Complaint Demand For Jury Trial
[387] Maxine Bernstein, "As Government Shutdown Continues, Oregon U.S. Attorney's Office Seeks Delays in Civil Cases, Reduces Staff," *The Oregonian*, January 3, 2019.
[388] While the burden of maintaining our attorney's retainer through this time was painful, we have been given the strength and comfort we prayed for.
[389] LaVoy Finicum, "Nevada Ranch Standoff One Cowboy's Witness," *YouTube*, April 26, 2014.
[390] LaVoy Finicum, Interview conducted by Glenn Beck, *The Glenn Beck Program*, April 14, 2014.
[391] Cami Cox Jim, "Battle for the West: Ranchers unite against Grand Canyon Watershed National Monument; STGnews Videocast," *St. George News*, May 2, 2015
[392] LaVoy Finicum, "June 25, 2015; LaVoy Publicly Announcing the Cancellation of His BLM Contract," *YouTube*, March 23, 2016.
Mori Kessler, "Arizona Rancher Follows in Bundy's Footsteps," *St. George News*, November 1, 2015.
[393] LaVoy Finicum, "BLM Update," *YouTube*, September 7, 2015.
[394] ibid.
[395] LaVoy Finicum, "BLM Stealing Water," *YouTube*, August 7, 2015.
[396] LaVoy Finicum, "Water Tank Sabotage," *YouTube*, September 10, 2015.
[397] LaVoy Finicum, "By Dang I'm Mad," *YouTube*, October 14, 2015.
[398] Marcus Mumford and J. Morgan Philpot.

399 "Watch Ammon Bundy Speak on Wildlife Refuge Occupation," *PBS NewsHour, YouTube*, January 4, 2016.

400 Kelly House, "Arrival of Rifle-toting 'Patriots' Breaks Relative Calm at Oregon Standoff Compound," *The Oregonian*, January 9, 2016.

401 Les Zaitz, "Kate Brown Presses Top Federal Officials for 'Swift' Action Against Occupiers," *The Oregonian*, January 21, 2016.

402 Shuf1111, "Burns Oregon—Ranchers Sign to End Their Contract with BLM," *YouTube*, January 25, 2016.

Maxine Bernstein, "Oregon Standoff: Ranchers, Including Ex-con, Renounce Grazing Permits," *The Oregonian*, January 24, 2016.

403 Rick Koerber, "Second Eyewitness: Chronicling the Tragic Ambush and Murder of LaVoy Finicum," *The Free Capitalist*, January 31, 2016.

404 Les Zaitz, "Oregon Standoff Spokesman Robert 'LaVoy' Finicum Killed, Bundys in Custody after Shooting Near Burns," *The Oregonian*, January 26, 2016.

405 Code of Federal Regulations (CFR), "Transfer of Grazing Preference" [4110.2-3], Title 43.

406 "Oregon Standoff Timeline: 41 Days of the Malheur Refuge Occupation and the Aftermath," *The Oregonian*, February 14, 2017.

407 ibid.

408 Maxine Bernstein, "Jury Finds All Oregon Standoff Defendants Not Guilty of Federal Conspiracy, Gun Charges," *The Oregonian*, October 27, 2016.

409 Maxine Bernstein, "Ammon Bundy's Lawyer Tackled, Tasered by U.S. Marshals in a Surreal Ending to the Oregon Standoff Trial," *The Oregonian*, October 28, 2016.

410 Maxine Bernstein, "Oregon's Top FBI Agent Greg Bretzing to Retire in January," *The Oregonian*, November 30, 2016.

"Greenbrier Enhances Senior Management Team with Addition of Experienced National Security Executive," *GBX*, February 7, 2017.

"Federal Register," 2014.

411 Kathy Gibson Boatman, "Sylvia Allen Holds Stakeholder Meeting on Federal Overreach," *Mogollon Rim News*, March 3, 2017.

412 "The Firing of FBI Director James Comey," *CNN*, 2017.

413 Maxine Bernstein, "LaVoy Finicum Shooting: Prosecutors Seeking Missing Shell Casings, Metal Fragment from Ryan Bundy's Shoulder," *The Oregonian*, August 3, 2017.

414 Steven Dubois, "Bundy Lawyer from Ore. Trial Agrees Not to Practice in State," *The Seattle Times*, January 8, 2018.

415 Glenn Thrush and Julie Hirschfeld Davis, "Trump Picks Christopher Wray to Be F.B.I. Director," *The New York Times*, June 7, 2017.

416 Brian Maffly, "Interior Boss Blasts Fired Utah BLM Law Enforcement Agent," *The Salt Lake Tribune*, September 25, 2017.

417 Special Agent L. Wooten, "Disclosure and Complaint Narrative in Regard to Bureau of Land Management Law Enforcement Supervisory Misconduct and Associated Cover-ups as well

as Potential Unethical Actions, Malfeasance and Misfeasance by United States Attorney's Office Prosecutors from the District of Nevada, (Las Vegas) in Reference to the Cliven Bundy Investigation," Letter to Andrew D. Goldsmith, Bureau of Land Management, 2017.

[418] Richard Pérez-Peña and Julie Turkewitz, "Mistrial Declared in Bundy Armed Standoff Case," *The New York Times*, December 20, 2017

[419] Maxine Bernstein, "Let Out of Jail after Nearly Two Years, Ryan Bundy Arrives to Court in Style," *The Oregonian*, November 14, 2017.
Sarah Childress, "In Surprise Ruling, Ammon Bundy Released on House Arrest," *PBS Frontline*, November 30, 2017.

[420] Laura Jarrett and Pamela Brown, "Ex-FBI Deputy Director Andrew McCabe is Fired—and Fires Back," *CNN*, March 17, 2018.

[421] "Hammonds Out of Prison After Presidential Pardon," *News Channel 21 KTVZ*, July 10, 2018.

[422] Maxine Bernstein, "Juror in FBI Agent Acquittal: 'It's Possible Someone is Lying,'" *The Oregonian*, August 11, 2018.

[423] Conrad Wilson, "DOJ Investigates FBI Agents Who Responded to Malheur Occupation," *Oregon Public Broadcasting*, October 25, 2018.

[424] Maxine Bernstein, "As Government Shutdown Continues, Oregon U.S. Attorney's Office Seeks Delays in Civil Cases," *The Oregonian*, January 3, 2019.

[425] *Tenorio v Pitzer*, 10th Circuit.

[426] LaVoy Finicum, "Freedom's Cry," *YouTube*, January 30, 2016.

[427] Jordan Page, "Ballad of LaVoy Finicum (Cowboy's Stand for Freedom)," *YouTube*, January 27, 2016.

[428] See story on how Dad came to be known as #tarpman in the extras section of the appendix.

[429] "Watch Ammon Bundy Speak on Wildlife Refuge Occupation," *PBS NewsHour*, *YouTube*, January 4, 2016.

[430] Delta City Council Meeting Minutes. August 2, 2016. Delta City Council.

[431] Pat Sunderland, "Residents Protest 'Sovereign Citizen' Label," *Delta County Independent*, August 10, 2016.

[432] See story on how Dad came to be known as #tarpman in the extras section of the appendix.

[433] James Madison, Speech presented at the Debates in the Several State Conventions of the Adoption of the Federal Constitution, 4:427-9.

[434] Ezra Taft Benson, "Prepare, Then Fear Not," Address given at the New England Rally for God, Family, and Country, July 4, 1966, p. 58-62.

[435] "Abrahamic Covenant," LDS KJV, Bible Dictionary, p. 602.

[436] "Israel," LDS KJV, Bible Dictionary, p. 708.

[437] Gen. 49:3-4

[438] "Abrahamic Covenant," LDS KJV, p. 602.

[439] W. Cleon Skousen, *5000 Year Leap*, 1981, p. 3, par. 4-7; p. 4 par. 1-2.

[440] Joseph Smith-History 1:5

[441] Joseph Smith-History 1:6

442 John Taylor, *The Government of God*, 1830, p. 3 par. 5.
443 "Apostasy," *True to The Faith: A Gospel Reference*, 2004, p. 13–14.
444 "The Gospel of Jesus Christ Was Restored through the Prophet Joseph Smith," *What We Believe*, LDS.org, December 2012.
445 See glossary for definition of *ordinances*.
446 "Restoration of the Gospel," *True to The Faith: A Gospel Reference*, 2004, p. 135–39.
447 Russel M. Nelson and Wendy W. Nelson, "Hope of Israel," Speech at Worldwide Youth Devotional, June 3, 2018.
448 "Temple List," *LDS.org*.
449 Moses 1:39
450 John Taylor, *The Government of God*, 1830, p. 94, 95-97.
451 Joseph Smith-History 1:53, 59
452 "Restoration of the Gospel," *True to The Faith: A Gospel Reference*, 2004, p. 135–39.
453 ibid.
454 Doctrine and Covenants 13, 128:20, 29:36-37; Joseph Smith-History 1:68-72
455 Doctrine and Covenants 109
456 Doctrine and Covenants 110
"Restoration of the Gospel," *True to The Faith: A Gospel Reference*, 2004, p. 135–39.
457 L. Tom Perry, Speech at Regional Conference, February 2014.
458 Ezra Taft Benson, "Prepare, Then Fear Not," Address given at the New England Rally for God, Family, and Country, July 4, 1966, p. 58-62.
459 "2017 Statistical Report for 2018 April Conference," March 31, 2018.
460 Mark 12:17
461 Ezra Taft Benson, "Prepare, Then Fear Not," Address given at the New England Rally for God, Family, and Country, July 4, 1966, p. 58-62.
462 Review the timeline of events.
463 The guards were so past feeling. I listened to each of Ammon and his brother Ryan's recorded phone calls that their wives posted to social media. These men were put in solitary confinement for unacceptable reasons. While each phone call I listened to outraged me, the blasphemous religious bigotry was the most insulting and witness of how past feeling those agents were. I know the Lord sustained these men as they were at the hands of tyrants.
464 Joseph Bauman, "'No More Moo by '92' on West Ranges May Be a Simplistic Approach," *Deseret News*, August 2, 1990.
465 April 12, 2014. Dad was there.
466 "Since the 1890s, cooperative federalists have been working toward collapsing political boundaries that safeguard life, liberty, and the pursuit of happiness. They have successfully changed the meaning of words (liberty and freedom) against those people who support the Constitution. LaVoy Finicum was label lynched as a domestic terrorist, a right-wing extremist on the verge of committing a Title 18, Section 2331 Act of Domestic Terrorism. As a result, local, state, and federal law enforcement, i.e. the FBI were engaged. LaVoy was profiled and

considered the top threat in the Oregon occupation. The outcome was the agents' trapping him and the others on that highway in Oregon. [It seemed] they felt justified because in their view, as local, state, and federal law enforcement, they were stopping a potential domestic terrorist act from being committed by a potential domestic extremist who was either considered anti-government and/or a sovereign citizen who was rejecting federal authority. This language, defining these buzzwords, is found in the Department of Homeland Security lexicon on domestic extremism, which is a result of the 2001 Patriot Act. This is when the definition for domestic terrorism was redefined and added to title 18 of the federal code" (Mark Herr, "Beyond the Matrix," Personal interview conducted by G. Edward Griffin, Red Pill University Expo, May 7, 2018).

This is how a person like LaVoy Finicum is shot in the back three times despite both hands being up in the universal sign of surrender. This is how good men like the Bundy boys are imprisoned for years.

Laura Myers, "Reid Calls Bundy Supporters 'Domestic Terrorists,'" *Las Vegas Review-Journal*, April 17, 2014.

[467] Dad was in this meeting.
[468] See glossary for definition of *adverse possession*.
[469] Ken Heaton, Audio recording of the funeral of LaVoy Finicum, Kanab, Utah, February 5, 2016.
[470] Tony Dokoupil, "Oregon Occupier LaVoy Finicum Warns FBI He'd Take Death Over Jail," *NBC News*, January 6, 2016.
[471] LaVoy Finicum, "Tarp Man," Personal interview conducted by Thara Tenney, 2016.
[472] Doctrine & Covenants 84:14; Abraham 1:2
[473] Doctrine & Covenants 131:1–4, 132:19, 29
[474] Genesis 17:5–6; Abraham 2:9, 3:14
[475] Abraham 2:9
[476] Abraham 2:11
[477] Genesis 17:7
[478] Galatians 3:26–29, 4:1–7; Doctrine & Covenants 84:33–40
[479] 3 Nephi 20:25–26
[480] *Lowery v. Garfield County*, 122 Mont. 571, 208 P.2d 478, 486
[481] *Field v. Sosby*, Tex.Civ.App., 226 S.W.2d 484, 486
[482] *Ryan v. Stavros*, 348 Mass. 251, 203 N.E.2d 85
[483] *Sertic v. Roberts*, 171 Or. 121, 136 P.2d 248
[484] *Field v. Sosby*, Tex.Civ.App., 226 S.W.2d 484, 486
[485] *U.S. v. Chatham*, D.C.N.C., 208 F.Supp. 220, 226
[486] "Adverse Possession," *Black's Law Dictionary*, 2019.
[487] 2 Nephi 2:27
[488] Moses 4:3
[489] "Agency," *True to the Faith*, 2004.

490 Edward Day Collins, *Committees of Correspondence of the American Revolution*, 2015, vol. xii, p. 245, par. 2.
491 Ibid., p. 271, par. 4
492 Mark Herr, Interview conducted by Thara Tenney, 2017.
493 Mark Herr, 2019
494 Mark Herr, et al., "Macro Understanding of Centralized Governance 3.4," 2015, p. 7, par. 2.
495 Thomas Jefferson, "Letter to Joseph C. Cabell," *The Jefferson Papers*, 1816.
496 Ibid., p. 1, par. 5.
497 LaVoy Finicum.
498 "Freedom," *Noah Webster Dictionary*, 1828.
499 Gen. 32:28
500 Gen. 35:10
501 2 Sam. 1:24, 23:3
502 Rom. 10:1, 11:7; Gal. 6:16; Eph. 2:12
503 "Israel," LDS KJV, Bible Dictionary, p. 708.
504 Mark Herr, *Anti-Label Lynching Act [LaVoy's Law]*, Bill draft, 2018.
505 Thomas Jefferson, "Letter to Isaac H. Tiffany," April 4, 1819.
506 "What is Natural-Born?" *Black's Law Dictionary*, 2018.
507 Mark Herr, 2019.
508 "Freedom," *Noah Webster Dictionary*, 1828.
509 Cicero, *De Legibus [On the Laws]*.
510 Abraham 3:25
511 2 Nephi 2:11,15-16
512 Doctrine and Covenants 29:39
513 Dallin H. Oaks, "Opposition in All Things," LDS General Conference, April 2016.
514 "Ordinances," *True to the Faith*, 2004, p. 109-110.
515 Moses 1:39
   "Priesthood," *True to the Faith*, 2004, p. 124-128.
516 John Locke, *Second Treatise of Civil Government*, 1689, ch. 16.
517 Exodus 20:15, 17
518 Scott Bradley, *To Preserve the Nation: In the Tradition of the Founding Fathers*, 2009.
519 George A. Peek Jr., *The Political Writings of John Adams*, 1954.
520 Bill Norton, "Understanding Your Most Fundamental Rights - part 3."
521 Mark Herr, et al., "Macro Understanding of Centralized Governance 3.4," 2015, p. 61, par. 1-4.

ABOUT THE AUTHOR

THARA TENNEY is the lucky wife of Tom Tenney and the proud mother of four boys. While she has a bachelor's degree in communications with an emphasis in marketing, her motivation never was to advance the 21st century's corporate ladder. Alongside many small projects, her sacred toil has forever been dedicated to raising her boys with the aim to train up strong sons of liberty. Through the years the battle of the balance has flitted between homeschooling, community self-care coach, fundraising chairman, children's sports, campaign messaging director, and more.

She is the oldest child of the LaVoy and Jeanette Finicum dozen. After the tragic murder of her father, for a year she had the opportunity to travel the country with her mother, speaking about what really happened January 26th, 2016.

Trauma's brutal course changed something within her the day LaVoy was shot three times in the back by out-of-control American agents while his hands were up in the universal sign of surrender. Yet, true to form, the motivation behind the toil this book demanded was her children. Her resolve was found in the reality that they deserve answers to their future adult questions.

Proceeds from this book will go to support the Finicum family's civil wrongful death case.